Ьӣ 617387

ECONOMIC RESEARCH CENTRE

REPORT OF THE
HUNDRED AND SIXTH ROUND TABLE
ON TRANSPORT ECONOMICS

held in Paris on 28th-29th November 1996
on the following topic:

INTERCITY TRANSPORT MARKETS IN COUNTRIES IN TRANSITION

EUROPEAN CONFERENCE OF MINISTERS OF TRANSPORT

EUROPEAN CONFERENCE OF MINISTERS
OF TRANSPORT (ECMT)

The European Conference of Ministers of Transport (ECMT) is an inter-governmental organisation established by a Protocol signed in Brussels on 17 October 1953. It is a forum in which Ministers responsible for transport, and more specifically the inland transport sector, can co-operate on policy. Within this forum, Ministers can openly discuss current problems and agree upon joint approaches aimed at improving the utilisation and at ensuring the rational development of European transport systems of international importance.

At present, the ECMT's role primarily consists of:

- helping to create an integrated transport system throughout the enlarged Europe that is economically and technically efficient, meets the highest possible safety and environmental standards and takes full account of the social dimension;
- helping also to build a bridge between the European Union and the rest of the continent at a political level.

The Council of the Conference comprises the Ministers of Transport of 39 full Member countries: Albania, Austria, Azerbaijan, Belarus, Belgium, Bosnia-Herzegovina, Bulgaria, Croatia, the Czech Republic, Denmark, Estonia, Finland, France, the Former Yugoslav Republic of Macedonia (F.Y.R.O.M.), Georgia, Germany, Greece, Hungary, Iceland, Ireland, Italy, Latvia, Lithuania, Luxembourg, Moldova, Netherlands, Norway, Poland, Portugal, Romania, the Russian Federation, the Slovak Republic, Slovenia, Spain, Sweden, Switzerland, Turkey, Ukraine and the United Kingdom. There are five Associate member countries (Australia, Canada, Japan, New Zealand and the United States) and three Observer countries (Armenia, Liechtenstein and Morocco).

A Committee of Deputies, composed of senior civil servants representing Ministers, prepares proposals for consideration by the Council of Ministers. The Committee is assisted by working groups, each of which has a specific mandate.

The issues currently being studied – on which policy decisions by Ministers will be required – include the development and implementation of a pan-European transport policy; the integration of Central and Eastern European Countries into the European transport market; specific issues relating to transport by rail, road and waterway; combined transport; transport and the environment; the social costs of transport; trends in international transport and infrastructure needs; transport for people with mobility handicaps; road safety; traffic management, road traffic information and new communications technologies.

Statistical analyses of trends in traffic and investment are published yearly by the ECMT and provide a clear indication of the situation in the transport sector in different European countries.

As part of its research activities, the ECMT holds regular Symposia, Seminars and Round Tables on transport economics issues. Their conclusions are considered by the competent organs of the Conference under the authority of the Committee of Deputies and serve as a basis for formulating proposals for policy decisions to be submitted to Ministers.

The ECMT's Documentation Service is one of the world's leading centres for transport sector data collection. It maintains the TRANSDOC database, which is available on CD-ROM and accessible via the telecommunications network.

For administrative purposes the ECMT's Secretariat is attached to the Organisation for Economic Co-operation and Development (OECD).

Publié en français sous le titre :

LE MARCHÉ DES TRANSPORTS INTERURBAINS DANS LES PAYS EN TRANSITION

Further information about the ECMT is available on Internet at the following address:
http://www.oecd.org/cem/

TABLE OF CONTENTS

SUMMARY OF DISCUSSIONS

GERMANY

Jan S. KOWALSKI
Head of the Section for International Economic Policy
Institute for Economic Policy Research
University of Karlsruhe
Germany

SITUATION IN EAST GERMANY

SUMMARY

Karlsruhe, March 1996

1. INTRODUCTION

East Germany is obviously a very special case of a country in transition. Usually we depict with this term a group of the former communist countries which, since the beginning of the decade, have been transforming their socioeconomic systems from mono-party, dictatorial structures and centrally planned command economies, toward multi-party parliamentary democracies and market-oriented economic systems. In the literature on transition economies, issues of privatisation and incentives structures dominate the discourse. Discussion on the degree of success of these transformations in Poland, the Czech and Slovak Republics, Hungary and elsewhere in the former Soviet bloc and their consequences for transport activities, remains outside the scope of this contribution (see, *inter alia*, Böttcher, Funck, Kowalski, 1993; Funck, Kowalski, 1995; Kowalski, 1993, 1995).

The former German Democratic Republic was almost a laboratory case of a communist economy, but it is doubtful if we can talk in its case of a "normal" transition. The Economic and Monetary Union, followed very closely by the formal unification of the two German States in November 1990, resulted in a totally different path of transformation of the socioeconomic structures in what came to be called the New Federal States (NFS).

It should be noted that changes in the transport infrastructure networks and flows, as well as in the functioning of transport enterprises, may be analysed from at least three perspectives:

i) The purely German context, pertaining to the area of the united Germany, influenced by the regulations and financial transfers from the western to the eastern part of the country and by the rapid legal, economic and social integration. This certainly is a decisive factor in determining consequences for transportation in this area.

ii) The Central and Eastern European area, apart from the former GDR, where the transformation from centrally-planned into market-oriented economies, as well as the high intensification of interactions with western Europe through association and membership in the EEC, brings about changes in the whole pattern of flows and the way of functioning of the transport sector.

iii) The European Union context, where the implementation of the Internal Market and further developments after the Maastricht Treaty change the overall framework of interregional competition throughout western Europe, influencing economic activities and transport flows.

In this contribution, we shall concentrate on the first perspectives, only occasionally introducing issues connected with the other two. It should also be borne in mind that, because the recording system for the New Federal States is still in the development phase, the reliability of the transport statistics is not always very good (as with most other statistical indicators for the NFS). We rely on official statistics and sources, supplemented by results from studies performed by or with the participation of the Institute for Economic Policy Research of the University of Karlsruhe (in particular, the research group headed by Professor Werner Rothengatter).

2. DEVELOPMENTS IN THE FORMER GDR SINCE 1990

As mentioned above, in contrast to the situation for the other former COMECON countries, economic reform and the necessary adjustment costs (such as the unemployment shock, closure of numerous unrentable enterprises, etc.) in the former GDR were and are supported financially and organisationally by West Germany. In 1991, about 140 billion and in 1992 around 180 billion DM were transferred to the eastern part of united Germany within the framework of various programmes. Since that time, it is estimated that approximately 200 billion DM of public transfers have been channelled every year from the West to the East, compared to a GDP level of approximately 343 billion DM in the NFS in 1994. Roughly the same amount of capital was provided yearly to the New Federal States (NFS) by private economic actors.

Even more importantly, it has also been possible to apply in the East most of the legal regulations pertinent to the functioning of the socioeconomic system from the West. This was a fundamental issue. It should be borne in mind that, according to leading scholars working on transition issues in central and eastern Europe, the lack or at least the inefficiencies, of legal market institutions and procedures are still considered to be one of the main barriers to transformation in the former communist countries apart from East Germany. In the NFS, the systemic transition to the market economy institutions and legal framework has been completed very quickly. This involved not only the adoption of the legal framework from West Germany, but also a human transfer of numerous experts in juridical, tax and commercial law matters, enterpreneurs, scholars, teachers, etc. Their activities sometimes led to personal tensions between the *"Wessies"* and the *"Ossies"* (i.e. people from the West and East of Germany) but without their individual commitment the rapid transformation would have been impossible.

In short, the Monetary and Economic Union created almost overnight a single, although very uneven, German economy.

This does not mean, of course, that the process of change was, is and will be devoid of problems, conflicts and setbacks. Indeed, the mass media are filled with negative reports on the psychological, social and economic consequences of rapid change, in particular the high unemployment level, which remains officially at about 15 per cent at the end of 1995, but is in reality much higher, as many of the unemployed are "hidden" in various social support and retraining programmes, thus not appearing in the unemployment statistics.

We do not take these hardships and resulting tensions within East German society lightly. We also consider all official statements, promising the citizens of the new German *Länder* that their standard of living will equal that of their western counterparts in another three to five years, to be either purely politically motivated or based on a complete ignorance of the impossibility of attaining the high growth rates of GDP necessary to fulfil such visions (growth rates in the range of 15 per cent per year would have to be reached in the NFS from 1992 onwards until the year 2000 in order to equalize per capita GDP in both parts of Germany by that year).

Where does East Germany stand now five years after the unification? Table 1 shows some relevant data on economic development (Junkernheinrich *et al.*, 1995). If we take GDP as a measure of the overall economic change, progress was significant between 1991 and 1994. Gross Domestic Product rose by 17. 4 per cent, from less than 17 000 to almost 20 000 DM per capita. It can be seen that the gap between the NFS and their western counterparts, although still a large one, diminished in all cases. On the other hand, it should be noticed that

11

the turnover per capita in construction and industry in the NFS, measured as a ratio of the level of relevant indicators in East Germany to that of the western States, lies significantly lower than that of the GDP. This shows again the role of transfers in the NFS economy. Also, the capital stock of the NFS enterprises amounts to about 10 per cent of the total German one, compared with about a 20 per cent share in population, which points to a distinct and pertaining capital gap (Junkernheinrich *et al.*, 1995, p. 361). Productivity levels of the NFS enterprises are still, on average, no higher than 50 per cent of the western level, but in some areas, like the Dresden region and in some activities, such as car production and optics, they even exceed the norms set by firms in the old States.

Also, as we already mentioned, the institutional transition is practically implemented, privatisation of the state enterprises concluded successfully (despite financial burdens left by the *Treuhand* at the end of this process). Unemployment levels remain unbearably high but exports, especially in the direction of the former trading partners in the East, show a rising tendency, promising revigoration of the economic flows interrupted by the political and economic upheavals of the early 90s.

3. FUTURE CHANGES WITHIN THE AREA OF EAST GERMANY

The future path of economic development in the NFS obviously depends on many side conditions, which lie to a large extent outside the influence of the decisionmaking powers of German politicians. During the preparation of the Federal Traffic Infrastructure Plan (1992), forecasts of socioeconomic development until the year 2010 have been formulated, which set out from the optimistic assumption that no major catastrophes will occur in central and eastern Europe, including Russia (see also Kowalski 1991 and Kessel *et al.*, 1990). Further, the following general premises have formed the basis for considerations about possible scenarios for the economic development of East Germany:

   i) In the year 2010, the GDP per capita will be roughly on the same level in both parts of the country. This does not preclude persistence of the interregional differentiation;

   ii) The sectoral structure of the East German economy in the year 2010 will correspond approximately to that in West Germany;

iii) Trading relations of the East German territory will undergo a total reorientation towards the West, in particular toward West Germany and western Europe.

Some of these premises seem to be doubtful, or at least merit more discussion from today's perspective (see Rothengatter, 1995).

Table 2 shows the main elements of the forecast from the BVWP (1992), Table 3 presents the results of several independent population forecasts for the New Federal States. On the whole, the economic developments in East Germany followed roughly a path which was expected five years ago (cf. Rothengatter, Kowalski, 1991). The scale and scope of the destruction of work-places in traditional sectors of industry in the GDR, however, even exceeded our pessimistic scenario (it has to be added that we were already considered to be "black" pessimists at that time). On the other hand, the vision of structural changes in production and trade presented five years ago has proved to be a fairly accurate one. The economic growth in both West and East Germany has been slower than predicted, so that the hypothesis of the equalisation of the GDP per capita levels by the year 2010 seems less probable today than five years ago.

Generally, the main source of difficulties in predicting the future economic development and relevant transport volumes in East Germany is connected with the uncertainty with respect to the migration behaviour of the area's inhabitants and potential inflows of people from western Germany and from abroad (obviously, a very politically sensitive issue). The data in Table 3 point to a large range of different expectations by various authors with regard to future population changes in the NFS. The BVWP forecast seems to postulate population levels in East Germany which seem much too high from today's state of knowledge. This is obviously the main source of possible deviations from economic development and transportation development scenarios postulated for the NFS. The newest population forecast, which is presently being prepared by the IFO Institute in Munich, was not yet available at the time of preparing this contribution. But it should be noted that all authors expect a further decline in the number of inhabitants of the NFS, coupled with rising productivity and per capita income levels.

Overall growth of the NFS economy will, however, be characterised by regional differentiations, which have already become very pronounced in the first part of the 90s.

We expect a particularly rapid growth in the Greater Berlin area, due to the internationalisation of the service sector and its expansion towards the eastern European markets, as well as to the increased administrative functions of the city as the capital of the whole Republic. We estimate the population of this area to reach about 5.5 million in the year 2010 as compared to 4.3 million at present. We also expect positive, albeit more modest growth for the Baltic coastal area around Rostock, due to its tourist potential and its role as a gateway to Scandinavia, the Baltic States and to St. Petersburg. Also, the large cities in the south, such as Dresden (university and administrative centre), Jena (R&D, university and optics industry) and Leipzig (research, industry, fairs and conference centre), can be expected to remain growth poles. In all probability, the existing airports in Leipzig-Halle and Dresden will be modernised and their facilities extended, strengthening their position as possible locations for corporate headquarters. Also, the regions in the south-west part of the former GDR, i.e. mainly in the Thuringian region, are expected to register above-average growth rates, due mainly to the favourable economic structure, dominated by increasingly innovative small and medium enterprises, coupled with their relative proximity to the old Federal States.

On the other hand, the peripheral rural areas in the North and East are unlikely to show much dynamism and will experience relative or even an absolute decline. The same applies to areas of single-sector industrial concentrations, specialising in metal extraction, brown coal, chemicals, heavy engineering and textile production. A very special problem is posed by the old industrial regions around Halle and Leipzig. Leipzig itself, as mentioned above, is in a relatively favourable position. But the areas around it and towards Halle will be blighted for decades by the closure of the old metal and chemical plants and an exodus of labour. The catastrophic environmental situation of this area also makes it extremely difficult for the enterprises from the West to take over and restructure the production capacities. Another problem region is the lignite mining area around Cottbus in the south-eastern part of Saxony, although the closeness to the Bohemian economic centres may prove to provide positive stimuli to growth in this area.

4. CHANGES IN THE TRANSPORTATION SECTOR

As was expected, the economic development in East Germany has already resulted in considerable changes in transport flows and modes in the NFS. Steep growth rates in individual mobility and motorisation levels have been observed in the last five years and less pronounced (due to increased efficiency in the market economy conditions) increases in goods transportation volumes. In comparison with scenarios developed at the beginning of the decade, the most important deviations of actual observed tendencies from these scenarios concern (Rothengatter, 1995):

-- The speed of motorisation, which exceeds scenario assumptions, despite the economic slowdown;

-- Transportation volumes in passenger transport, which in West Germany exceed the forecast levels by about 10 per cent; in East Germany, however, they lie below these scenario levels.

Further economic growth will be accompanied by more changes in transportation. Obviously, increased transport flows call for new investments in the transport infrastructure networks, changes which are already being undertaken. In this chapter, we shall first provide some information about the evolutions in flows which took place since the unification of the Germanys, as well as some forecasts for the future, and then sketch the developments in the infrastructure networks.

4.1. Transport sector activities and volumes

Table 4 shows changes in employment in the railways and in the rest of the transport sector for the old and new Federal States of Germany. Not surprisingly, the number of employed declined strongly in the overstaffed East German railways (united since 1st January 1994 with their western counterparts in the framework of the privately-run Deutsche Bahn AG). This decline was less pronounced in the other parts of the transport sector. In part, this reduction in employment reflected improved management and organisation but also corresponded to a reduction in railway services. From Table 5, it can be seen that in the case of rail passenger transport this decline was not very pronounced and an increase was even recorded in 1993; in the case of goods transport, the shrinking production levels in manufacturing and the expected modal split evolution resulted in a considerable reduction in demand for railway

15

services. The exception is provided by combined transport, which increased, albeit from a relatively negligible starting level. It should be noted that the decline in goods transport services by the railways is not limited to East Germany. It has also been recorded in West Germany, thus deriding many of the proclaimed aims of transport policies in this country.

Table 6 provides information about public road transport services in West and East Germany for passengers and for goods transport volumes. The volume of services of public road transport enterprises diminished in East Germany between 1991 and 1994, that of private companies recorded a considerable increase. The volume of long-distance road freight transport increased dramatically in the first phase after unification, reflecting a change in modal split, but it has stagnated since 1992, due to the economic difficulties of many East German firms.

Another transport mode which gains in service volumes in East Germany is air passenger traffic (Table 7), reflecting both business and public administration oriented trips, mainly between West and East Germany, and private tourist flights.

In the case of private mobility related to individual car ownership, as expected, this was a fast-growing part of East German transport flows. Table 8 shows the development of car ownership and registration, Tables 9 and 10 provide indicators of the amount of travel performed by these cars. As expected, individual passenger transport by car increased considerably. Also, the amount of goods transport by cars must have increased considerably, judging from petrol consumption. Bearing in mind that long-distance road freight transport stagnated, after the initial explosion between 1990-91 (Table 6), this points to increased short-haul goods transport in East Germany.

Figures 1, 2 and 3 show the tendencies in the modal split for passenger transport, confirming the increasing role of individual car transportation.

On the whole, it must (unfortunately) be noted that the preferences and travel behaviour of people in East Germany seem to follow patterns copied from the West. This means that, both in goods and passenger traffic, the share of road traffic will increase to the same high western levels at the expense of the railways, which in the past, as in the other COMECON countries, carried about 70 per cent of goods and passengers. The BVWP estimated that in 2010, the share of the railways in long-distance passenger transport would sink to about 8.5 per cent, that of air traffic would reach 4 per cent and the share of private road traffic in the modal split would rise to 87.5 per cent. It should be noted that even this very high share for road traffic in East Germany remains below the share of this mode predicted for West Germany, thus expressing the past long-term preferential treatment accorded to the railways in the East. That this forecast is realistic seems to be more and more doubtful.

Tables 11 and 12 present BVWP92 (Federal Traffic Infrastructure Plan, 1992) statistics and Figure 4 shows the slightly revised (as compared to BVWP92) forecast for the number of personal trips within and outside of East Germany, expressing a very strong increase in transport volumes. Figure 5 provides some more in-depth data for traffic with various parts of the globe, showing particularly fast growth rates in the direction of eastern Europe.

With respect to the volume of traffic, the *Bundesverkehrswegeplanung* expected by the year 2010 a sevenfold to tenfold increase in long-distance passenger trips between the eastern European countries and the whole of Germany, as well as in the transit traffic through Germany. About a twofold increase in the tonnage of transported goods was postulated by the scenario.

This prediction is made with the assumption that no major change in transport policy in favour of rail transport will occur. It is, of course, possible to influence modal split away from road transport. The past and present experiences in the Federal Republic of Germany in this respect show, however, that the pressure of the road and car lobby is hard to stop and that cars continue to exert an almost magical pull on the citizens of the NFS.

4.2. Transport infrastructure

The network of transport infrastructures in East Germany was relatively dense but in a neglected condition. The state of the motorways seemed reminiscent of the era of the Third Reich. Smaller roads and streets (apart from prestigious large city centres) were full of potholes and in a general state of decay. The railways were old, the gauge permitting only low speeds. But the railway network comprised around 14 000 km of lines, that of roads about 120 000 km. The density of the railway network was slightly higher than in West Germany, that of the road network lower. Also, the network of inland waterways was relatively well developed (2 300 km).

Thus the problem of infrastructure in East Germany was and is not so much that of quantity but of quality, so that the main thrust of investment activities within the so-called "German Unity" (*Deutsche Einheit*), Transport Infrastructure Programme, elaborated and proclaimed in 1990-91, concerns the upgrading and renovation of the existing infrastructure networks. Many additional links must, of course, be newly constructed as, for example, the motorway alongside the Baltic coast from Lübeck through Rostock towards Szczecin, motorways from Dresden to Prague and from Kassel to Leipzig and some others (see Figures 6, 7, 8 for an overview of the German Unity programme projects).

One very significant element both in railway and road investment projects implemented within the framework of the programme is the possibility of accelerated planning and implementation procedures, which permit the average planning period to be shortened from the typical twenty years which were necessary in the old Federal States to start real work on an infrastructure project, to about two to five years for the NFS at present. Needless to say, these accelerated procedures are also heavily criticised by opponents of NFS transport policy.

For the ten railroad projects foreseen in the "German Unity" programme, approximately 30 billion DM has been foreseen. In view of the serious strains on the German state budgets, it seems doubtful if this sum will be fully devoted to infrastructure projects. The quality and quantity of service increased dramatically for the intercity and interregional train connections. The institutional merger of the West and East railways resulted in a uniform service level and integrated timetables. (Discussion of the Hamburg-Berlin magnetic train will be omitted for the sake of space in this report.)

For the seven road transport projects, planning and construction are well advanced and partial stretches could very soon be opened to traffic. The following measures have been completed (*Strassenbaubericht*, 1995, pp. 15-17):

-- The extension of the southern Berlin motorway ring to six lanes (A10);
-- The border crossing Neisse bridge near Görlitz (A4);
-- The A4 between Eichelborn and Weimar;
-- The Hermsdorf motorway cross (A4 A9); and
-- The A9 between Grosskugel and Droyssig and between the state border of Thuringia/Bavaria and Berg/Bad Steben.

By the end of 1994, the overall degree of advancement of implementation of the "German Unity" projects (which altogether amount to 1 968 km of modernised and newly constructed roads), was about 60 per cent for the elaboration of technical blueprints, about 15 per cent for implementation of planning procedures and obtaining necessary permits, 9 per cent under construction and 5 per cent already opened to traffic. By the end of 1995, the relevant figures were supposed to reach 80 per cent for technical blueprints, 25 per cent for conclusion of planning procedures and permits, 25 per cent under construction and 10 per cent opened to traffic. By the end of 1994, seven road projects of the "German Unity" programme received 2.2 billion DM in investments. In 1995, 1.5 billion should have been additionally realised (of about 23.5 billion DM originally foreseen in the Programme for the whole implementation).

The degree of realisation of various projects varies significantly from the very initial stages for Project 10 (motorway Lübeck-Szczecin) to much further advanced stages for Projects 12 (Berlin-Nuremberg) and 13 (Göttingen-Halle) or 14 (Magdeburg-Halle).

The "German Unity" programme includes one internal waterway project *Mittellandkanal*, which was expected to cost approximately 4 billion DM to implement. On the Elbe River section, difficulties caused by very variable water flow have slowed progress, but in the other parts of the project work on technical improvements of sluices, etc., is well advanced.

Figures 9 and 10 show in greater detail the infrastructure projects overall (i.e. not only the special projects from the "German Unity" programme) implemented or being implemented since 1990. The story they tell (Figure 9) is that we can indeed observe a priority in assignment of money to projects, and the advantaged situation of the NFS compared with the OFS. From Figure 10, it can be seen that, apart from the well-known and prestigious projects such as those from the "German Unity" programme, an enormous amount of work has been done on numerous small stretches of roads around, within and between cities, removing the most troublesome bottlenecks and resulting traffic jams (although, needless to say, they are still a major nuisance for travellers in East Germany). Also, the inclusion of infrastructure projects concerning transport in the direction of central and eastern Europe should be noted (both border crossings and links to major cities). Indeed, since the early 90s, German traffic infrastructure planning includes explicit consideration of the evolution of demand for transport in the neighbouring countries in transition.

With respect to air traffic infrastructure in the NFS, very strong politically-dominated discussion is still underway in Germany. The probable extension and modernisation of the Schönefeld Airport by Berlin depends on the outcome of the plan to merge the Federal State of Brandenburg with the City of Berlin. The airports in Leipzig-Halle and Dresden will be modernised and, in the former case, extended (*Luftverkehrsprognose*, 1995).

5. SOME GENERAL QUESTIONS ON REFORMS IN EASTERN EUROPE, UNIFICATION OF GERMANYS AND TRANSPORTATION ISSUES

In this contribution, we have focused our attention on the specific situation of transportation activities in the area of the former German Democratic Republic. We have tried to make clear the reasons why East Germany cannot be treated in the same manner as the other countries in transition. In this chapter, some pertinent issues for all Central and Eastern Europe Countries in transition are briefly addressed.

The experiences gathered during the first five years after the overthrow of the communist governments in central Europe, as well as the forecasts on manifold increases in passenger and goods traffic flows between East and West Europe, point to the particular importance of the development of adequate transportation links from the transforming countries to the West as well as within these countries themselves. It is obvious that the provision of such adequate transport networks is financially beyond the capacities of the central European countries at present. Various schemes to solve this problem are discussed below.

Many authors, especially those who devote themselves exclusively to transportation research, maintain that the transport sector was and remains the most backward sector of the overall economy of the former communist countries. It is held that the reason for the sorry state of this sector was the insufficient level of investment expenditures in transport infrastructure as compared to other spheres of economic activity.

It could, however, be argued that the situation of the transport sector was no better and no worse than that of other sectors of the economy (Funck, Kowalski, 1987, 1989). The underdevelopment of the transport sector reflected the overall underdevelopment, experienced in all parts of the economy since the mid-70s. At present, two phenomena can be observed, one of which increases and the other decreases strains in the transport sector. On the one hand, the volume and share of investments in transport infrastructure declined even further as compared with the other sectors of the economy. On the other hand, due to hardening budget constraints on enterprises as a result of the reforms started in 1990, demand for transport services per unit of output declined considerably for all segments of this sector. Paradoxically, this means that, in the short term, despite the economic decline and reduced investment levels, the pressure on the transport sector decreased as compared with the past, not only during the initial phase of shrinking GDP levels in the transition countries but also in the subsequent period of high rates of real growth experienced in Poland, the Czech and Slovak Republics and Hungary. The modal split, especially in the case of goods transport, shows similar evolutions to those observed in East Germany.

The transition to a market economy has already resulted in major structural adjustments in the economies concerned. First of all, the share of services in employment and the generation of GDP increased and continues to rise fast: service activities were traditionally underdeveloped in eastern countries, due mainly to reasons related to the communist doctrine. The share of manufacturing has diminished strongly and will continue to do so, that of agriculture and forestry will diminish more slowly.

Within the manufacturing sector, significant shifts have occurred, namely, an increase in the importance of activities concerned with consumer goods production, at the expense of those branches devoted to investment goods, especially primary materials and heavy machinery. Also, in the very near future, more diversity in the composition of household consumption will probably evolve with increasing incomes, and reduced subsidies for collective consumption, following western patterns.

The political and economic upheavals in eastern Europe and the dissolution of the COMECON have also resulted in significant geographical adjustments in the patterns of trade and flows of people. In the past, the geographical distribution of foreign trade in socialist countries could be described by the "one-third" rule, i.e. about one-third of the turnover was conducted with the Soviet Union, one-third with the rest of COMECON and one-third with the rest of the world. The share of hard currency countries was kept artificially low for doctrinal reasons, but also because of the insufficient availability of means of payment.

In the wake of transformations in eastern Europe, the share of trade with the rest of the world, in particular with western Europe, increased considerably, reflecting a need for a more intense economic interaction with these highly-developed countries. In the early 90s, one possible barrier to the growth of East-West trade was seen in the high degree of indebtedness of eastern Europe in recent years. Real developments point to the comparative irrelevance of this issue for trade. The payments problem was, to some extent, solved by schemes like the Polish debt reduction, agreed on in 1991 (when the Polish debt to the public lenders was halved), which then enabled intensified East-West trade flows, partly by ignoring the issue in practical policy. One of the reasons for this may be the fact that, for the last few years, the transforming economies ran considerable trade deficits with the European Union and yet were able to finance them.

It should, however, be noted that the extent of the adjustment toward an increase in trade with western Europe, which could be observed immediately after the disruption of the communist system, was probably artificially high, firstly because of the breakdown of eastern European (and former Soviet) markets, due to the currency problems experienced in the first phase of transition from rouble-based to convertible systems, secondly, because of the psychological inclination of most consumers to choose, in the early days of transition, western goods over eastern commodities.

This phenomenon, especially marked in East Germany in 1990, was also observed in Hungary, Poland and the CSFR. But already, five years after the opening of the East German and Polish economies, there are numerous indications that consumers are starting to search for cheaper goods of eastern European origin. We expect, therefore, that in the perspective of five to ten years, the geographical proximity of the former communist countries will, again, play a considerable role in the determination of the spatial structure of commodity flows. Data for foreign trade flows in 1994 and what is known about 1995 already point to a significant increase in trade flows between the Visegrad countries, and between them and the former Soviet republics, such as the Ukraine, Belarus and Russia itself.

In addition, strong growth in intrasectoral, as opposed to intersectoral, trade is to be expected. In the past, the COMECON agreements enforced a high degree of sectoral specialisation in the foreign trade structures of eastern European countries (for example: Bulgaria specialised in certain kinds of electronic data processing products, Poland was "responsible" for most radiolocation equipment, the Soviet Union for certain kinds of raw materials, etc.). Under free market conditions, the patterns of trade will most probably move towards more intrasectoral specialisation and thus exchange patterns which are well known from western experience. This will have consequences for goods transport volumes and contents.

A special phenomenon, which started to receive attention from statistics very recently, is the enormous amount of cross-border, "grey zone" trade between some NFS of East Germany and areas of western Poland. Most of the transactions involve imports of foodstuffs and consumer durables from Poland to East Germany. Prudent estimates of the extent of this trade put it at about 3 billion DM, the upper range of evaluations puts it at almost 6 billion DM. In the border areas, this informal trade activity has serious transport consequences in the form of congestion and queues at the border crossings. Macroeconomically, the positive balance of these transactions helps to more than compensate for the officially-recorded negative trade balance of Poland.

Coupled with these changes in the pattern of commodity flows, we expect some shifts in the movements of people, namely, a considerable increase in West-East exchanges. As is well known, in the past most of the eastern European countries (with the one notable exception of Poland) restricted the free flow of people, especially the travel of their own citizens to the West. Since the opening of eastern Europe, the number of private and business-related journeys has increased manifold, and will increase even further in the future. This evolution, of course, finds its strongest expression in the heart of the European continent, namely, in the area of the unified Germany, but flows with all the eastern European countries will grow too.

With the probable enlargement of the European Union to the East, the volumes and directions of transport flows, as well as the legal framework of the transport sector will evolve even more strongly towards western European patterns. But even before this step is taken, the EU association agreements with the transition countries have resulted, as we discussed above, in a high degree of economic and transport integration between western and eastern Europe.

6. PRIVATISATION OF INFRASTRUCTURE VERSUS PRIVATISATION OF TRANSPORTATION ENTERPRISES

In this final chapter, we shall briefly comment on the discussion concerning the potential and scope of privatisation processes in transportation activities in the countries in transition.

Experiences from western Europe point to a rather limited potential for privatising transport infrastructure in the reforming countries of eastern Europe. There are some examples of privately built and operated highways, railways, bridges, tunnels, airports and seaports but, on the whole, the share of privately constructed and operated infrastructure is very low. The time horizons of the private transport infrastructure projects are as a rule very long, profitability very often doubtful. The long and painful story of the Channel Tunnel is well known in central and eastern Europe.

Considering that lack of private and public investment capital for all sorts of projects is an acute problem at present in the countries in transition, and that the purchasing power of the potential customers will remain relatively low for a long time, the prospects for the private construction of new and taking over of the existing infrastructure networks are very slim (for a more general discussion of the privatisation issues in transition countries, see Kowalski, 1990; Lipton, Sachs, 1991; Kowalski, 1993). In practice, the only way we can envisage private gauge and road networks is through international financing of some projects by the IMF, the World Bank and similar organisations and by choosing the form of a private company for them. Of course, various specific solutions are possible in such a case, but again, due to the overall low income levels in this part of Europe, the prospects for profitable operation of such endeavours seem doubtful to this author.

With respect to the transport enterprises using the infrastructure, the privatisation potential is certainly higher, but different in various sectors. In Poland, Hungary and the Czech and Slovak Republics, most of the shipping, haulage and dispatching companies have already been privatised, either through employees' and management buy-outs, liquidation of the "old" firms, or through joint ventures with foreign capital. Many new firms have also been created. In Polish sea-shipping, even large, formerly state companies have been privatised, in the sense of having a private company charter, but a large stake in their capital is, as a rule, owned by various public institutions.

In the case of the railways, while the potential for privatisation is obviously high in the service areas (such as catering), the privatisation of entire railway companies seems dubious in the short to medium term. The same applies to the national airlines, where it is easy (and in part already being done) to privatise some elements of the firms, leaving however the bulk of the enterprises in public hands. But it should be mentioned that numerous privately-owned small airlines have started operating since the early 90s in the fastest reforming countries.

In conclusion, we are of the opinion that the most promising way to privatise national carrier companies is to change their status to private companies, while retaining public ownership of the majority stake of shares. Even such a "minor" change can result in economic behaviour which will be more oriented towards profit, efficiency or subsidy minimisation than is the case with the wholly state companies.

TABLES

Table 1. **East-West Germany - An economic comparison**

AREA	GDP per capita 1991	E. Germany % of given area	GDP per capita 1994	E. Germany % of given area	Turnover per capita in manufacturing	E. Germany % of given area
Baden-Württemberg	43 802	38.8	43 054	46.3	32 000	27.1
Bayern	41 915	40.5	43 118	46.2	27 372	31.7
Bremen	51 614	32.9	51 954	38.4	48 018	18.1
Hamburg	67 270	25.2	67 097	29.7	25 976	33.4
Hessen	48 499	35.0	49 812	40.0	23 914	36.3
Niedersachsen	34 617	49.0	34 633	57.5	24 516	35.4
Nordrhein-Westfalen	38 402	44.2	38 105	52.3	27 218	31.9
Rheinland-Pfalz	34 865	48.7	34 653	57.5	25 278	34.3
Saarland	35 445	47.9	34 906	57.1	26 656	32.5
Schleswig-Holstein	34 417	49.3	34 981	57.0	17 557	49.4
West Germany excl. West Berlin	40 895	41.5	41 040	48.6	29 989	32.1
East Germany (incl. West Berlin)	16 979	100	19 930	100	8 671	100

Table 2. **Structural data for the New Federal States (NFS)**

	1987-88	**2000**	**2010**
Population (millions)	16.70	15.70	16.00
Employment (millions)	8.69	6.76	7.24
Gross value added in bill. DM (1980)	252.70	406.80	713.80
of which:			
primary sector	22.7	18.7	15.0
secondary sector	149.0	200.4	302.7
tertiary sector	81.0	187.7	395.9
GDP per capita (in DM)	15 160	25 895	44 610
Productivity in comparison to Old Federal States in %	55.0	74.3	100.0
Car park (millions)	4.0	6.6	8.2

Source : BVWP, 1992.

Table 3. **Population forecasts for NFS in millions**

	2000	**2010**	**2020**	**2030**
Sta BVA	3 variants 15.3 - 15.5	15.0 - 15.6	14.4 - 15.5	13.3 - 14.8
DIW	15.2 - 14.9	15.0 - 15.6	14.4 - 15.5	13.3 - 14.8
Prognos	14.3	13.7		
Förster		14.8		12.6
Münz/Ulrich	22.7	12.9 - 14.1	15.0	15.0

Source : *Luftverkehrsprognose für den Flughafen Dresden*, p. 34, 1995.

Table 4. **Employment in the transport sector (in 1 000)**

	1991		**1992**		**1993**	
	OFS	**NFS**	**OFS**	**NFS**	**OFS**	**NFS**
Railways	243	208	237	186	227	138
Rest of transport	776	-	779	110	770	104

Note: OFS = Old Federal States; NFS = New Federal States
Source : Verkehr in Zahlen, 1995.

Table 5. **Railways**

	1991		1992		1993	
	OFS	**NFS**	**OFS**	**NFS**	**OFS**	**NFS**
Person-km (mill.)	46 096	10 323	46 867	9 844	47 704	9 969
Goods transport (mill. t-km) *of which*	67 592	18 663	60 967	14 745	55 202	13 900
combined goods ('000)	13 614	793	13 370	854	14 184	1 204

Note: OFS = Old Federal States; NFS = New Federal States
Source : Verkehr in Zahlen, 1995.

Table 6. **Road transport**

	1991		1992		1993		1994	
	OFS	**NFS**	**OFS**	**NFS**	**OFS**	**NFS**	**OFS**	**NFS**
Public road transport (mill. person-km)								
public enterprises	34 644	14 035	35 163	10 953	35 830	9 571	34 871	10 443
private enterprises	30 678	320	30 995	1 436	30 755	1 576	28 271	2 793
Road goods transport (bill. tonne-km)								
longhaul	62.5	1.9	64.3	8.5	57.5	8.7		
shorthaul	24.0	2.8	25.0	3.6				

Note: OFS = Old Federal States; NFS = New Federal States

Table 7. **Air transport**

	1991		1992		1993		1994	
	OFS	**NFS**	**OFS**	**NFS**	**OFS**	**NFS**	**OFS**	**NFS**
Air passengers ('000)	77 595	2 155	85 570	3 670	91 405	4 644	97 591	5 453

Note: OFS = Old Federal States; NFS = New Federal States
Source: Verkehr in Zahlen, 1995.

Table 8. **Cars**

	1991		1992		1993		1994	
	OFS	**NFS**	**OFS**	**NFS**	**OFS**	**NFS**	**OFS**	**NFS**
No. of cars (mill.)	27.60	4.94	27.97	5.36	28.30	5.60	28.40	5.99
New cars registered (mill.)	2 844	666	2 576	704	2 063	569	2 029	538

Note: OFS = Old Federal States; NFS = New Federal States
Source : Verkehr in Zahlen, 1995.

Table 9. **Road traffic (billion km)**

	1991		1992		1993		1994	
	OFS	**NFS**	**OFS**	**NFS**	**OFS**	**NFS**	**OFS**	**NFS**
All vehicles	502.5	71.7	507.2	82.7	505.7	91.8	496.8	94.2
Passenger car	437.3	59.1	440.7	69.3	444.4	76.5	428.3	77.4
Trucks	39.9	3.5	40.6	5.8	38.1	9.0	40.9	10.1

Note: OFS = Old Federal States; NFS = New Federal States

Table 10. **Petrol use (million tonnes)**

	1991		1992		1993		1994	
	OFS	**NFS**	**OFS**	**NFS**	**OFS**	**NFS**	**OFS**	**NFS**
Passenger cars	40.556	5.176	40.681	5.890	40.778	6.314	38.923	6.505
Goods transport	13.848	1.613	14.040	2.303	13.399	3.235	14.291	3.603

Note: OFS = Old Federal States; NFS = New Federal States

Table 11. Transport volumes in personal long-distance transport Trips per year (in mill.)

	Internal	West Europe	East Europe	Intercontinental
NFS 2000	522.93	17.21	36.76	3.53
OFS 2000	2 224.54	309.99	14.83	16.58
NFS 2010	606.13	29.09	52.95	6.10
OFS 2010	2 263.14	354.66	24.26	20.85

Note: OFS = Old Federal States; NFS = New Federal States
Source : BVWP, 1992.

Table 12. Transport volumes in NS in personal long-distance transport Trips per year (in mill.)

	NFS (internal)	OFS	Abroad
2004	581.0	257.8	64.0
2010	584.2	259.9	83.1
2030	542.9	244.1	176.8

Note: OFS = Old Federal States; NFS = New Federal States
Source : BVWP, 1992.

FIGURES

Figure 1. **Passenger transport in the new *Länder* in 1991 in billion passenger-km**

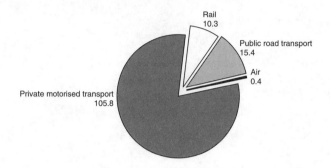

Figure 2. **Passenger transport in the new *Länder* in 1992 in billion passenger-km**

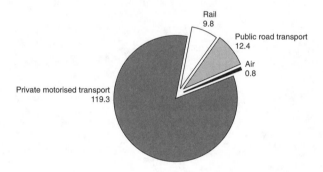

Figure 3. **Passenger transport in the new *Länder* in 1993 in billion passenger-km**

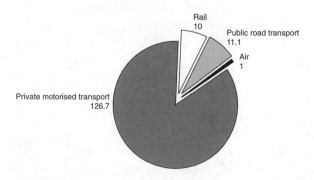

Figure 4. Number of long-distance journeys in 2010 from and to the new *Länder*

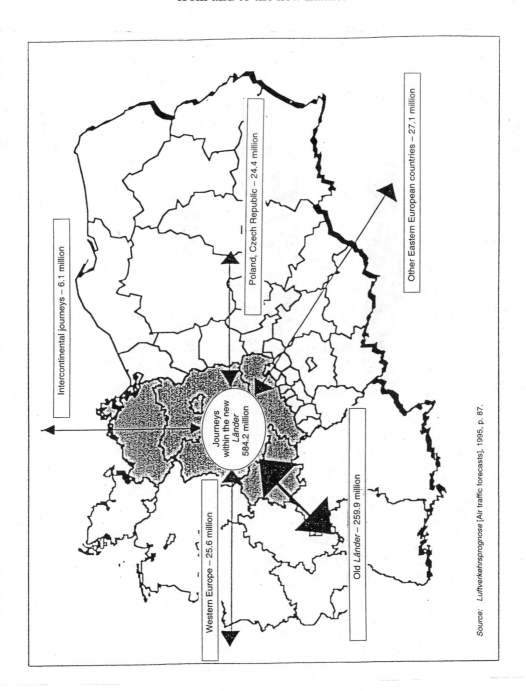

Source: *Luftverkehrsprognose* [Air traffic forecasts], 1995, p. 87.

Intercontinental journeys – 6.1 million

Poland, Czech Republic – 24.4 million

Other Eastern European countries – 27.1 million

Journeys within the new *Länder* 584.2 million

Western Europe – 25.6 million

Old *Länder* – 259.9 million

Figure 5. Long-distance passenger transport between the new *Länder* and abroad

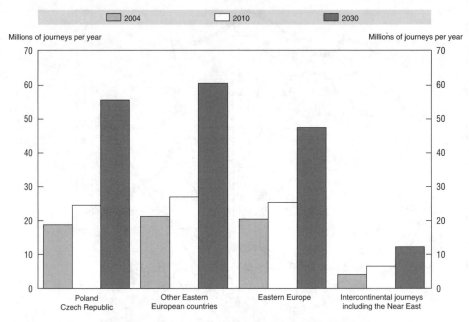

Source: *Lufverkehrsprognose* [Air traffic forecasts], 1995, p. 88.

Figure 6. **Rail network development projects between the old and new *Länder***

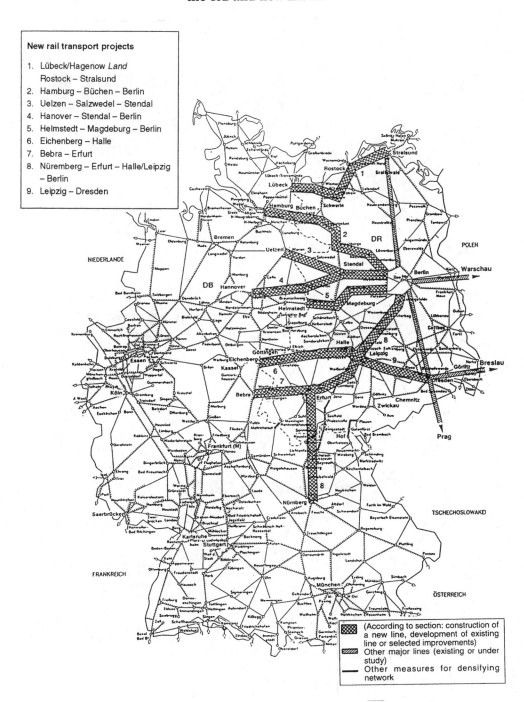

New rail transport projects

1. Lübeck/Hagenow *Land*
   Rostock – Stralsund
2. Hamburg – Büchen – Berlin
3. Uelzen – Salzwedel – Stendal
4. Hanover – Stendal – Berlin
5. Helmstedt – Magdeburg – Berlin
6. Eichenberg – Halle
7. Bebra – Erfurt
8. Nüremberg – Erfurt – Halle/Leipzig
   – Berlin
9. Leipzig – Dresden

(According to section: construction of a new line, development of existing line or selected improvements)
Other major lines (existing or under study)
Other measures for densifying network

Figure 7. Road network development projects between the old and new *Länder*

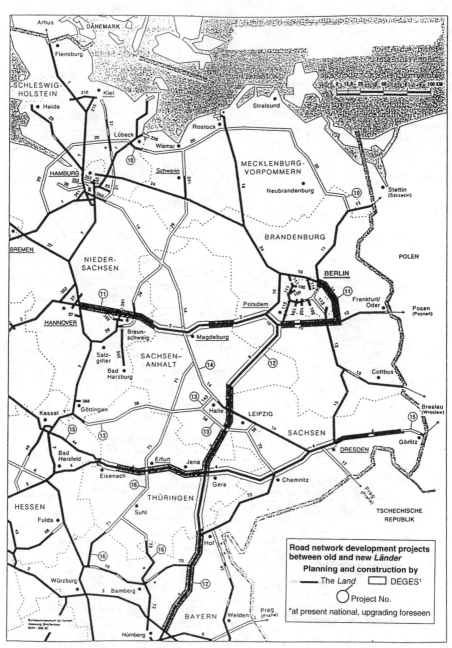

Figure 8. Inland waterway network development projects between the old and new *Länder*

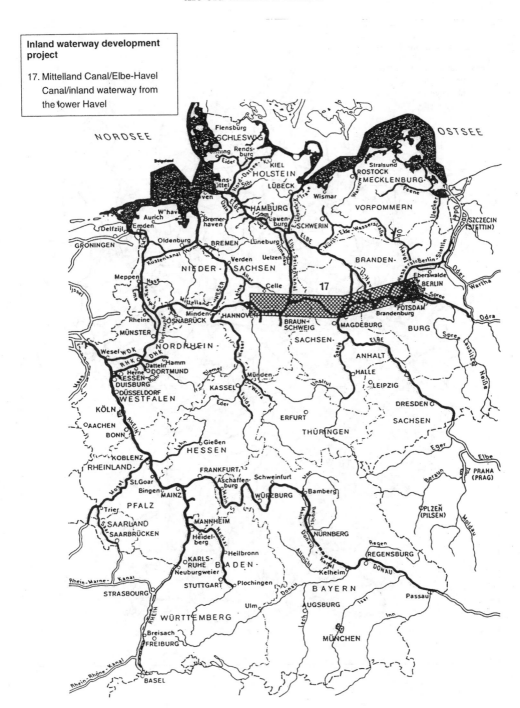

Inland waterway development project

17. Mittelland Canal/Elbe-Havel Canal/inland waterway from the lower Havel

Figure 9. **German road network**

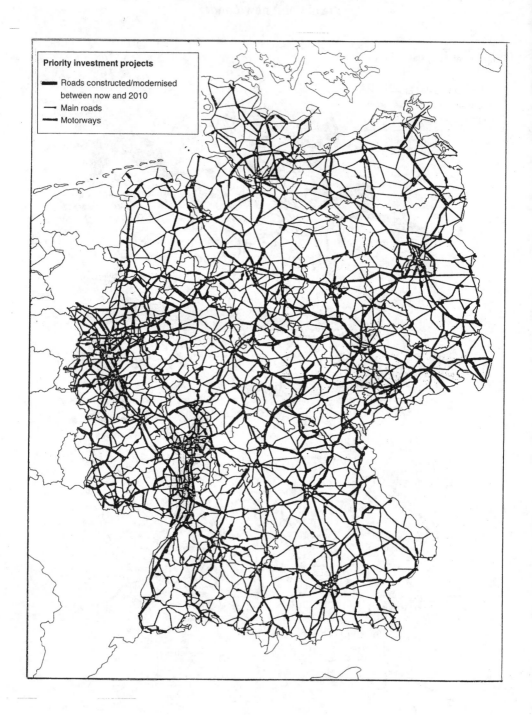

Figure 10. **German road network (detail)**

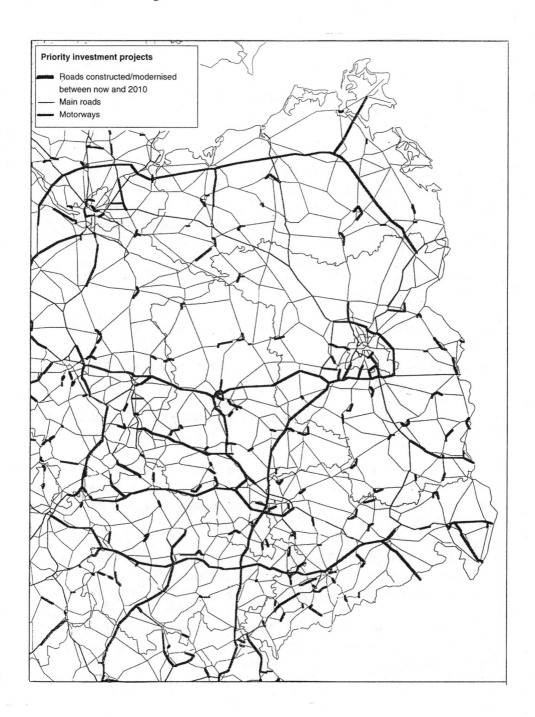

41

BIBLIOGRAPHY

Böttcher, H., R. Funck, J. Kowalski (1993), *"The New Europe: Political, Social and Economic Changes in Eastern European Countries and their Impacts on the Spatial Division of Labour"*, in: Hirotada Kohno, Peter Nijkamp (Eds.), Potential and Bottlenecks in Spatial Development, Springer Verlag, Berlin, pp. 89-107.

Deutsches Institut für Wirtschaftsforschung (1995), *Verkehr in Zahlen 1995*, Federal Ministry of Transport, Bonn, Berlin.

Federal Ministry of Transport (1991), *Verkehrsprojekte Deutsche Einheit*, Bonn.

Federal Ministry of Transport (1992), *Federal Transport Infrastructure Plan 1992*, Bonn, July.

Federal Ministry of Transport (1995), *Strassenbaubericht*, BT-Drucksache 13/2682, Bonn.

Funck, R., J. Kowalski (1987), *"Impact of transportation bottlenecks on production -- the Polish case"*, in: Tismer, J. *et al.* (Eds.), Transport and Economic Development -- Soviet Union and Eastern Europe, Duncker und Humblot, Berlin, pp. 292-305.

Funck, R., J. Kowalski (1989), *"Einige Thesen zur Bewertung von Ost-West Verkehrsprojekten"*, in: Verkehrskooperation in Ost und West. Proceedings of a Conference at the Technical University of Berlin, 9-10 March, pp. 103-118.

Funck, R., J. Kowalski (1995), *"Innovative behaviour, research and development activities and technology policies in the countries in Transition: the case of Central Europe"*, in: P. Nijkamp (Ed.), Innovative Behaviour and Spatial Structures.

Junkernheinrich, M., G. Heimpold, R. Skopp (1995), *"Der schwerige Weg Ostdeutschlands zur selbsttragenden Entwicklung"*, in: Wirtschaftsdienst, 1995, Vol. 7, pp. 359-365.

Kessel, P. *et al.* (1990), *"Szenario zur Verkehrsentwicklung mit der DDR und Osteuropa"*, Untersuchung im Auftrag des Bundesministers für Verkehr (FE-Nr. 98105/90), Bonn.

Kowalski, J. (1990), *"Privatisierungsstrategien in Polen: eine ordnungspolitische Aufgabe"*, in: Zeitschrift für öffentliche und gemeinwirtschaftliche Unternehmen, 1990, B.13, H.3, pp. 337-343.

Kowalski, J. (1991), *"Strukturdaten für die RGW-Länder und für Skandinavien, Ergebnisse zum Forschungsauftrag Verkehrsuntersuchung für Deutschland"*, IWW, Universität Karlsruhe.

Kowalski, J. (1993), *"Transport implications of German unification"*, in: Derek Hall (Ed.), Transport and Economic Development in the New Central and Eastern Europe, Belhaven, London, New York, pp. 82-92.

Kowalski, J. (1995), *"Wirtschaftsentwicklungen in Polen und die Chancen von westlichen Investoren"*, in: P. Friedrich, J.W. Tkaczynski (Eds.), Auslandsinvestitionen in Polen -- Chancen für Joint-Ventures, Berlin Verlag, Berlin, pp. 25-38.

Lipton, D., J. Sachs (1991), *"Privatisation in Eastern Europe: the Case of Poland"*, in: Brookings Papers on Economic Activity, 1, pp. 293-341.

(1995), *Luftverkehrsprognose für den Flughafen Dresden*, Endbericht, Arthur D. Little, MKmetric GmbH, IWW, July.

(1995), *Luftverkehrsprognose für den Flughafen Leipzig-Halle*, Arthur D. Little, MKmetric GmbH, IWW, July.

Rothengatter, W. and J. Kowalski (1991), *"Development prospects for European transport between East and West: Passenger transport"*, in: Prospects for East-West European Transport, ECMT, Paris, pp. 189-225.

Rothengatter, W. (1995), *"Szenarien für die Verkehrs- und Wirtschaftsentwicklung"*, in: Am Verkehrskollaps vorbei?, Technische Universität Berlin, Proceedings of the Conference 1 TUB - Verkehrstagung, 29 June, Berlin, pp. 37-44.

AUSTRIA

Gerd SAMMER
Institut für Verkehrswesen
Universität für Bodenkultur
Vienna
Austria

Jürgen HAMADER
Gerald PFEIFFER
Karl REITER
Forschungsgesellschaft Mobolität AMOR
Graz
Austria

SUMMARY

Vienna and Graz, June 1996

1. INTRODUCTION

1.1. General

Transport plays a major role in economic and environmental developments. In the transition from a planned to a market economy, such as the one now taking place in the former eastern bloc countries, many initiatives are being taken which will determine future developments. By means of government regulatory action, these countries have given precedence to public transport for both passengers and freight. Contrary to the situation in western industrialised countries, this has led to a very high market share for public transport. After the long phase of decline in public transport and growth in private road transport, western European countries are now trying, for ecological reasons, to reverse the trend by improving the share of public transport (by rail). An important question therefore has to be asked with regard to the transport sector in the European transition countries:

Can the eastern European countries benefit from the experience of western Europe and for ecological reasons avoid the downtrend in public transport?

This possibility should be considered even though it appears extremely unlikely in the light of developments in recent years. This report analyses the past transport trend in two transition countries, the Slovak Republic and the Czech Republic. Economic development scenarios are used to show the scope for development in the transport sector. The basis for this report is a study on the possibilities of improving energy efficiency in the transport field in the Slovak Republic and the Czech Republic. This study, commissioned by the Austrian Energy Utilisation Agency and the Austrian Environment Ministry in Vienna, was completed in 1994. The study findings were used by the Federal Austrian Government in its project to support the conversion of the energy sector in these two countries. The data used for the analysis therefore end with the year 1992. The forecasting period runs to the year 2011. When this report

49

was being prepared, it was checked how far the forecasts corresponded to the actual trend in the years 1993 and 1994. This check brought out the following points:

-- The volume of available transport statistics has become smaller since the separation into the Slovak and Czech Republics;
-- The data which are available show a good degree of correlation within the usual tolerance range for a forecast.

1.2. Basic data

The following should be noted with regard to the accuracy of the data used and the forecast results:

-- The basic data were compiled by Slovak and Czech experts. The problem emerged during compilation work that only a few key data were primary data. As was to be expected, the public transport sector provided the best material since it was exclusively controlled by government until 1989. Accordingly, the statistical records for rail and buses are extremely extensive although, as a result of the central planning system, many data cannot be seen as a reflection of reality. The focus was on achieving a target, and frequently the target was achieved in statistical terms if not in actual practice.
-- Forecasts are estimates that are difficult to make when conditions are stable. It is all the more difficult to forecast possible developments when countries are in a transition phase. This fact should be taken into account when interpreting the results.

1.3. Scope of the report

The transport demand data in this report refer to annual traffic and cover the following transport modes and types of traffic:

-- Passengers

  • Private motorised transport [private cars (PC) and motorcycles (MC)];
  • Bus transport;
  • Rail transport;

- Local urban public transport;
- Air and sea transport.

Although this report focuses on intercity transport, urban passenger transport has to be included for comparison and data requirements. Local urban public transport is therefore considered separately. Owing to the lack of other data, private motorised traffic was determined from the vehicle fleet so that it is not possible to differentiate between urban and intercity traffic.

-- Freight

- Road haulage;
- Rail transport;
- Air transport;
- Sea transport.

2. KEY DATA FOR TRANSPORT DEMAND

2.1. Car ownership

Car ownership has risen continually since 1975 and by a factor of five in the last twenty years. In the last two years, car ownership in the Slovak Republic has marked time.

As an important indicator for private transport, car ownership over the same period has risen from 74 cars per 1 000 inhabitants to 183 (Figure 2.1-1). It is interesting that no change in the trend has occurred in the early years of transition. The indicator started to mark time only in the last two years. The figure for the Czech Republic is about 30 per cent higher.

An international comparison of car ownership is given in Figure 2.1-2.

Figure 2.1-1. **Car ownership in the Slovak Republic and
the Czech Republic compared with Austria**

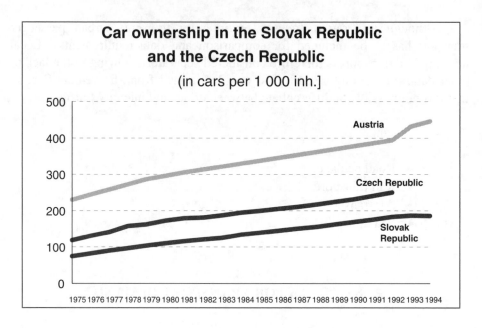

Figure 2.1-2. **Car ownership in 1991 for selected European countries**
(*Welt-Strassen-Statistik*, 1992)

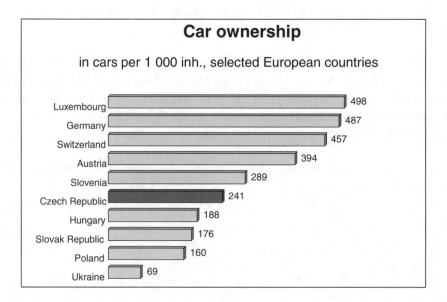

Average vehicle age in the Slovak Republic declined from 10.9 years in 1975 to 9.7 years in 1992. In Austria, the average vehicle age is about six years.

In the last ten years, the average annual distance travelled per car has been about 8 000 km and is therefore about 40 per cent lower than in western European countries.

Average car occupancy in the Slovak Republic decreased from 1975 (two occupants per journey) to 1.7 occupants per journey in 1992 and is gradually declining to the western European average (Austria 1.2).

2.2. Motorcycle ownership

After annual average growth of about 0.5 per cent, without any marked fluctuations from 1975 to 1988, motorcycle ownership has risen considerably since 1988, although growth has levelled off in the last few years (Figure 2.2-1).

Figure 2.2-1. **Motorcycle ownership in the Slovak Republic and the Czech Republic**

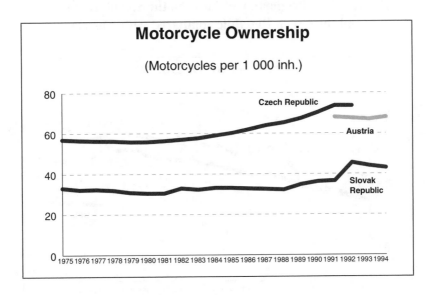

The value for Austria in 1991 has also been shown by way of comparison (67.2 motorcycles per 1 000 inhabitants). A wider comparison for Europe is given in Table 2.2-1.

Table 2.2.-1. **Motorcycle ownership in selected European countries in 1991** (*Welt-StraßenStatistik*, 1992)

Italy	121	Bulgaria	54	Poland	37
Switzerland	110	Germany	37	Hungary	36
Austria	67	Slovak Rep.	37	Slovenia	8

2.3. Proportion of buses (excluding urban public traffic)

The proportion of buses rose until 1990 and is now declining.

The very high proportion of buses compared with western countries can be explained by the objective of making it possible to reach any place with a public transport mode. This social policy goal is based on the ideological rejection of private car traffic and cannot be maintained in the future.

Figure 2.3-1. **Proportion of buses in the Slovak Republic and the Czech Republic compared with Austria**

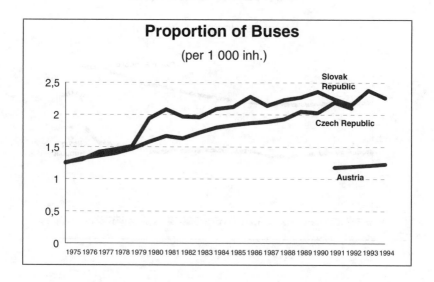

54

Figure 2.3-2 compares the traditionally high proportion of buses in the former eastern bloc countries with the situation in western European countries.

Figure 2.3-2. **Proportion of buses in selected European countries in 1991** (*Welt-Straßen-Statistik*, **1992**)

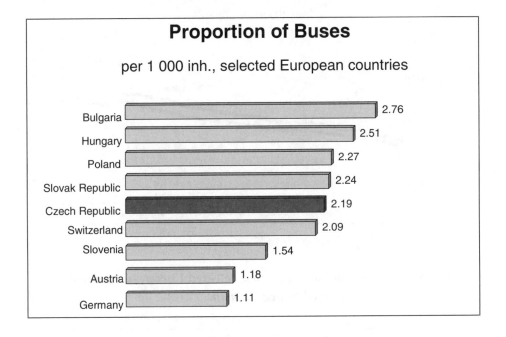

2.4. Proportion of lorries

Figure 2.4-1. **Proportion of lorries in the Slovak Republic and the Czech Republic**

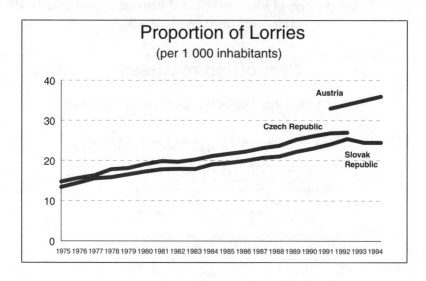

Figure 2.4-2. **Proportion of lorries, selected European countries, (*Welt-Straßen-Statistik*, 1992)**

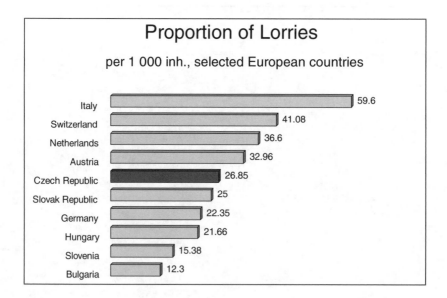

The proportion of lorries in the Slovak Republic amounted to 25 per 1 000 inhabitants in 1994, as compared with 33 in Austria. Most freight traffic has been traditionally carried by rail. However, marked shifts are to be expected in this area in the next few years. Figure 2.4-2 again gives a comparison with selected European countries.

3. KEY TRANSPORT INFRASTRUCTURE DATA (SLOVAK REPUBLIC)

3.1. Road network

The total length of the road network (Figure 3.1-1) in the Slovak Republic has not changed to any great extent in the last twenty years, although there has been an improvement in road categories.

Figure 3.1-1. **Slovak road network, 1975-92**

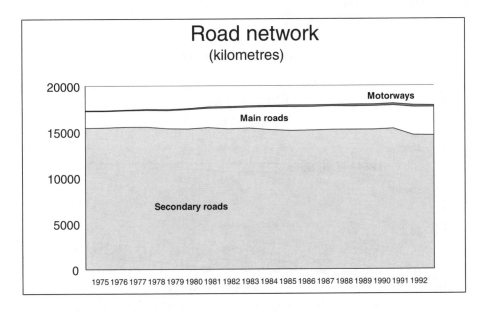

The road network has been upgraded almost exclusively by converting secondary roads into main roads. Although the motorway length has increased by a factor of 4, it is still only about 200 kilometres. The total network length amounted in 1992 to 17 855 km, as compared with about 105 000 km in Austria, which is roughly twice the size of the Slovak Republic. A limited increase to 18 274 km (up 2.3 per cent) is forecast for the next few years.

3.2. Rail and bus network (long-distance and regional transport)

There has been very little change in the total length of the rail network in the Slovak Republic in the last twenty years (Figure 3.2-1). However, it has been gradually electrified, with some 38 per cent of the network being converted by 1992. By comparison, about 55 per cent of Austria's network is electrified. The Slovak Republic's rail network was 3 661 kilometres long in 1992. According to a recent paper on the development of the Slovak rail network, there will be no new works before the year 2010. Owing to the poor financial situation, only extremely urgent maintenance and modernisation operations can be carried out in the next few years. The bus route network has been extended since 1975 by 2 per cent a year on average and in 1991 was 124 916 kilometres long.

Figure 3.2-1. **The Slovak Republic's rail network, 1975-92**

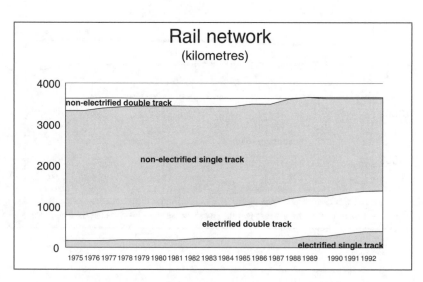

4. THE COST PICTURE IN THE TRANSPORT FIELD

4.1. Fares and freight rates

Public transport fares were not subject to any market or commercial pressures under the former centrally-planned economic system. Fares therefore remained unchanged in the twenty years to 1992. Fares for the various public transport modes are compared in Figure 4.1-1.

Figure 4.1-1. **Public transport fares in the Slovak Republic and the Czech Republic**

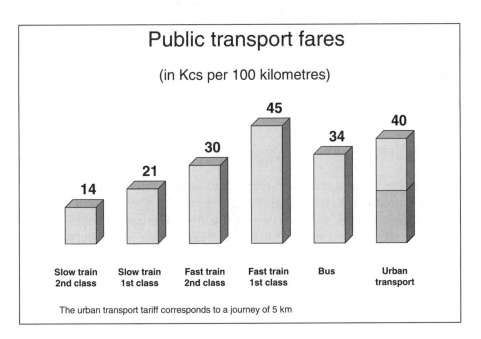

The only increase was in urban transport prices, which were doubled in 1990 (from Kcs 1 to 2 per journey).

Rates were also kept constant over a long period in freight transport, although ongoing adjustments have been made since 1984 (Figure 4.1-2). Rail freight rates have been deregulated since November 1993.

Figure 4.1-2. **Freight rates in the Slovak Republic and the Czech Republic**

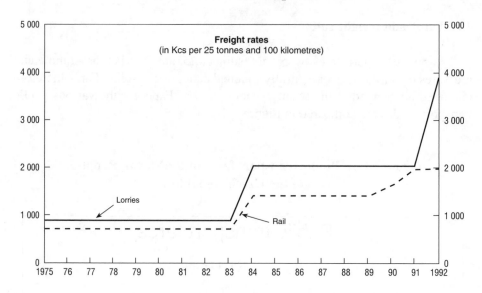

4.2. Energy and fuel prices

Under the planned economy, electricity and fuel prices were not geared to market and production costs. Figure 4.2-1 shows the price trend in the private and rail sectors. Prices did not rise to a level consistent with the market until about 1991. The fuel tax rate in 1992 was 55 per cent for petrol and 68 per cent for diesel.

Figure 4.2-1. **Electricity and fuel prices in the Slovak Republic
and the Czech Republic**

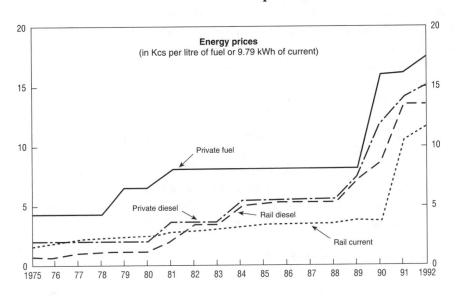

5. COMMENTS ON THE METHODOLOGY FOR FORECASTING THE TRAFFIC TREND

5.1. Scenario technique

The traffic trend forecast was based on an analysis of traffic data for the years 1971 to 1992. Another important input required for a transport forecast is usually an assessment of the economic trend. It was not possible to obtain an economic forecast exceeding a year for the Slovak Republic and the Czech Republic from either national sources or international organisations.

As a means of offsetting this problem to some extent, a three-scenario model, based on three different possible transport trends, was developed for the traffic forecast. The framework for the three scenarios is as follows: they describe the probable trend subject to three different kinds of basic economic conditions, assuming that currently unforeseeable government measures influencing the transport trend will not be taken. In other words, these three scenarios describe the transport and energy trends which should be seen if there is no marked change with regard to foreseeable transport policy and government measures. In principle, these three scenarios describe the transport trend that has been recorded in western Europe in the last twenty years. Since it is very difficult to foresee economic developments in the medium and long term, forecasts have also been worked out for the "prosperity" and "stagnation" variants as well as for the "reference" trend.

-- *"Reference" trend scenario*

This scenario, which from now on is referred to as the reference trend, is based on slow but steady economic growth in the Slovak Republic. It is marked by a gradual reversal in the next few years of the present downtrend in economic indicators and by subsequent moderate economic growth. In the case of car ownership, this scenario corresponds to a continuing uptrend.

-- *Extreme scenario I: "Prosperity"*

It is the most optimistic variant of economic development and is based on a rapid reversal of the pattern in the last few years. This economic prosperity is associated with economic growth that is already high in the next few years.

-- *Extreme scenario II: "Stagnation"*

This scenario is based on a continuation of the economic stagnation which started in 1989 and points to a long-lasting recession. In the stagnation scenario, an economic recovery is not to be expected in the next ten years.

The year 2011 has been selected as the target year for the forecast since comparable forecasts for this period are available in other countries. The most important sources used for comparisons were the transport trends in the last fifty years and the forecast data for them up to the year 2011 in Austria and other western European countries.

5.2. Procedure

The forecasts were worked out separately for passengers and freight on the basis of the breakdown for vehicle types and transport modes defined in Section 1.3. In relation to transport modes, they were constructed in hierarchical form, as shown in Figure 5.2-1.

Two different models were used for the forecasts for both passengers and freight. Figure 5.2-1 shows the bottom-up procedure used for all transport modes in which vehicle ownership or numbers is a key indicator. This mainly applies to private transport modes such as private cars, motorcycles or lorries. Taking private cars as an example, this figure shows the input data and the various steps leading to the result. Total data, such as passenger-km performed or total energy consumption, were brought in for control purposes or calibration of the system.

Taking into account the shares in traffic performed already obtained from the bottom-up forecast, the share of the remaining modes was determined in the top-down method by means of a forecast for total passenger and goods traffic performed. This is illustrated by Figure 5.2-2, using bus transport as an example.

Figure 5.2-1. **Bottom-up forecasting model with private car traffic as an example**

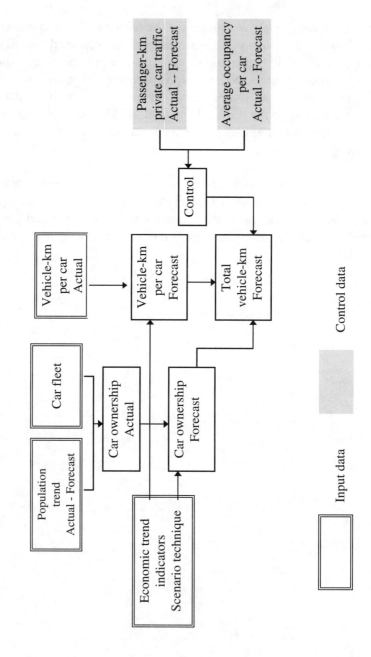

Figure 5.2-2. **Top-down forecasting model with the bus as an example**

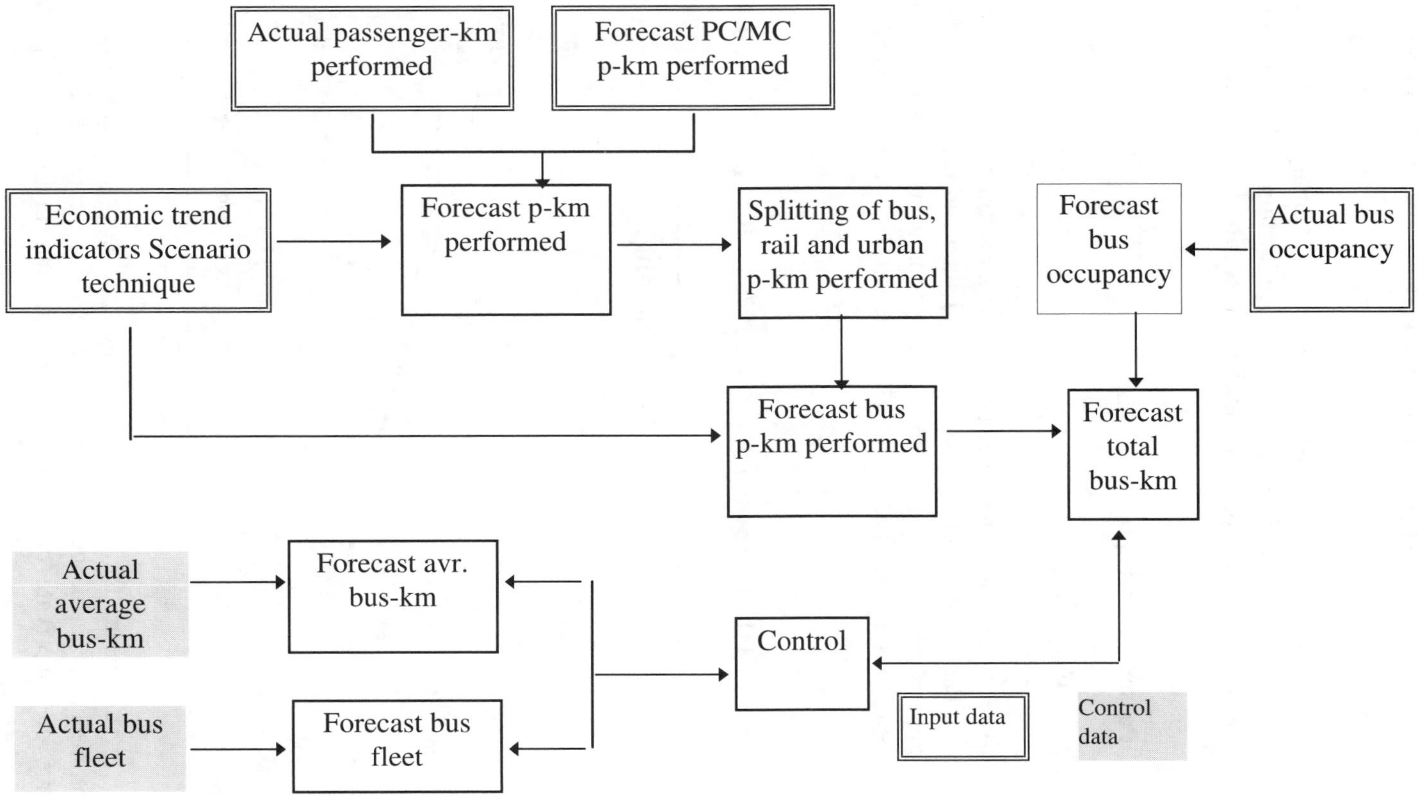

6. ANALYSIS RESULTS AND FORECAST FOR THE TRAFFIC TREND IN THE SLOVAK REPUBLIC

For reasons of space, the detailed transport analysis and forecast results are given by using the Slovak Republic as an example. The overall results for the Czech Republic are provided in the next section.

6.1. Passenger transport

6.1.1. Private cars

The starting point for forecasting private car traffic is car ownership. The trend in car ownership is similar worldwide and can therefore be forecast with the greatest reliability. The trend corresponds to a saturation curve in which the peak is specific to a country and depends on topographical, social and economic factors.

Figure 6.1.1-1. **Car ownership from 1975 to 2011 in the Slovak Republic**

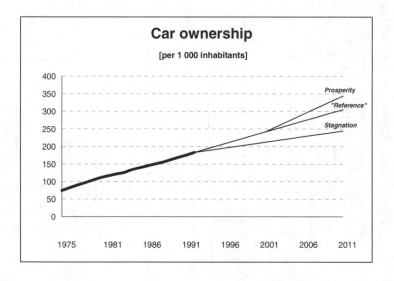

At present, there are 183 private cars per 1 000 inhabitants. In the reference scenario, the trend since 1971 will continue with an annual increase rate of 6.4 private cars/1 000 inhabitants and in 2011 reaches a level of

66

305 cars/1 000 inhabitants, or roughly that of Austria in 1981. In the stagnation scenario half the previous increase rate is assumed (3.2 cars per 1 000 inhabitants a year). The prosperity scenario corresponds to the reference trend up to the year 2001 and then keeps to the same annual increase rate as Austria (10.3 cars/1 000 inhabitants per year) (Sammer, 1989). The values for the year 2011 are therefore 244 cars/1 000 inhabitants (this value corresponds to that of Austria for 1976) or 344 cars/1 000 inhabitants (the value for Austria in the year 1986). The figure shows that a decline towards the saturation point in the Slovak Republic does not occur by the year 2011. This point is to be expected at about 500 cars/1 000 inhabitants.

Annual vehicle-km and annual passenger-km for private cars can be worked out from car ownership on the basis of population numbers, average annual vehicle-km and average car occupancy.

In all three scenarios, an increase in total vehicle-km is to be expected. It ranges from 45 per cent with the stagnation trend to 240 per cent with the prosperity trend up to the year 2011.

Figure 6.1.1-2. **Total private car-km from 1975 to 2011 in the Slovak Republic**

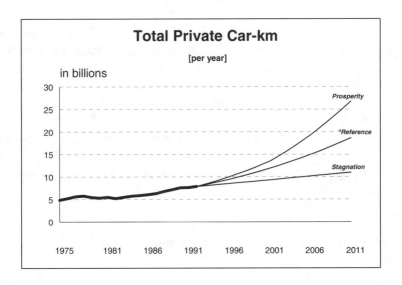

67

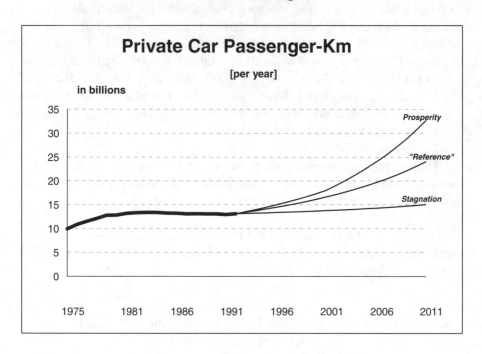

Smaller increase rates (stagnation + 16 per cent, reference trend + 85 per cent, prosperity + 150 per cent) are to be expected for passenger-km than for kilometres performed. This is to be explained by the marked decline in occupancy, for which the trend is closely connected with car ownership. This means that, without taking improved engine technology into account, several factors contribute simultaneously to increased emissions and energy consumption in private car traffic. Wider car availability (car ownership) does not only have a marked influence in this respect, but also leads to higher average mileages and lower occupancy, which again raise the energy and consumption levels.

Table 6.1.1-4 summarises all the key transport data:

Table 6.1.1.-4. **Trends in key data for private cars in the Slovak Republic**

	Scenario	1981	1991	2001	2011
Car ownership	Prosperity			241	344
(cars/1 000 inh.)	Reference	116	176	241	305
	Stagnation			212	244
Fleet	Prosperity			1 305 000	1 911 000
	Reference	583 982	929 118	1 305 000	1 694 000
	Stagnation			1 149 000	1 356 000
Avr. annual	Prosperity			10 300	14 000
vehicle-km	Reference	9 412	8 200	9 100	11 000
	Stagnation			8 100	8 100
Total annual	Prosperity			13.4m	26.8m
vehicle-km	Reference	5.50m	7.62m	11.9m	18.6m
	Stagnation			9.3m	11.0m
Occupancy	Prosperity			1.34	1.22
(travellers/car)	Reference	2.40	1.70	1.40	1.29
	Stagnation			1.48	1.37
Annual	Prosperity			18.0m	32.6m
passenger-km	Reference	13.19m	12.95m	16.6m	24.0m
	Stagnation			13.8m	15.0m

6.1.2. *Motorcyles*

The starting point is, again, vehicle ownership which is closely connected with car ownership (Figure 7.1.2-1). Growth is to be expected up to a certain level of car ownership, although subsequently it will level off or even decline. In the Slovak Republic, however, growth in all three scenarios is to be expected up to the year 2011, as the comparative saturation values for western countries are higher.

Motorcycle ownership will double from about the year 1991 to the year 2011 (reference trend) and its growth figures will still exceed those for the private car.

Figure 6.1.2-1.   **Motorcycle ownership from 1975 to 2011
in the Slovak Republic**

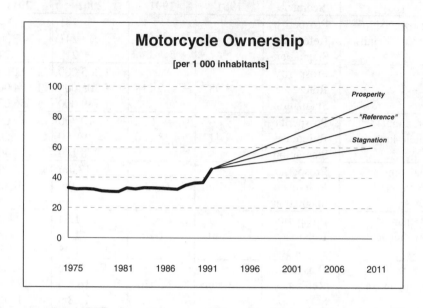

Figure 6.1.2-2.   **Total motorcycle-km from 1975 to 2011
in the Slovak Republic**

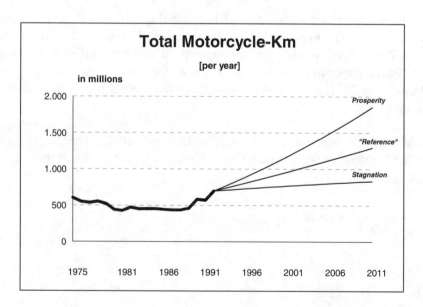

In the reference scenario, total motorcycle-km will rise by a factor of 1.5 up to the year 2011 (stagnation 45 per cent, prosperity 250 per cent) as a result of the steep increase in the fleet and in the rise in average distance travelled.

Table 6.1.2-1. **Trend in key data for motorcycles in the Slovak Republic**

	Scenario	1981	1991	2001	2011
Ownership (motorcycles/ 1 000 inh.)	Prosperity			66.6	90.0
	Reference	30.5	36.6	59.5	75.0
	Stagnation			52.4	60.0
Fleet	Prosperity			361 000	501 000
	Reference	153 750	193 744	323 000	417 000
	Stagnation			284 000	334 000
Avr. vehicle-km (per year)	Prosperity			3 270	3 700
	Reference	2 787	2 958	3 000	3 100
	Stagnation			2 700	2 500
Total vehicle-km (per year)	Prosperity			1 180m	1 850m
	Reference	428m	573m	965m	1 290m
	Stagnation			770m	834m
Occupancy (traveller/vehicle)	Forecast	1.2	1.0	1.1	1.1
Passenger-km (per year)	Prosperity			1 300m	2 040m
	Reference	490m	580m	1 060m	1 420m
	Stagnation			850m	920m

6.1.3. *Buses (excluding urban public traffic)*

The top-down model was used for bus traffic. Starting from a forecast for total passenger-km performed, the share of bus transport was estimated from comparative values for other countries on the basis of vehicle numbers (Figure 6.1.3-1). In the prosperity scenario, bus passenger-km declines faster than in the reference and stagnation scenarios.

Figure 6.1.3-1. **Bus passenger-km from 1975 to 2011 in the Slovak Republic**

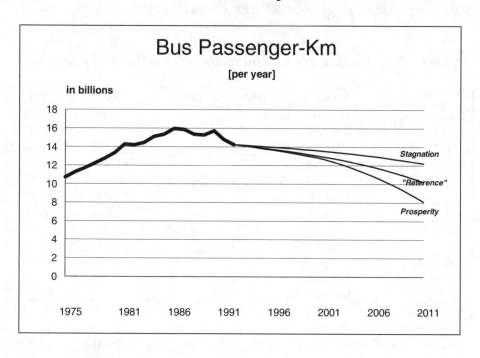

In the centrally-planned system, public transport was governed by the ideal of catering for the entire population. The Slovak Republic therefore still has a dense bus network, since every Slovak citizen should have access to public transport. The decline in bus passenger-km already started in 1989 with the collapse of the old government order. This trend will continue up to 2011, but it will vary with the economic situation. The fall will be between 18 per cent (stagnation scenario) and 45 per cent (prosperity scenario) as compared with 31 per cent in the reference scenario.

Total bus-km will keep to much the same trend as bus passenger-km, but with a lower range of reductions owing to changing occupancy rates.

Figure 6.1.3-2. **Total bus-km performed from 1975 to 2011 in the Slovak Republic**

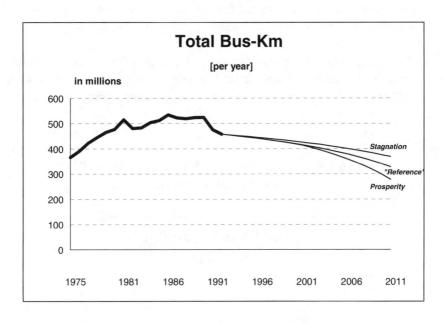

Table 6.1.3-1. **Trend in key bus transport data for the Slovak Republic**

	Scenario	1981	1991	2001	2011
Number of buses (per 1 000 inh.)	Prosperity			1.91	1.25
	Reference	2.08	2.24	1.91	1.47
	Stagnation			1.96	1.65
Fleet	Prosperity			10 357	6 949
	Reference	10 482	11 857	10 385	8 188
	Stagnation			10 646	9 202
Avr. bus-km (per year)	Forecast	49 129	40 096	40 000	40 000
Total bus-km (per year)	Prosperity			415m	278m
	Reference	515m	475m	416m	328m
	Stagnation			426m	368m
Occupancy (travellers/buses)	Prosperity			30.6	29.1
	Reference	27.95	31.13	31.1	31.1
	Stagnation			31.8	33.1
Bus pass.-km (per year)	Prosperity			12.7b	8.1b
	Reference	14.3b	14.8b	13.0b	10.2b
	Stagnation			13.5b	12.2b

6.1.4. Rail transport

As in bus transport, the forecast for rail started with passenger-km. This was again derived from forecast total passenger-km (Figure 6.1.4-1).

Rail passenger-km also falls sharply up to the year 2011. In the reference trend scenario, the decline which started in 1989 continues until 2011 with a fall of 28 per cent (stagnation scenario 15 per cent, prosperity scenario 42 per cent).

Figure 6.1.4-1. **Rail passenger-km from 1975 to 2011 in the Slovak Republic**

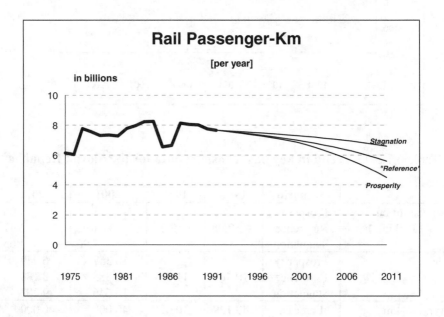

Table 6.1.4-1. **Trend in key data for rail passenger transport in the Slovak Republic**

	Scenario	1981	1991	2001	2011
Avr. electric locomotive-km [per year]	Forecast	171 879	155 103	152 000	145 000
Avr. diesel locomotive-km [per year]	Forecast	109 299	104 372	96 000	92 000
Occupancy electric [travellers/train]	Prosperity			261	192
	Reference	312.23	286.33	265	226
	Stagnation			272	254
Occupancy diesel [travellers/train]	Prosperity			127	93
	Reference	148.74	139.01	129	110
	Stagnation			132	124
Passenger-km [per year]	Prosperity			6.86b	4.5b
	Reference	7.273b	7.746b	6.99b	5.6b
	Stagnation			7.30b	6.6b

6.1.5. Urban public transport

Although this report is not concerned with local public transport, the results for this activity are given in this section to permit comparisons and complete the picture.

Urban public transport comprises all public urban transport modes -- trams, buses and trolley-buses. Owing to its great flexibility when the network is to be adjusted, either by extending or reducing it (no additional road infrastructure is required), the diesel bus is mainly behind all changes. The results for non-motorised traffic are not included because of the lack of basic data.

Annual passenger-km is derived from the forecast for total passenger-km and is given in Figure 6.1.5-1.

Figure 6.1.5-1. **Urban passenger-km performed from 1975 to 2011
in the Slovak Republic**

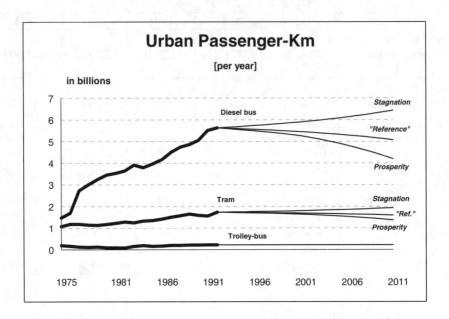

The bus accounted for 41 per cent of urban public passenger-km in 1991. Since 1975, the bus network had been greatly developed while, relatively speaking, only small increases in bus and tram passenger-km performed were recorded. Up to the year 2011, the trend in urban public transport will vary with the economic situation. While traffic performed declines by 5 per cent in the reference scenario, it rises by almost 20 per cent in the stagnation scenario. Urban public transport is not subject to the same laws as the other forms of public transport and depends closely on population and settlement structures.

The trend in the occupancy of the three urban public transport modes is similar to that for national bus transport. The changes expected in the settlement structure are mainly responsible for the occupancy trend. In the prosperity scenario, municipalities mainly expand in the transitional zone between town and region, where private transport obviously plays a greater role than public transport. In the stagnation scenario, a higher settlement density and lower car ownership have the opposite effect and raise the occupancy level.

The resulting total vehicle-km performed is shown in Figure 6.1.5-2. In the trend scenario, total vehicle-km will decrease by 5 per cent, almost entirely as a result of the decline in bus transport.

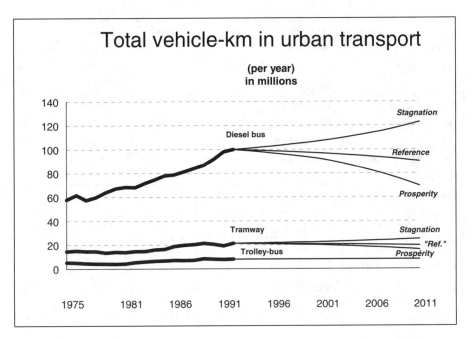

The trends in key data for urban public transport are given in Table 6.1.5-1. The actual position of the trolley-bus has been extrapolated since it plays only a very minor role.

Table 6.1.5-1. **Trend in key data for urban public transport in the Slovak Republic**

	Scenario	1981	1991	2001	2011
Total bus-km [per year]	Prosperity			91.9m	69.5m
	Reference	68.5m	97.8m	96.8m	90.1m
	Stagnation			107.3m	123.0m
Total tram-km [per year]	Prosperity			20.0m	16.0m
	Reference	13.8m	19.2m	21.0m	20.0m
	Stagnation			23.0m	25.0m
Total trolley-bus km [per year]	Forecast	4.29m	7.78m	8.1m	8.1m
Bus occupancy [occupants/bus]	Prosperity			57.3	60.3
	Reference	51.49	56.27	56.3	56.3
	Stagnation			55.0	52.3
Tram occupancy [occupants/tram]	Prosperity			82.6	85.6
	Reference	86.04	81.58	81.6	81.6
	Stagnation			80.3	77.6
Trolley-bus occupancy [occupants/trolley]	Forecast	22.55	28.26	28.3	28.3
Bus p-km [per year]	Prosperity			5.269m	4.194m
	Reference	3.526m	5.506m	5.450m	5.074m
	Stagnation			5.898m	6.434m
Tram p-km [per year]	Prosperity			1.646m	1.377m
	Reference	1.227m	1.564m	1.692m	1.597m
	Stagnation			1.803m	1.937m
Trolley-bus p-km [per year]	Forecast	96.8m	219.7m	229m	229m

6.1.6.   Air transport

Air traffic includes both the Slovak Republic's domestic and international traffic. In air transport, the forecast was derived from the volume of passenger traffic (Figure 6.1.6-1). The starting point for the exercise was a forecast up to the year 2010, which was worked out by the Zilina Transport Research Institute and included an optimistic and a pessimistic variant.

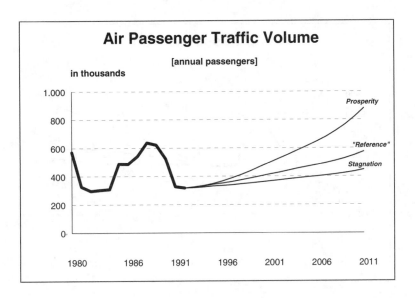

Following the steep fall in traffic volume after 1988, a rapid recovery is to be expected in the future. The level of passenger traffic of the late 1980s, however, will no longer be achieved in the reference trend scenario up to 2011.

Owing to the declining average stage length, passenger-km will rise more slowly than passenger numbers and in 2011, according to the reference trend scenario, will be 25 per cent under the 1988 peak but up considerably from today's level.

Figure 6.1.6-2. **The Slovak Republic's air passenger-km
from 1975 to 2011 (domestic and international traffic)**

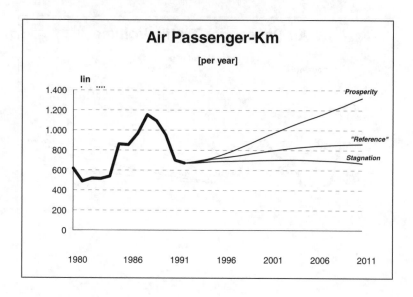

Table 6.1.6-1. **Trend in key air passenger traffic data for
the Slovak Republic (domestic and international traffic)**

	Scenario	1981	1991	2001	2011
Passenger numbers [passengers/year]	Prosperity			496 000	879 000
	Reference	326 000	326 000	413 000	574 000
	Stagnation			365 000	446 000
Average stage length [km/flight]	Forecast	1 491	2 144	1 900	1 500
Passenger-km [per year]	Prosperity			950m	1 320m
	Reference	486m	699m	790m	860m
	Stagnation			700m	670m

6.1.7.   Sea transport

Sea transport accounts for about 0.3 per mille of total passenger-km.
Since this current marginal contribution to traffic is expected to last, there was
no point in making a detailed forecast for sea transport. The present situation
has simply been extrapolated for the calculation of total results.

6.1.8. Total passenger traffic

Figure 6.1.8-1. **Trend in p-km and increase rates in the Slovak Republic**

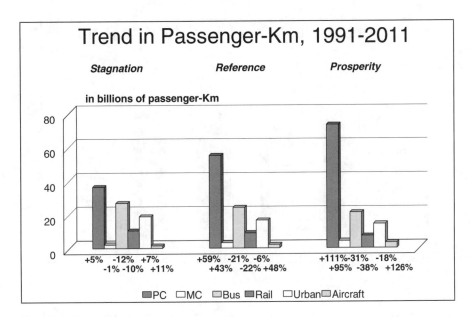

Marked passenger-km increases are to be expected for both private cars and motorcycles. In the reference trend scenario, this means that today's traffic will be roughly doubled by the year 2011. By contrast, marked decreases are to be expected for public transport modes. In the reference trend scenario, bus traffic is down by 31 per cent and rail traffic by 28 per cent. Much smaller decreases are only to be expected in urban public transport (reference trend minus 5 per cent). An increase is even forecast in the stagnation scenario.

Figure 6.1.8-2 shows the trend in total passenger-km up to the year 2011.

Figure 6.1.8-2. **Trend in total passenger-km in the Slovak Republic**

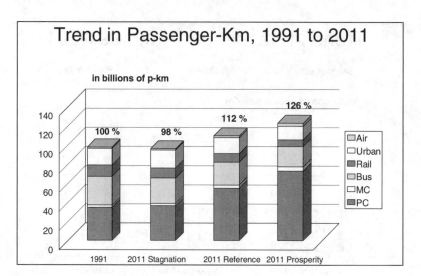

In the stagnation scenario, there is no increase in passenger-km performed by 2011, although structural changes are to be expected. A trend can be seen towards the replacement of public by private transport modes. It is most apparent in the prosperity scenario, although passenger-km rise by "only" about a quarter. Here, the close connection between economic development and private transport becomes clear. Although the share of private transport (private car + motorcycle) in total passenger-km was still 31 per cent in 1991, it is already up to 52 per cent in the year 2011 in the reference trend scenario (36 per cent in the stagnation scenario and 65 per cent in the prosperity scenario).

6.2. Freight transport

6.2.1.   Lorries

Figure 6.2.1-1. **Total lorry-km from 1975 to 2011 in the Slovak Republic**

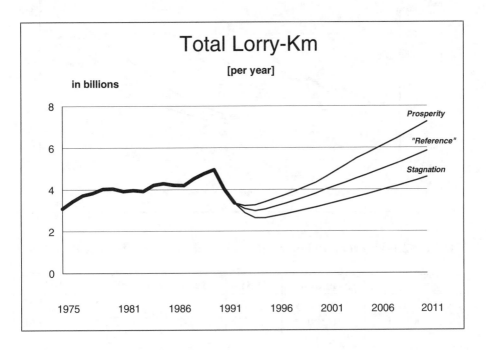

Following a downtrend lasting until about 1994, total lorry-km is expected to rise to 5.8 billion kilometres by 2011 in the reference trend scenario. This value exceeds the 1990 peak by 18 per cent (decrease of 8 per cent in the stagnation scenario and an increase of over 46 per cent in the prosperity scenario).

The trend in the freight load was also forecast so that traffic in tonne-kilometres (6.2.1-2) could be calculated. After the steep decline since 1989, it is expected that the freight load will again rise to the 1989 level by the year 2011 (2.58 t per lorry). The downtrend in tonne-km is also expected to be reversed by 1994 and to exceed the 1989 level by 2011 in the reference trend scenario. All the key data for lorry transport are given in Table 6.2.1-1.

Figure 6.2.1-2. **Lorry t-km from 1975 to 2011 in the Slovak Republic**

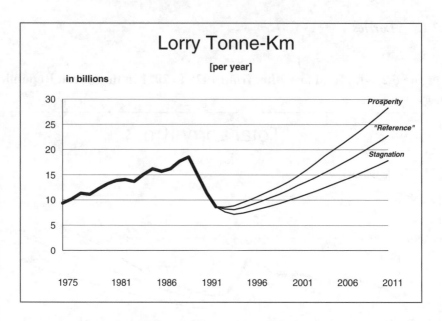

Table 6.2.1-1. **Trend in key road haulage data for the Slovak Republic**

	Scenario	1981	1991	2001	2011
No. of lorries	Prosperity			34.4	40.7
[per 1 000 inh.]	Reference	17.84	24.1	32.8	37.6
	Stagnation			29.7	34.4
	Prosperity			187 000	226 000
Lorry fleet	Reference	89 858	127 467	178 000	209 000
	Stagnation			161 000	191 000
Avr. lorry-km	Prosperity			24 700	32 000
[per year]	Reference	43 653	31 584	22 500	28 000
	Stagnation			20 400	24 000
Total lorry-km	Prosperity			4.6b	7.2b
[per year]	Reference	3.92b	4.03b	4.0b	5.8b
	Stagnation			3.3b	4.6b
Freight load [t/lorry]	Forecast	3.54	2.83	3.2	3.9
Lorry t-km	Prosperity			14.8b	28.2b
[per year]	Reference	13.89b	11.38b	12.9b	22.8b
	Stagnation			10.5b	17.9b

6.2.2. *Rail*

The first step in forecasting rail freight traffic was to work out an overall forecast for freight tonne-km performed by using the results obtained for lorry traffic. The starting point in this exercise was the modal split for freight. It was assumed that by the year 2011 the present modal split into 20 per cent road and 80 per cent rail would be equivalent to that of Austria (Herry, 1990) -- 45 per cent road and 55 per cent rail. On this basis, it was then possible to work out rail tonne-kms (Figure 6.2.2-1).

Figure 6.2.2-1. **Rail tonne-km from 1975 to 2011 in the Slovak Republic**

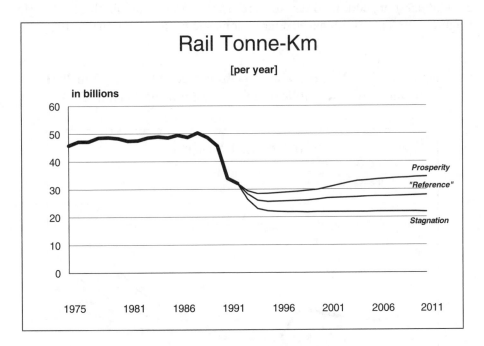

In the case of rail t-km, there will be no return to the peak values of the 1980s. In the reference trend scenario, the level will probably decline further until 1995 before rising slightly to 27.8 billion tonne-kilometres by the year 2011. An important reason for this decline is also to be seen in the probable structural change in freight transport (less bulk freight). The key data are given in Table 6.2.2-1.

Table 6.2.2-1. **Trend in key rail freight data for the Slovak Republic**

	Scenario	1981	1991	2001	2011
Traffic performed [t-km/year]	Prosperity			30.7b	34.5b
	Reference	47.3b	33.9b	26.7b	27.9b
	Stagnation			21.8b	21.9b

6.2.3. *Air transport*

A freight volume forecast by the Zilina Research Institute was used in the case of air transport in order to forecast the trend for all three scenarios (Figure 6.2.3-1). The tonnages refer to domestic plus international traffic.

Figure 6.2.3-1. **Volume of air freight recorded from 1975 to 2011 by the Slovak Republic (domestic and international traffic)**

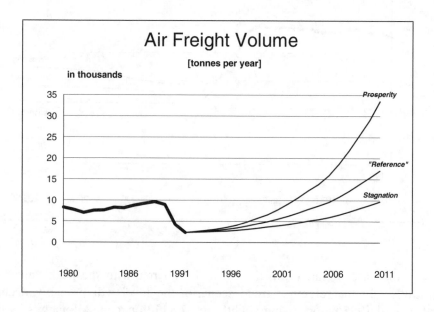

In the reference trend scenario, the volume of freight rises by a factor of 4 from 1991 to 2011 (by a factor of 8 in the prosperity scenario, an increase of 130 per cent in the stagnation scenario).

Using the average stage length, which is assumed to be constant at 3 100 km, it is possible to calculate freight tonne-km (Figure 6.2.3-2). With constant stage lengths in the next twenty years, the increases correspond to the tonnage increases. Table 6.2.3-1 gives all the key data for air freight.

Figure 6.2.3-2. **Air freight t-km recorded from 1975 to 2011 by the Slovak Republic (domestic plus international traffic)**

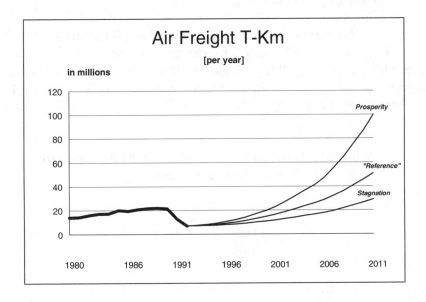

Table 6.2.3-1. **Trend in key air freight data for the Slovak Republic (domestic plus international traffic)**

	Scenario	1981	1991	2001	2011
Freight volume [t/year]	Prosperity			7 700	33 500
	Reference	7 778	4 210	5 500	17 000
	Stagnation			3 900	9 700
Average stage length [km/flight]	Forecast	1 846	2 982	3 000	3 000
Freight t-km [per year]	Prosperity			23.0m	99.9m
	Reference	14.4m	12.6m	16.5m	50.8m
	Stagnation			11.8m	28.9m

6.2.4. Sea transport

In 1991, sea transport accounted for 5 per cent of total freight traffic performed. Since, in practice, this share will not change greatly in the next twenty years, it was considered pointless to work out a detailed forecast for sea freight. The values for the year 1991 were extrapolated for the total calculation.

6.2.5. Freight traffic results

Figure 6.2.5-1 shows the trend in t-km performed for all freight transport modes. The picture is similar to that for passenger transport. Road traffic will expand, while rail traffic will fall. But the most impressive increase rates are to be expected in air transport. In the reference trend scenario, lorry traffic is doubled and air traffic rises by a factor of 4, while rail is down by 18 per cent.

Figure 6.2.5-1. **Trend in freight traffic and its increase rates in the Slovak Republic**

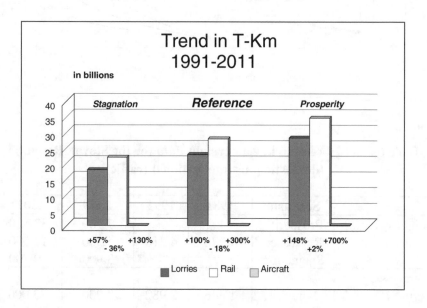

Figure 6.2.5-2. **Trend in the total freight traffic of the Slovak Republic**

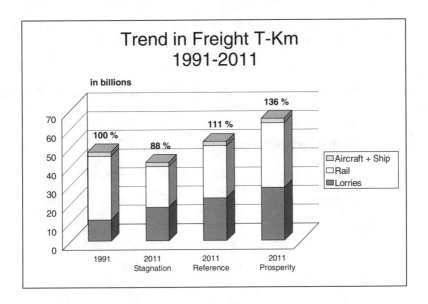

Figure 6.2.5-2 shows the trend in total freight t-km. In freight transport, total growth rates are more dependent on the economic trend than in passenger transport. In the stagnation scenario traffic performed falls to 88 per cent compared with the year 1991. In the reference trend scenario traffic performed rises by 11 per cent as in passenger transport. A marked shift from rail to road transport is to be expected. Although rail in 1991 still accounted for 71 per cent of traffic, its share in 2011 is only 53 per cent.

7. RESULTS FOR THE TOTAL TRAFFIC TREND IN THE CZECH REPUBLIC

7.1. Passenger transport

Figure 7.1-1 shows the increase rates for the various transport modes from 1991 for all three scenarios. Marked increases in traffic performed are to be expected for the two private modes (PC and MC) and for air transport. In the reference trend scenario, this means an increase of some 50 per cent compared with current passenger-km. By contrast, sharp falls can be expected for public transport modes. In the reference trend scenario, bus traffic is down by 21 per cent and rail traffic by 22 per cent. Only in urban public transport are considerably smaller decreases to be expected (reference trend: -6 per cent). An increase is even to be foreseen for the stagnation scenario.

Figure 7.1-1. **Trend in passenger traffic performed in the Czech Republic**

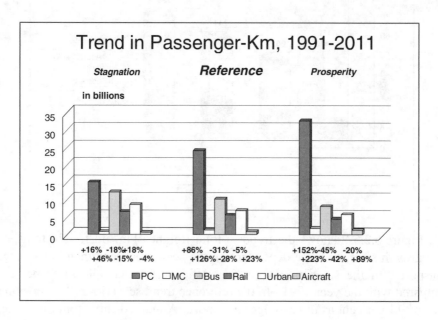

Figure 7.1-2 shows the place of each transport mode vertically and total passenger-km performed up to the year 2011. In the stagnation scenario, there is no increase in passenger-km by that year, although structural changes are to be expected. There is movement towards the replacement of public transport by private transport modes. This trend is the most obvious in the prosperity scenario, although passenger-km are up by "only" about a quarter. Here, the close connection between economic development and private transport becomes apparent. Although the share of private transport in total passenger-km (car + motorcycle) was still 38 per cent in 1992, it is expected to be 53 per cent in the year 2011 in the reference trend scenario (40 per cent in the stagnation scenario, 63 per cent in the prosperity scenario).

Figure 7.1-2. **Trend in the passenger-km of the Czech Republic**

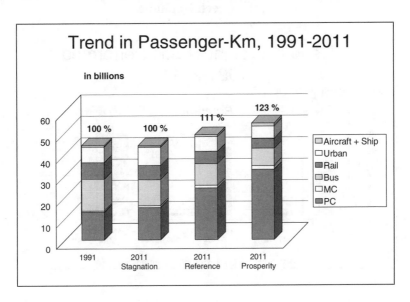

7.2. Freight transport

Figure 7.2-1 shows the trend in freight t-km performed by all transport modes. The results are similar to those for passenger transport. Road traffic will increase and rail traffic will be compressed. But the most impressive increase rates are to be expected in air transport. In the reference trend scenario, lorry traffic rises by about 86 per cent and air traffic by a factor of 4, while rail is down by 39 per cent and sea traffic declines slightly (decrease from 1991 to 1992).

Figure 7.2-1. **Trend in freight t-km and their increase rates in the Czech Republic**

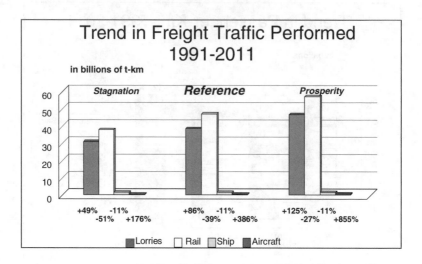

Figure 7.2-2. **Trend in the freight traffic of the Czech Republic**

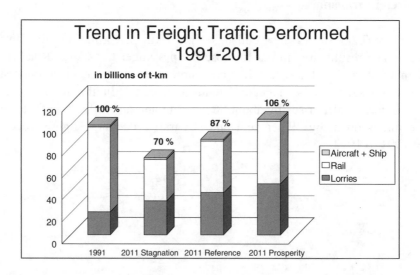

Figure 7.2-2 shows the trend in total freight t-km and its structure. In freight transport growth rates depend more closely on economic development than in passenger transport. In the stagnation scenario, traffic

performed falls to 70 per cent compared with the year 1991. In the reference trend scenario, traffic declines by 13 per cent and rises only in the prosperity scenario, by 6 per cent. A marked shift from rail to road transport is to be expected. Although the share of rail in traffic performed was 78 per cent in 1992, it is only 52 per cent in 2011 in the reference trend scenario.

8. FINAL COMMENTS

8.1. Comparison of results

A comparison of traffic peformed by transport mode in the Czech Republic, the Slovak Republic and Austria, which is taken as an example of a highly-developed European country, leads to the following conclusions:

-- So far, public transport has played the main role in transport activity in the Slovak Republic and the Czech Republic;
-- Rail has predominated in the freight field;
-- Sharp increases in private transport and marked declines in public transport are to be expected up to the year 2011;
-- The marked development of road transport will result in a steep increase in environmental degradation, accidents and fuel consumption in these countries if it is not checked;
-- The forecast trend is already underway.

Figure 8.1-1. **Passenger-km performed
(excluding non-motorised transport)**

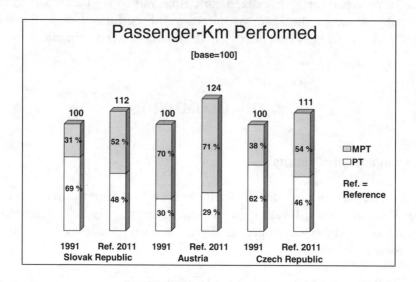

Figure 8.1-2. **Freight t-km performed
(excluding aircraft and pipelines)**

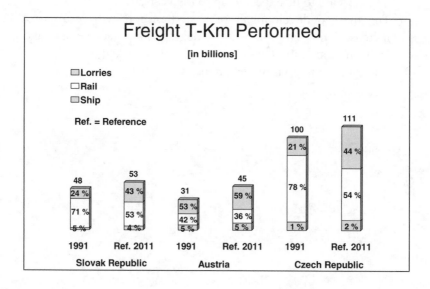

8.2. Conclusions

The findings of this report show that transport is also in a phase of radical change in the former eastern bloc countries. The trend is away from a centrally-planned policy which gave precedence to government-regulated public transport and rail transport over private transport and road transport, and towards one giving precedence to road transport. This trend is due to the removal of restrictions on the creation of private transport undertakings, the abolition of subsidies for public transport and the promotion of investment in road development while, at the same time, public rail transport is being starved of finance and not being restructured in any way. Despite the cost of fuel, which is high considering the population's income, this trend is leading to the situation which we have experienced in the last thirty years in western European countries.

If this transport trend, which is also being countered in western countries, is to be avoided for environmental and transport policy reasons with the aim of setting up an economically and ecologically efficient transport sector, the following strategies should be recommended:

-- Traffic limitation strategies (without endangering necessary economic growth);
-- Stabilization strategies ranging from traffic transfer strategies to environment-friendly and energy-efficient transport modes;
-- Improvement of vehicle energy efficiency and a reduction in environmental degradation through new technologies and driver behaviour.

For financial as well as for political reasons, it is not possible to introduce all the measures by means of the instruments described below immediately and at a single stroke. The following two arrays of measures are therefore recommended:

-- "Immediate measures" comprise all those which should be the most effective without being very costly;
-- "Development measures" cover those areas which are either costly or are based on politically unpopular decisions and therefore involve a longer discussion process. The timeframe for these measures should begin today, but ranges from the medium to the long term.

These two arrays of measures could modify the response to the question asked and answered in Section 1.1.

8.2.1. *"Immediate measures"*

"Immediate measures" are mainly intended to stabilize the actual situation with regard to the modal split. In order to attenuate the environmentally undesirable trend in transport revealed by forecasts, a few measures are needed which should be implemented rapidly, do not destroy existing structures and serve as a run-up to many other measures and instruments.

The policy of flexible adjustment was included as the second criterion for the selection of immediate measures. Owing to the need for speedy implementation, immediate measures should be handled with the required flexibility and not create a prejudicial scenario, as may be done by all kinds of development action.

The limited financial cost of immediate measures was selected as the third criterion. Owing to a tight central government budget, cost restraint is a must for municipalities and transport undertakings.

"Immediate measures" consist of the following components:

Component 1:   Encouraging awareness and providing information

Objective: Encourage awareness of the need for an energy-efficient and environment-friendly system, prepare a positive climate for decisions, drive home the environmental connection in the minds of decisionmakers and citizens so that private cars will be used in a way compatible with the environment.

It is possible to change attitudes to transport and environmental protection, improve acceptance of unpopular measures and influence behaviour in the long term through public relations work that heightens awareness, i.e. through measures for the "mind" (e.g. specialised surveys on environmental protection in the transport field, planning of public awareness programmes, training and briefing sessions, instruction in schools, training of mobility advisers).

Component 2: **Increased regulation of car parks and making public transport attractive**

Short-term objective: Stabilize the current modal split between public and private transport.

With its still extensive capacity, public transport should be made more attractive through immediate action to reduce further shifts from public transport to private modes. Such measures comprise municipal and regional transport plans, maintaining the important role of public transport, speeding it up and making it more attractive, giving it priority over transport by car, restrictive measures against private cars and motorcycles, regulating parking space, etc.

The proceeds from car park operation should also be used for funding. This instrument has already been adopted in some eastern European countries and, when used consistently, can produce considerable financial resources that should be earmarked for additional measures. The privatisation of car park management is, however, imperative.

Component 3: **Reorganisation of rail and local public transport**

Objective: Adjust the type of organisation to a management system meeting today's needs and to new types of funding.

The present structure of public transport undertakings must be converted to a privately-managed system. At the same time, a new type of funding is urgently needed for modernisation purposes. Privatisation models are also to be discussed in this connection.   If restructuring is not successful, competitiveness with regard to road transport can in no way be maintained.

Component 4: **Incorporating energy-savings goals and environmental protection in urban and regional planning**

Short-term objective: Safeguard public transport's existing chances.

Urban and regional planning is one of the most important inputs in transport and settlement policy. Its importance is illustrated by the chances which have been missed in western European countries, where public transport structures have been counter-productive owing to regional planning deficiencies. This component covers the definition of objectives in regional planning laws and development programme planning.

8.2.2. *"Development measures"*

Development measures are recommended as medium- and long-term measures for which the preparatory phase should be started at the present time. First, as they require an often high financial outlay, their speedy implementation at present is hardly feasible. Second, the need for their discussion with the population, which must be properly planned beforehand, is obviously an obstacle to immediate implementation.

These measures also consist of components:

Component 5: Improvement of public transport infrastructure and rolling stock

Objective: Make public transport and rail freight more competitive.

The development of transport infrastructure and of modern rolling stock is one of the costliest but also one of the most advantageous operations from the economic policy viewpoint. Infrastructure is to be seen not only as track, but also its stations, stops and technical equipment, in other words, as an overall plan for long-distance public transport which is to be made more attractive, speeded up and given priority over transport by private car.

Component 6: Balanced improvement of road infrastructure

Objective: Improve road infrastructure while maintaining the competitiveness of rail.

Taking environmental protection into account, road infrastructure should be developed, particularly where there is no or little possibility of developing rail. Strong competition from rail corridors should be avoided.

Component 7:   Organisational measures

Objective: Exploit existing potential for organisational measures.

In the case of measures to heighten awareness, organisational measures also belong to the "software" category.   By intelligently planning basic transport conditions, costly "hardware" can in many cases be avoided, for example, by using traffic regulations to reduce speeds to 100/80/50/30 km/h, stepping up speed-limit enforcement on roads, speeding up public transport, giving priority over car traffic (brief-interval timetables, sophisticated types of operation) and taking measures concerning private cars and motorcycles (driving and access restrictions, efficient use of cars).

Component 8:   Combined freight traffic and intercity logistics

Objective: Orderly development of freight transport.

The present trend towards small carriers operating obsolete vehicles is counter-productive from the environmental and energy policy viewpoints.   In addition to improving the quality of rail freight, the development of a modern combined transport system, which has been declared a major area of research by the EU, would be a good start to a new integrated freight transport system for the countries in transition.

BIBLIOGRAPHY

Hamader, Pfeiffer, Reiter, Sammer *et al.* (1994), *Möglichkeiten der Energieeffizienzsteigerung in der Slowakischen Republik, Bereich Verkehr;* im Auftrag der Energieverwertungsagentur und des Umweltministeriums (study carried out on behalf of the Austrian Energy Agency and Ministry of the Environment), Vienna.

Hamader, Pfeiffer, Reiter, Sammer *et al.* (1994), *Möglichkeiten der Energieeffizienzsteigerung in der Tschechischen Republik, Bereich Verkehr:* im Auftrag der Energieverwertungsagentur und des Umweltministeriums (study carried out on behalf of the Austrian Energy Agency and Ministry of the Environment), Vienna.

Sammer G., K. Fallast, .R. Lamminger, G. Röschel, T. Schwaninger (1990), *Mobilität in Österreich 1983-2011;* Herausgeber ÖAMTC, Vienna.

FRANCE

Gautier CHATELUS
INREST-DEST
Arcueil
France

SUMMARY

Arcueil, August 1996

1. INTRODUCTION

The transport sector in central Europe has seen radical changes in recent years. These have followed and sometimes preceded economic developments but, in any case, reflect the transition underway. As a sector supporting the economy, transport has a crucial role to play in this transition. Changes are underway in the sector at every level. Broadly speaking, the very nature of mobility has altered, with changes in the pattern of flows, the reasons for travelling and the role of transport itself. At the same time, the economic system has been transformed. The former planned economies -- which were based on integrated relations and monopolistic principles, on both the domestic front and in the international division of labour within the eastern bloc's foreign trade grouping, the CMEA -- have been opened up extensively to a much more competitive system in which the marketplace has replaced planning. Even if the microeconomic transformation is by no means over, the new economic rules governing the economy have been adopted in most sectors. The very structure of the economy and the type of production are changing, thereby modifying the type of goods carried.

Accordingly, there has been a change in what the economy and society expect of the transport system. Like the economy in general, the transport sector has moved from an integrated, supply-driven, goal-oriented system to a decentralised system driven by demand. The choice of trade relations quantities and destinations and the actual type of goods (and therefore of transport demand) are no longer dictated by planning but by the market. In the same way, the choice of a transport mode is no longer subject to goal-oriented policy rules but rather to market laws, with the customer selecting the carrier offering the best service at the lowest price.

Unlike freight, passenger transport was considered non-productive until 1990. It was, therefore, a consumer good which did not have priority over a production good. The market for this consumer good was therefore regulated by scarcity, which resulted in priority for freight and public transport and in

105

particular a very limited number of private cars. Here again, there has been a turnaround in the situation in 1996, since the passenger transport market is now regulated by prices and is marked by a steep increase in demand for personal mobility.

These comprehensive changes in transport demand have occurred in a context of deep economic recession which has had a considerable effect on total demand for both freight transport (marked reduction in volumes) and passenger transport (decrease in daily mobility as a result of unemployment, cuts in personal transport budgets).

At the microeconomic level, the transition involves the reorganisation of business enterprises, the break-up of monopolistic conglomerates and the more or less gradual privatisation and restructuring of transport undertakings. There has been a radical change in the organisation of the sector and the role played by the various actors. Like the undertakings themselves, the institutional environment has to adapt to a new context. The hard budget constraints typical of market economies have mostly replaced the soft constraints of undertakings which were more concerned with maximising their turnover than their profit. Transport undertakings must therefore adjust to a new context, requiring them to seek profits in an environment that has become extremely competitive within modes (excluding rail) and especially between modes.

In this report we try to analyse in detail the recent trend in the transport market in central Europe and to see how the transition is reflected in the transport field. The report is in several parts. After a general review of the economic situation in the last two years in central Europe, we shall evaluate the overall trend in mobility by analysing passenger and freight traffic by mode. We shall then consider a number of key factors in these developments: the trend in international flows, growth in combined transport and changes in vehicle fleet.

2. ECONOMIC AND POLITICAL DEVELOPMENTS IN CENTRAL EUROPE

2.1. The deep recession following the collapse of the planned economies

The Central European Countries (CECs) have been in a very deep recession since 1989. The standard macroeconomic indicators have greatly deteriorated, as seen particularly in the early transition period. Initially, between 1989 and 1992-93, inflation in central Europe soared to close on or over 100 per cent (sometimes with hyperinflation peaks at over 1 000 per cent) and then GDP fell by 20 per cent or more as industrial output plummeted (by 30 to 60 per cent); unemployment, starting from an official rate of almost zero, has risen a little more slowly within four or five years to levels close on or exceeding those of the European Union (between 10 and 18 per cent). This trend started a couple of years later in the countries of the former Yugoslavia (affected by war) and in the Baltic States (see Table 1 and recapitulative tables in Annex 1).

These free-falling macroeconomic indicators mainly reflect the disintegration of the planned economy as markets are opened up to competition and the emphasis in the economy is redirected from the supply to the demand side. Accordingly, prices rise as long as supply is not adjusted to demand, while no customers can be found for primary goods, resulting in a sudden drop in industrial output and GDP. Older firms then have to adapt by restructuring, cutting their wage bills or in some cases opting for privatisation. As the last solution takes longer, unemployment rises less quickly.

The various countries have embarked on in-depth institutional reforms to initiate and back up this radical change in the economy and society. At policy level, these reforms are resulting in a more democratic form of public life and, at the economic level, in the adoption and implementation of open-market and adjustment policies. These policies are mainly intended to open up the market for goods and services and financial markets, liberalise foreign trade, provide a legal basis for private activities and restructure or prepare enterprises for privatisation. The aim is to carry out these different policies while at the same time maintaining economic stability, which can be done only by maintaining a minimum amount of equilibrium in the key sectors of the economy. In particular, this means that government intervention in the welfare and public service fields has to be reviewed in order to limit public spending. Some budgetary restraint has therefore had to be applied (with varying stringency and success), particularly in the countries with a heavy foreign debt -- which is the case of most of them, with the notable exception of the Czech and Slovak Republics.

Table 1. **ECONOMIC DEVELOPMENTS IN THE CEECs**
1989 (91) = 100

Bulgaria	Romania	Slovenia	Estonia
Hungary	Russia	Czech Republic	Latvia
Poland	Slovak Republic	Croatia	Lithuania

GDP trend   Industrial output trend

Source: Deutsche Bank Research Review.

2.2. Stabilization and recovery in 1994-95: end of the first transition phase

After this very deep recession, the period 1994-95 was one of stability or even marked economic recovery for the CECs. GDP growth in all countries was flat or positive (2 to 6 per cent), hyperinflation was brought under control everywhere and inflation (although higher than in the European Union) was reduced to reasonable levels, usually to between 8 and 25 per cent. Industrial output stabilized and even picked up considerably in some countries (excluding the Baltic States). Unemployment levelled off at between 8 and 14 per cent, with a reduction in rates in countries where it had been highest and a continuous rise in those where the adjustment had started later. The main exception as regards unemployment is the Czech Republic, which still seems to have a very low rate (4 per cent).

Democracy has become the rule almost everywhere, as reflected in several countries by the first multi-party elections (often won by offshoots of the former communist parties). At the institutional level, the first wave of major reforms seems to be over and the focus is now more on finalising the implementation of the institutional provisions for the new economic system.

It therefore does seem that the first stage in the transition process has been reached (or completed in the Czech Republic, Poland and Hungary, which were even admitted to the OECD in 1996). The obsolete part of the former system's macroeconomic legacy seems to have been eliminated.

2.3. Varying prospects for the CEECs

It now remains to be seen how far this transition has gone at microeconomic level, within enterprises and in which new direction the various countries are heading. A number of possibilities are open. Firstly, which system will be adopted: all-out liberalism (as in the United States), the social liberalism more typical of western Europe, or a more interventionist and protectionist government system, as has been the case in the South-East Asian countries? Other systems, perhaps specific to the region, might also emerge from this transition.

Another question is how successful this transition will be, for although many economists consider that the CEECs' development will be in the form of a U or J curve, nothing is really certain and the strong growth which should follow the period of recession and stabilization will not be automatic, especially in the context of global economic difficulties and increased competition between the different parts of the world. It is possible to anticipate substantial growth buoyed by the prospects of European integration, as was the case of Spain in the 1980s (with growth peaks alternating with periods of stagnation). But it is also possible to envisage very fragile growth which could be very soon reversed, as has happened in some Latin American countries. Lastly, it is not to be ruled out either that some countries will stay in a downward spiral of economic recession and political unrest and will simply not manage to put the adjustment phase behind them[1].

Even if the tendency is to view the transition process as a uniform whole, it can be expected to take increasingly different forms in the various countries. It now seems clear that all countries will not develop in the same way. The initial situation was already quite different from one country to another (even if the basic aim was to break with the centrally-planned economy and become integrated in the world economy)[2]. But the approaches taken by the countries further accentuate the differences, particularly as regards the rate of reforms, their depth, the level of social protection and the degree of government intervention to be maintained, etc. The macroeconomic results differ in the same way.

Moreover, these macroeconomic data must be treated carefully, since they are not very precise, owing to the volume of unofficial economic activities. The figures provided by the economic research bodies are thus adjusted regularly and substantially, sometimes several years after the period to which they refer. In addition, in transition periods, macroeconomic aggregates conceal microeconomic trends and complex, varied institutional and social changes. Indirect measurements and less quantitative appraisals are therefore sometimes useful for obtaining a more detailed view of the actual situation.

Lastly, although the economic aspect is often seen as the most important, the social acceptability of the transition process is increasingly becoming one of the main factors in policy options, as shown by the return to power of the former communist parties in a number of countries. It is now clear that everybody will not benefit to the same extent from the change in political systems. A number of major values (such as democracy, freedom of speech and movement, etc.) are certainly to everybody's benefit, but society as a whole is now affected by other negative developments, such as violence or job insecurity. But the main threat to societies is the increase in inequalities (which are now highly visible). In countries nurtured for forty years or more on the egalitarian myth, it is all the more difficult to accept that some gain a great deal from the transition process while others may lose out. In particular, the rise in unemployment combined with the decline in community services and welfare standards is a cause for discontent, as is the adjustment of the cost of basic necessities to world prices. It is then very difficult to have drastic austerity measures accepted and fully implemented[3], as shown by the Hungarian plan of 1995 for fiscal consolidation. As in the European Union, this ambiguity is reflected in the treatment of public transport, which has very high deficits and costs but is vital in social terms.

Moreover, as the transition process is having quite different effects within one and the same country, regional and local inequalities are becoming very pronounced. While in most capitals the trend is very positive as a result of the new private economy and foreign investment, the situation is quite different in other regions. The industrial structure in certain areas where the economy was geared exclusively to one heavy industrial enterprise (which controlled sub-contracting, the social services, etc.) is turning them into stricken zones because of the bankruptcy threat to the enterprise, whose output is usually not adapted to the new economic system. At the other end of the regional spectrum, some border regions are recording spectacular informal economic growth, owing to their geographical position. Activity will then be in the form of sub-contracting work for richer neighbours (Germany, Austria) or will be based on the service and trading activities encouraged by differences in living standards and prices on either side of the borders[4]. These differences are due to very different levels of openness of the economy and of taxes and customs duties. A vast number of cross-border journeys are therefore being recorded (over 220 million involving Poland in 1994), which are, to a large extent, connected with this transborder trade (often informal). This heterogeneity is quite obviously reflected in the transport sector with, for example, a huge increase in car ownership in major towns, whereas in some regions mobility is declining as a result of the population's relative impoverishment and the rising prices of the various transport modes. Freight transport is also developing in the same way, mirroring closely the changes in the economic system.

2.4. Still far to go towards restructuring and privatisation

But it is especially at the microeconomic level that one has to look in order to understand the mechanisms underway more clearly and to analyse the results to be expected of them. An analysis of the structural changes in the economy makes it possible to identify the problems which are still to be resolved and understand the general trend in the various countries. It will then be possible to draw conclusions on the present trend in total transport demand and on developments in this market. Such an analysis also gives a more detailed picture of the changes affecting firms, their trade relations, their production and therefore their transport needs. When applied to transport undertakings themselves, this procedure makes it possible to focus on their development and see how the sector is adapting to the new situation.

Although the transition process is proceeding rapidly, it is now starting to enter the second phase, in which obsolete government enterprises with heavy deficits have to be restructured. An initial improvement in macroeconomic structures has led to the formation of a real market, the creation of many new private enterprises and the overhaul of the most profitable existing enterprises. But a problem that often remains is the complete restructuring of the major industrial conglomerates, which requires the injection of new capital and especially a substantial reduction in the wage bill if normal profitability standards are to be achieved. Privatisation has usually been the approach used to tackle this problem and speed up the transition process. All countries are endeavouring to privatise, in various ways, including direct sales, take-overs by employees and the distribution of vouchers (shares) to the public[5,6]. But when large, inefficient enterprises are to be denationalised, either by selling them off (assuming a purchaser can be found) or by employee buyouts or mass privatisation (in which case there is no real owner or injection of new capital), the restructuring problem remains. Restructuring operations, business wind-ups and redundancies are therefore still required, even in countries which now seem to be finding their feet, such as Poland and the Czech Republic.

Transport undertakings are in the same situation. This sector is, in fact, quite representative of the changes underway and the difficulties which still have to be resolved. The transport field in the planned economies was traditionally based on major National State Enterprises (NSEs) which controlled entire sectors and also on large lorry fleets integrated within industrial enterprises for own-account, short-distance transport. The opening-up of the economy has resulted in a number of developments. In road transport, this was seen in the great number of very small private undertakings (one to two lorries) which suddenly sprang up. Their fragmented structure is typical of the development of a new private sector in the economy. But these undertakings are still very weak, not ready to compete with foreign operators and very poorly co-ordinated. The next step in the transition process for these undertakings will therefore be to establish themselves by creating alliances and by adopting a more suitable institutional framework, which in many cases is being set up.

The main approach in the case of major national road transport undertakings has been to split them up into regional or specialised entities (the PKS in Poland broken up into over 140 undertakings and Volan in Hungary into over 60). But even when this is done, it is difficult to find private purchasers, especially in the public passenger transport field. Other undertakings have been completely dismantled by selling the vehicles to their drivers (as in Romania). However, international road haulage NSEs have often been kept as they are, with the aim of privatising them (Hungarocamion is up for sale, Somat in Bulgaria sold to the German operator, Vili-Betz, etc.)

Restructuring the other modes is much more difficult, particularly as regards the railways, where overmanning is rife and on the increase with the decline in traffic. It is therefore still very difficult to reorganise and privatise rail (as is the case of firms in the not very competitive heavy industrial sectors). Lastly, owing to the strategic importance attached to certain modes and to air transport in particular, governments try to keep a minimum stake in them when they are put up for sale.

The diversity of these situations reflects fairly well the progressive restructuring at microeconomic level, with the emergence of a real private sector which has to be consolidated, the privatisation of a few major national enterprises by selling them to foreign investors and major restructuring difficulties for unprofitable public enterprises.

2.5. Regional integration

A major objective for CECs is regional integration, which will have a considerable impact on economic development but also on the main international transport flows. The main issue for these countries is their association with -- and subsequently integration in -- the European Union, which has endorsed this ambition. The impact of this association will be seen not only in traffic flows but also in the economic structure of the countries concerned. They will have to adapt to European standards and rules. Markets will be harmonized and opened up completely to international competition. This also requires infrastructure improvements in central Europe so that needs similar to those in the EU can be met.

But, as has been said, closer regional integration at central European level is also essential and the countries in the region are trying to strengthen their co-operation. Three major groupings stand out: one in the North around the Baltic (supported by the Scandinavian countries in the EU), one in the South around the Black Sea (encouraged by Turkey and incorporating the Caucasian States) and, on a more formal basis, one in the centre with the creation of the Central European Free Trade Agreement (CEFTA), which is aimed at setting up a free trade zone in 1997 for Poland, the Czech and Slovak Republics, Hungary and, more recently, Slovenia. Although these alliances have little impact in terms of total trade (for trade relations between the countries concerned are quite limited), they do give the possibility of taking a joint approach to a number of regional problems and, in particular, to the organisation of transport (especially combined transport). They also contribute to progress towards the harmonization and standardization of rules[7].

Two or three groups of countries can be defined. There are the Baltic States, whose main characteristic is that they were part of the former USSR and therefore have to reconstruct their national economies on a more autonomous basis. These countries are, however, still very close to Russia, which remains their leading and indeed a vital trading partner. To the West, these countries turn especially to Scandinavia and Germany as natural partners around the Baltic. In their case, the transition did not really start until about 1991.

The other countries, which from now on we shall refer to as the CECs are those which were not an integral part of the USSR. Even if some of them came into being as a result of secessions (from Yugoslavia and Czechoslovakia), they turn more naturally to the West as a result of their central position. Moreover, they started their transition in 1989-90 with economies that were less dependent on the Soviet bloc. Of these CECs, it is possible to single out the CEFTA countries (Poland, Hungary, the Czech and Slovak Republics and Slovenia), which seem to have made greater progress in their reforms and economic development.

3. TRANSPORT MARKET TRENDS

The transition in the transport field is taking place in this context of very rapid change followed by relative stability (against a backdrop of austerity measures) in the socioeconomic situation. When the overall figures for mobility in central Europe are analysed, they suggest that this mobility is on the same curve as the economic trend, i.e. that traffic is stabilizing following a general decline in the early years of transition. The shift in trade relations is resulting in a marked change in the direction of traffic flows and, as a result of the market being opened up, the share of road transport is rising.

3.1. Unreliability of statistics

Before going any further with the analysis of transport markets in central Europe, the recurrent problem of the availability and reliability of statistics must be stressed. This weakness of the statistical system does not apply only to the transport field but to economic data as a whole. Broadly speaking, it can be said that the bulk of statistics under the former regime was provided by the national enterprises, which often held monopolies on specific markets. These enterprises produced the figures which were used to draw up national statistics.

Since 1989, this system has collapsed with the opening-up of economies, which very soon led to the development of a new private sector and eliminated monopolies. Moreover, the purpose of statistics and therefore the information to be obtained and the main aggregates to be measured are no longer the same. A new system for the compilation and processing of statistics has therefore to be created. But this is a difficult task requiring new resources in a critical budgetary context. In addition, the difficulty of this task is compounded by the informal sector, which may account for 30 to 40 per cent of economic activity in certain countries.

These problems were identified quite soon in central Europe (the subject comes up regularly in the *Economic Bulletin for Europe*, published by the UN/ECE[8] and has been stressed since 1990-91 in the case of the transport field[9]). Solutions have been proposed[10], but no serious steps have yet been taken at regional level and only a few countries provide quite a full range of data. The Czech Republic has just set up a complete statistical system (1995) and Hungary has always provided quite a full range of data. The statistics for Poland and Bulgaria are also quite exhaustive. But, owing to the lack of resources, surveys are often unsatisfactory and to a large extent the statistics are more in the form of estimates than figures actually recorded. In particular, it is difficult to obtain data on the traffic of major infrastructure systems and their reliability is often doubtful, as is the case of aggregate figures for the transport of passengers by private car and road haulage on own account. The figures for road haulage for hire or reward may also be approximate in many cases, owing to the volume of informal activity.

3.2. Trend in mobility in central Europe and the Baltic States

As we have said, it is difficult to give a real analysis of flows, in particular passenger flows, owing to the lack of data. We can, however, identify some trends. Generally speaking, the curve showing the slump in traffic carried (both passengers and freight) at the start of the transition period is tending to level off as the economy stabilizes (see Table 2 and Annex 2).

Table 2. **FREIGHT CARRIED**
1989 = 100 (t-km)

Source: ECMT.

3.2.1. Slump in freight traffic

The sharp downtrend in freight is therefore levelling off in almost every country. There was even a marked recovery in Poland, the Czech Republic and Romania as well in 1994. It is, in fact, only in Lithuania that total traffic carried is still declining. The pick-up in traffic therefore closely reflects the economic recovery.

116

--   *Despite the fall, the traffic carried/GDP ratio is still high.*

However, traffic carried (t-km) per $ of GDP (according to the ECMT[11] and the World Bank[12]) is still much higher than in countries of the European Union (such as France), despite a marked improvement in ratios (cf. Table 3 and Annex 2). Although the figures given cannot be considered extremely accurate, they do reflect a high freight transport rate.

A number of explanations can be given for this fact. First, the GDP of the countries concerned is low in absolute terms and does not necessarily reflect the actual standard of living and the level of industrial ouput. The ratios are therefore obviously higher (see Annex 2). Second, the economic structure of the countries concerned is still greatly influenced by intermediate and heavy industrial production. In fact, in trade with the European Union (see below), the average weight per unit value of exports from the CEECs is far higher than that of their imports, which does reflect the fact that their products tend to have a lower value added[13].

Table 3.   **T-KM PER $ OF GDP, FRANCE = 1**

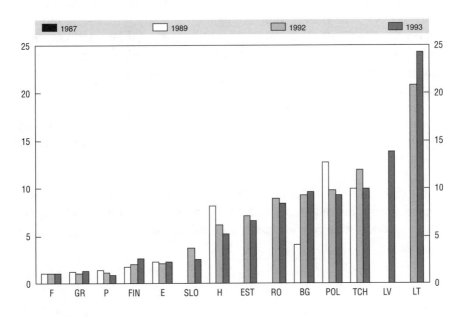

Source: ECMT, World Bank.

117

Moreover, some countries have a transit role which obviously accentuates their transport activity. But, as we shall see, the volume of this transit traffic is, to some extent, overestimated in most CECs. The Baltic countries, however, have a very important transit role, as shown by the activity of the main ports, where 80 to 90 per cent of traffic is in transit to or from the CIS (see below). Overall, therefore, the volume of transport activity is out of proportion to the economic activity of the countries handling this transit traffic.

Another more direct reason for this high ratio is the low productivity of transport. This low productivity, which is mainly seen in road haulage, can be explained as follows. First, as has already been stressed, the market is extremely fragmented and its structures are still shaky. Second, information on the possibilities of freight (in particular, return freight) is often inadequate since the transport intermediary sector has not been sufficiently developed (especially in the case of domestic freight), while on international markets, the carriers of the CEECs do not have easy access to return freight in third countries. Accordingly, lorry load factors are lower than in the European Union. For example, a traffic survey[14] on the Via Baltica in 1992 showed that over 20 per cent of lorries run empty on this major international corridor.

The low transport productivity is also connected with the structure of the fleet (see below). The fleet is in poor condition -- many vehicles are more than ten years old. Above all, its structure is not adapted to current demand, since it was inherited from the former centrally-planned economic system. Under this system, the supply of utility vehicles was mainly geared to the production of medium-sized lorries (taking loads of 3 to 5 tonnes), to the detriment of heavier lorries (in particular semi-trailer or light utility vehicles[15,16]. This category of intermediate vehicles is therefore overrepresented, which means that only a small part of their capacity is used or a number of vehicles are needed to carry a single consignment.

Lastly, in the rail field, the fall in traffic carried without the railway companies being restructured no doubt contributes to low productivity in freight transport as trains are not run at their full capacity.

--   A shift in the modal split to the detriment of rail

With regard to the modal split, ECMT data show a sharp fall in rail traffic in central Europe in general, although rail has kept high shares in the Baltic countries and Croatia. While the fall in rail traffic and market shares in central Europe is an established fact and seems inevitable up to a certain point, the results for the Baltic countries and Croatia call for some explanation.

In every case, the reliability of road traffic statistics, which certainly underestimate some of the traffic, can be questioned. In particular, the transport of small loads in private cars is not taken into account at all, although the highly fragmented structure of the new private sector and the size of the informal sector would suggest that such transport is widespread, involving in particular deliveries of goods in towns, as well as transborder traffic generated by the significant differences in price for a large number of products, whether in the frontier zones of the European Union or of the CIS (or even the CECs).

In central Europe, the share of rail is still declining while the total transport market is expanding. The result is -- as seen for the first time in 1994 -- that rail is maintaining its volume of traffic in most countries, with even a slight increase in absolute terms in Hungary, Poland and Slovenia. The last country has also seen an increase in the relative share of rail (Table 4, Table 5 and Annex 2).

Table 4. **RAIL FREIGHT CARRIED**
1989 = 100 (t-km)

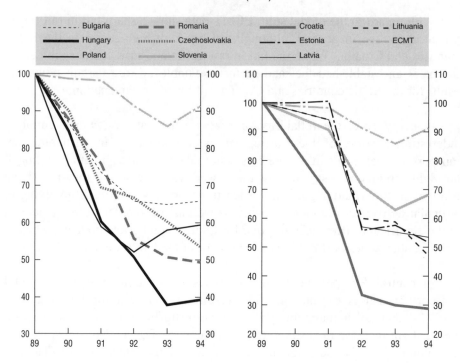

Source: ECMT.

The quality of statistics must also be very poor for Yugoslavia's successor states, especially for Croatia. In the case of that country, it is not possible to draw definite conclusions as the figures are very unreliable, owing to the extremely tense international political situation. The decline in the share of rail has been quite limited in Slovenia, for two reasons. First, the level of rail traffic was initially lower than in the other CECs. Second, it is a small country with substantial south-north and east-west transit flows that are to the advantage of rail. In addition, it is a neighbour of Austria, whose policy is to encourage rail, particularly by restricting east-west road transit traffic, which means that some of Slovenia's international traffic has to be carried by rail and combined transport.

The role of transit is even more important in the Baltic countries since, as we have stressed, these countries compete for transit to and from the CIS. They serve as entry and especially as export ports, particularly for Russia. Lithuania is also a transit region between Russia and the Russian enclave of

Kaliningrad, a route on which traffic is also tending to expand. For these East-West traffic flows, road infrastructure is of very poor quality, the distances are long and the roads are not very safe. Rail is therefore usually the natural choice and can keep a very high modal share.

Although rail traffic has plummeted since 1989 (down 40 to 60 per cent), its share has decreased to a lesser extent (since traffic has also fallen sharply). But this share, of between 40 and 80 per cent in 1994 [except in Hungary (29 per cent)], is still much higher than in the ECMT's western European Member countries as a whole (16 per cent). Rail's share has even been maintained in overall terms in the Baltic countries (66 to 87 per cent of t-km recorded).

Table 5. **TREND IN THE SHARE OF RAIL IN THE CECs (T-KM)**

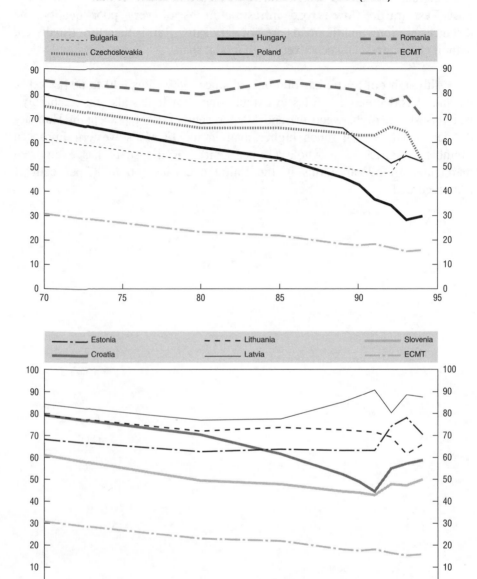

Source: ECMT.

The high share of rail shown in Table 5 (even if it is probably overestimated) seems enviable in the European Union from an environmental viewpoint. However, it probably points to difficulties for the future. The shift in trade flow patterns and the stabilization of total traffic carried are, admittedly, positive factors, suggesting that the automatic and structural fall in traffic, due to the major macroeconomic changes in the initial transition phase, is more or less at an end. This initial phase has, therefore, resulted in a steadier rail freight trend. Moreover, as has already been said, as production in central Europe is geared more to heavy and intermediate industrial products, rail should also be able to keep a relatively higher modal share than in the West, all other things being equal.

But, for a number of reasons, it may be difficult in the future to sustain this level of traffic, or at least the same modal share. At first sight, a comparison with the European Union, to which the CECs are seeking admission, suggests that rail's share is still excessively high in central Europe for historical reasons but that, in the long term, traffic flows in these countries should be more like those of the EU (with rail, even so, still in a slightly stronger position if output is still geared more to heavy industry).

Furthermore, owing to the very slow pace of its resructuring and its chronic deficits, rail is becoming less competitive and less adaptable to demand[17]. It is very difficult for rail to attract capital to upgrade and modernise a deteriorating network. Freight, admittedly, does not require the same quality of service and network standards as passenger traffic, but the increasing obsolescence of railway lines will be a major obstacle. At the same time, (scant) financial resources are being allocated to the upgrading of road networks or even to the construction of motorways, while road freight is being rapidly restructured. The market is still poorly organised and the vehicle fleet is old and obsolete, but modernisation is taking place gradually and much more rapidly than in the case of rail. Competition from road haulage should therefore speed up considerably in the coming years, which will enable it to increase its market shares.

At the microeconomic level, the progressive restructuring of firms and, in particular, of the major national industrial enterprises, the modernisation of manufacturing techniques and means of production and the increase in subcontracting work for major multinational groups should, in time, have an impact on transport demand, owing to the gradual introduction of modern logistical systems and to the streamlining of production and warehousing. Transport demand might therefore become more selective and less concentrated, focusing on quality of service, reliability and flexibility in the transport system. At the microeconomic level, demand will therefore inevitably increasingly shift to road haulage, since rail, especially in its present state, is not structured to provide the same quality of service.

One solution for rail will therefore be to provide new freight services geared more closely to demand, more up to date and more competitive, while maintaining its role on its traditional markets (transit to the East, heavy consignments). The focus is therefore on the development of combined transport, for which a number of possibilities can be mentioned. There was, traditionally, a large volume of containerised traffic between the CECs and the USSR (owing to transhipment requirements at the frontier) until it collapsed with the decline in trade relations. Black Sea traffic was also containerised to some extent. Two national markets could also be developed in Poland and Romania (the other countries are too small). The other markets with a high potential are those involving traffic to and from the European Union and intercontinental traffic via the North Sea ports. In this case, combined transport has been quite successful in the last three years with the development of good rolling road services and non-accompanied combined transport to and from Germany and Austria.

But here again, although this combined transport market seems very promising for rail, its present success is due more to external factors than to the efficiency of the available services, since the distinctive feature of east-west freight routes on either side of the CECs is the difficulty of crossing frontiers, with waiting times of perhaps up to several days at the main customs checkpoints. As for transit through Austria, the Eco-credit system, aimed particularly at reducing East-West flows, also limits road traffic. Restrictions on road haulage therefore contribute considerably to the development of combined rail transport. In time, with the prospects for free trade and then integration in the European Union plus the modernisation of infrastructure and customs procedures, the constraints on road traffic should ease considerably, indirectly making combined transport less competitive than road haulage.

The sharp fall in rail freight has therefore levelled off for the first time, marking the end of the initial transition phase of macroeconomic adjustment. But the second transition phase of microeconomic modernisation and restructuring and the prospects of European integration may well result in another fall in rail freight demand unless a proactive policy for rail is implemented.

3.2.2. Passenger transport: towards greater personal mobility and difficulties for public transport

-- *A mobility trend that is more difficult to assess.*

The development of personal mobility in central Europe is quite difficult to assess. The trend in these countries is probably just as, if not more varied than for freight transport, while available statistics are even scarcer. Data for mobility by private car are well-nigh inexistent and are often obtained from estimates that have not been based on detailed surveys. Moreover, the major aggregates for personal mobility mainly reflect daily local mobility, which is not the subject of this report.

-- *Conflicting developments*

Traffic seems to have declined overall since 1990. Although the figures are difficult to process, a number of more or less conflicting developments are to be seen. While the prices of all transport modes have risen considerably for a population whose incomes have often declined after the initial years of transition, public transport is losing custom and car ownership is rising sharply in all countries. But this car ownership, to which we shall come back subsequently, is not necessarily accompanied by greater use of private cars.

-- *A marked decrease in public passenger traffic*

Although the highly-developed public transport system is still important from the social viewpoint, its traffic has slumped during the transition period; it has been seriously affected by the gradual increase in transport prices which were formerly heavily subsidised. Whether in rail or bus transport, traffic in most countries has therefore fallen by about 40 to 60 per cent since 1990 (in passenger-km, according to the ECMT[18]). In some cases, the trend was checked in 1994 but not reversed (cf. Table 6, Annex 2). The downtrend is often more pronounced for intercity than urban traffic.

Table 6. **PASSENGERS-KM PERFORMED**
1989 = 100

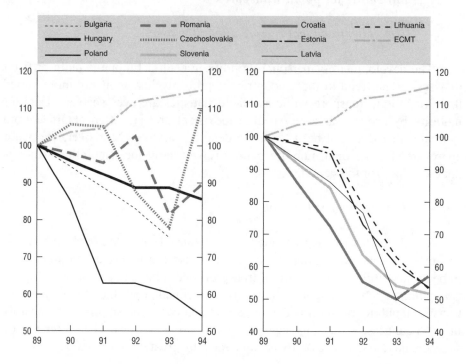

Notes: Passenger traffic: excluding private cars (except Hungary and Bulgaria).
Czechoslovakia = Czech Rep. + Slovak Rep. as from 1993. Change in series in 1994.
Source: ECMT.

This drop in traffic can be explained by purely economic factors, since economic adjustment and the very tight budget constraints on the authorities have obliged public transport operators to increase their fares in real terms and do away with special subsidies and free travel for certain social categories (workers, students, pensioners, etc). The cost of public transport has therefore risen considerably for most users, who also have less to live on. The use of public transport has therefore been restricted to necessary travel (mainly daily mobility in cities), whereas recreational or personal travel (on the intercity network) has been reduced.

Another -- geographical -- factor as seen in the break-up of states, whether the former republics of Czechoslovakia and Yugoslavia or the USSR, may also have had an effect in a number of countries. A frontier has been introduced where unimpeded travel was possible, which has probably created obstacles to travel in some cases (either by limiting the opportunities for travel or increasing its costs).

Lastly, the liberalisation of the transport market and, in particular, free access to the private car market, has considerably increased the competition from private cars. A car usually provides flexibility and comfort standards with which public transport can seldom compete. This competition has become greater owing to the poor quality of public transport[19]. Rail services are still poor and are tending to deteriorate, with commercial speeds which seldom exceed 100 km/h. Ancillary services are often not very efficient (although they can be improved in some cases). Rolling stock is increasingly out of date and does not provide sufficient comfort either.

In fact, it would seem that the only substantial increase has been in international bus passenger transport, owing to the opening of frontiers to central European tourists wishing to visit western Europe on very low budgets. One reason for this is that the cost of using a private car is still too high over long distances, particularly in the EU countries. Another is that accommodation costs can be reduced by using coach tour operator services. The train is seldom a good alternative, for there are few international rail package services and they are often still very expensive, as are air packages. International rail passenger traffic in the Czech Republic, for instance, has been reduced by a factor of four, mainly to the benefit of road transport (bus and private car), particularly as bus services are now better and cheaper[20].

-- *Development of car fleets and prospects for very high growth in personal mobility*

One of the main reasons for the decrease in public transport is competition from private cars. The opening-up of the economy has suddenly ended the shortages for which the car markets in central Europe were so well known. Very rapid growth in fleets has thus been recorded (see below). But this does not necessarily mean that private car traffic has developed to the same extent, for although the traffic jams in the major central European capitals testify to this increase in car ownership, intercity traffic seems to have developed less. In fact, in many countries, average vehicle mileages have declined considerably, as in Hungary, where private car travel has marked time since 1989, while car ownership has risen from 168 to 212 vehicles per 1 000 inhabitants[21]. The same applies, for example, to Bulgaria. In the Czech Republic and in Poland, however, the official national statistics show that growth in mobility is comparable to that for car ownership.

This limited growth in mobility compared with that of the car fleet is partly attributable to overestimation of the size of the fleet (see below) but mainly to economic reasons, since in relative terms it has become very expensive to run a car owing to the increase in petrol prices. This is particularly true of Hungary where petrol costs more than FF 5 per litre, while it is slightly cheaper in the Czech Republic and Poland. In other less advanced countries (Romania, Bulgaria, the Baltic States), falling living standards have brought the figures for mobility down. For example, Latvia's transport plan[22] shows that total personal mobility fell between 1990 and 1994 to the same extent as GDP and purchasing power (down by 45 and 60 per cent), whereas the car fleet was up by about 30 per cent in the same period.

Although this strong growth in car ownership is not yet reflected in equivalent growth in traffic, it still provides great future potential for personal mobility, provided that, as a result of improved purchasing powers, households can afford to use the car to a greater extent, as seems to be the case in Poland and the Czech Republic.

3.3. Towards very high growth in international freight

3.3.1.   The end to the shift in trade patterns

As we have already said, the geographical structure of trade has stabilized at the end of this initial transition phase. The CECs' main economic objective at the start of the transition process had been to rejoin the world economy by restructuring their foreign trade, not on a centrally-planned basis as had been the case in the days of the CMEA, but on a free trade basis, with each country taking its place according to its economic power and its production structure[23].

The first few years therefore saw a sharp fall in foreign trade in volume and, to some extent, in value terms (inasmuch as trade based on prices fixed arbitrarily in non-convertible roubles can be compared with prices charged freely on the world market). When the trends for foreign trade worked out by the UN/ECE[24] are looked at closely, it can be seen that foreign trade started to pick up again in 1992-93 in almost every country, following a more or less general decline (Table 7). Admittedly, the figures have to be qualified, since they vary greatly from one source to another[25] and values are expressed in current dollars. The changes therefore include changes in the rate for the dollar, not to speak of the difficulty of comparing the value of trade in roubles and dollars in the early years. The results given, however, do reflect the general trends in foreign trade.

Table 7. **TREND IN THE FOREIGN TRADE OF THE CEECs (VALUE)**
1989 =100

------- Bulgaria	— — — Romania	Slovenia	— · — Estonia
Hungary	■■■■■■ Russia	Czech Republic	Latvia
Poland	ιιιιιιιιι Slovak Republic	Croatia	– – – Lithuania

Imports **Exports**

Source: Deutsche Bank Research Review.

This decline, followed by a rise in foreign trade, clearly reflects this shift in trade patterns, with a marked decrease in trade with the USSR and the other former socialist countries and growth in trade with the West. Initially, as trade with the East was much greater, there was an overall fall in volumes and then, as the shift in patterns took place, growth in trade with the West predominated.

The present breakdown in trade seems to have steadied at its 1994-95 level, with growth in all the CECs' trade flows, whether to the West or East (see Table 8 and Annex 3). The OECD countries (mainly the European Union) account for about 70 to 75 per cent of the CEFTA countries' foreign trade and slightly less in the case of Romania and Bulgaria (the latter has still quite close ties with Russia), whereas in the Baltic States (where the shift in trade patterns has perhaps not yet stabilized), the former socialist countries still account for 25 to 50 per cent of trade, while the Scandinavian countries and Germany take most of the remainder.

Table 8. **Geographical breakdown of the CECs' trade**

	Bulgaria		Czech Republic		Hungary		Poland		Romania	
1989	Imp	Exp	Imp	Exp	Imp	Exp	Imp	Exp	Imp	Exp
Transition countries	47%	64%	51%	51%	41%	42%	41%	44%	40%	25%
Developed countries with a market economy	36%	20%	40%	39%	52%	49%	50%	46%	18%	47%
Developing countries	17%	16%	9%	10%	7%	9%	9%	10%	42%	28%

	Bulgaria		Czech Republic		Hungary		Poland		Romania	
1995	Imp	Exp	Imp	Exp	Imp	Exp	Imp	Exp	Imp	Exp
Transition countries	32%	31%	35%	20%	22%	20%	16%	15%	19%	10%
Developed countries with a market economy	51%	38%	59%	73%	73%	74%	71%	78%	56%	65%
Developing countries	17%	32%	6%	8%	4%	5%	13%	6%	25%	25%

Source: UN/ECE, INRETS-DEST Tables, 1996.

It is, therefore, now to be expected that central Europe's trade will expand rapidly to the East and West with much the same patterns as at present, but at a rate which might considerably exceed economic growth, since the countries concerned are being progressively integrated in the global economic system.

The prospects of association with the European Union should further consolidate trade. International flows will, therefore, be expanding regularly in the years to come.

3.3.2 *International bilateral traffic heavier than transit traffic despite the countries' central geographical position*

Owing to its geographical position, central Europe is often seen as a future hub for European transport. Great interest is being shown in the international transport corridors crossing the region as they will be carrying and distributing its main international traffic flows. Available data on the international traffic of the countries in the region show that transit flows are usually quite limited and exceeded by bilateral flows. Such a generalisation must obviously be qualified as at least two zones still play a major transit role (Slovenia and the Baltic States). Nonetheless, an analysis of the available, non-homogeneous, data suggests that transit traffic is not yet greatly developed in central Europe.

Thus, the data for Hungary and the Czech Republic provide interesting information (even if the latter country is a special case in that its foreign trade is still considerably influenced by its special ties with Slovakia). In both cases, transit activity accounts for only 25 per cent of total international traffic (but 35 to 50 per cent of road traffic). It has even slightly declined since 1991 in Hungary (when it was 31 per cent) (see Annex 3).

In Hungary, road transit traffic rose to 5.8 million tonnes in 1994, carried on about 500 000 to 550 000 lorries (which gives an idea of their low freight load), or about 1 500 lorries per day. The figures are twice as high for the Czech Republic. By way of comparison, in 1994, the Brenner road tunnel alone took a traffic of 1 160 000 lorries carrying 17.6 million tonnes.

The figures for transit in central Europe are therefore still quite modest, for which a number of reasons can be given. In the case of traffic between south-eastern Europe and the European Union -- for which transit through Hungary is unavoidable as long as it is difficult to cross Yugoslavia -- the distances involved (the main markets are Turkey and Greece or even more distant destinations), the poor quality of road and rail networks, the difficulties of crossing frontiers and the restrictions on transit through Austria are such that short sea shipping and direct connections via Italy have to be used for some traffic to avoid the central European overland route.

Similarly, on East-West routes between Russia and the European Union, central Europe is still a logistical barrier[26]. Overland transport is still difficult on these routes owing to poor quality networks and problems at frontiers. This difficult situation is compounded by the need for rail transhipment operations at the frontiers of the CIS, the number of different states on the routes (the Slovak/Czech split-up, creation of Ukraine and Belarus) which adds to the administrative workload and the increasing insecurity of inland transport in the former USSR. It must not be forgotten that great distances have to be covered between the economic centres in the European Union and those in Russia. The tendency will therefore be to make the most of the Baltic and Black Sea ports for a high proportion of Russia's traffic, rather than to use inland routes.

The last factor is directly economic and political, as Russia and the other republics of the former USSR are still in an uncertain and shifting situation. Although everybody agrees that Russia is one of the world's very great future markets, the present situation is still difficult and doing business in Russia is still very risky. Trade relations are therefore still limited compared with Russia's potential. However, the CECs, which have made greater progress in the transition process, have higher living standards than the rest of the region and are recording substantial economic growth, still have very close trade relations with the European Union even if they are small countries.

In the countries in the heart of central Europe, it is therefore bilateral trade with the EU rather than transit traffic which forms the basis of international transport. This bilateral traffic is carried on both major routes and on short-distance transborder routes.

3.3.3. Some major transit countries (Baltic States, Slovenia)

Although the volume of transit traffic in central Europe is still limited compared with what is often said, some countries do have an important transit role. These are mainly Slovenia and the Baltic States. All four of these countries are small (1.7 to 3.7 million inhabitants), have access to the sea and are located on major routes which cannot be avoided. For instance, Slovenia is a country via which Italy can be connected with the whole of eastern Europe. In addition, it provides an alternative to transit via Austria, which is expensive and regulated, for certain transalpine traffic flows. Lastly, it is the gateway to central Europe and the Mediterranean, since it is on a transit route giving access to its own port at Koper, or to the competing Italian ports (Trieste, etc). Slovenian transport policy is therefore geared to this transit role, in which the aim is to maximise the benefits obtained from transit (and therefore to attract traffic), while at the same time achieving sustainable growth without environmental damage being caused by traffic[27]. In providing access to the sea for the CECs, however, the Adriatic ports will (like those in the western Mediterranean) have to face up to fierce competition from the North Sea ports, whose influence is starting to spread to the centre of Europe and even to the Balkans.

The case of the Baltic States is slightly different, for their ports were traditionally entry and exit ports for the USSR. The situation has not greatly changed with the independence of the Baltic States, since no alternative can be really proposed for northern Russia, as the port of Saint Petersburg is not suitable for these flows. The Baltic ports have therefore remained vital for Russia and East-West transit is still a key factor in the transport system. There is a very marked East-West imbalance in this transit traffic. For example, in Latvia, over 90 per cent of port traffic consists of outbound shipments (of mainly Russian raw materials) as against under ten per cent of inbound cargo.

In Latvia[28], rail still accounts for over 50 per cent of the inland tonnage recorded, but of this total, 61 per cent consists of transit traffic from or to Russia, 12 per cent of North-South transit, 12 per cent of imports and 3 per cent of exports (and only 12 per cent of domestic traffic). Comparable figures are found in the other Baltic countries: in Estonia[29], transit accounts for almost 40 per cent of rail tonnage and imports/exports for 20 per cent, whereas on Lithuania's main East-West routes (Minsk-Vilnius-Kaunas-Klaipeda and Kaunas-Kaliningrad), 85 per cent of flows consist of transit traffic[30]. A special transit corridor is the one via Lithuania which connects Russia with the Kaliningrad enclave.

A very high proportion of the traffic handled by the Baltic ports consists of heavy bulk freight (raw materials from Russia and a small amount to that country). In 1994, the Estonian ports handled about twelve million tonnes of freight, mainly consisting of grain bound for Russia and coal from that country. In 1993 the Lithuanian ports handled 16 million tonnes of cargo, mainly comprising petroleum products (fuel oil) and Russian imports of grain and sugar. In 1994, the Latvian ports handled 35 million tonnes of cargo, mainly comprising exports of petroleum products (19.5 million), chemicals (six million) and metals and wood (five million) and imports of grain (0.2 million) and containers (0.7 million).

The structure of transport in the Baltic countries therefore very largely depends on Russian imports and exports of mainly heavy products requiring the use of traditional transport modes (pipeline or conventional train). But these transport markets, which were declining in 1994 (decrease in Russia's grain imports and petroleum product and coal exports), should be boosted in the coming years by strong growth in combined transport, which is more in line with current demand for transport services. Moreover, the Ro-Ro markets which were just starting up a few years ago are now going strong, whether in the case of ferry services for the rapidly developing links with Finland and Sweden or for transport to and from Germany and beyond.

In Lithuania, for example, Ro-Ro transport (road vehicles and rail wagons) doubled to 3.3 million tonnes between 1992 and 1994. In the case of road haulage only, the ferry boats carried 77 000 units, or a fivefold increase in two years. Despite recent rapid growth, container transport is still limited (7 500 TEU, but should increase to 135 000 by the year 2000, according to projections). Estonia's traffic is rising very fast on routes to and from Finland. In order to develop a modern freight transport system, the various countries are seeking new solutions by improving port infrastructure (quays for combined transport) or by devising new combined services (in particular, block trains running to Moscow).

The three countries, which are all trying to increase their transit traffic, seeing it as a factor in economic growth, are competing keenly for this role as a port gateway to Russia. There is a degree of geographical specialisation (with Tallin geared more to Saint Petersburg and Helsinki and Lithuania serving as a transit corridor for Kaliningrad), or in terms of the goods carried (oil port in Latvia). But the importance of this role as a gateway to Russia may continue (or may increase considerably if political and economic stability is achieved in Russia), for a number of reasons. First, the European Union is very far from Moscow and Saint Petersburg and sea transport still has a price advantage for the bulk of existing heavy freight. Second, owing to the poor quality of networks and all the technical and administrative obstacles in road and rail transport between Russia and Germany, sea transport is more reliable and more advantageous for higher-value goods (typically, those carried in swap bodies). Third, in the case of international container traffic, which often has to be broken up at the major northern ports (from Antwerp to Hamburg), carriage via the Baltic seems more logical.

The volume of this transit traffic will therefore probably remain stable or rise, with a marked increase in combined, container and Ro-Ro traffic, while heavy goods will maintain or increase their share of traffic. In this context, competition between the various ports should be keen and greater specialisation of traffic in terms of routes or products will probably be seen.

3.4. Development of combined transport

3.4.1. *High growth potential on five markets*

Combined transport's high potential in the coming years is, however, probably even greater for the central European than for the Baltic States. In addition to the usual arguments given in the EU countries -- admittedly to little avail so far -- for sustainable transport growth and respect of the natural and human environment which justify the development of combined transport, there are other reasons for promoting the use of this mode in central Europe.

First, the railway networks which are highly developed have, overall, not been running to capacity since the start of the transition period and the return to the total volumes of conventional freight traffic comparable to those of the 1980s is unlikely. The development of road haulage is still very limited and subject to very many constraints (in particular, waiting times at frontiers) in a market which is still not operating very efficiently, given the lack of intermediaries and the fact that customers are not yet opting automatically for road transport. The customers' transport needs are also based on a logistical system which often does not require the same quality of service as in the European Union. Lastly, the sharp increase in road traffic forecast for the coming years would be difficult to absorb, owing to the poor quality and low capacity of the road network. Combined transport should therefore have a high potential.

Combined transport is, in fact, starting to develop in many CECs and in the Baltic States. Broadly speaking, five types of market can be identified. The first consists of routes between CECs and Russia which once carried a high volume of container traffic, owing to the change of gauge at the borders of the USSR. Long distances, the possibility of pooling flows to the major cities (especially Moscow), the risks involved in road haulage and the poor quality of roads, as well as difficulties at frontier crossings, are so many factors in favour of combined transport.

135

A second market is that of the rolling road (with use of the Ro-Ro technique for wagons and road vehicles), especially for Baltic Sea and Black Sea traffic (see above). The third market is for transport in the two "major" CECs (Poland and Romania), where, owing to their topography and seaboard, combined transport could be used for domestic traffic. A fourth market is that for routes to and from the European Union and the last one is a maritime market for intercontinental flows via the North Sea ports.

It is not always easy to say what the actual traffic on these markets is, for, once again, the data are insufficient. Little is known about combined traffic to the East (CIS). Only the data provided by Intercontainer have been analysed and these give a total flow involving the CIS of 39 484 TEU in 1994 (about 700 000 t), or an increase of 14.8 per cent. But the value of this market is highlighted by the fact that Intercontainer is investing in the equipment needed for its development, despite the political and economic uncertainties[31].

Table 9. **Combined transport in three CECs**

Romania	Swap bodies		Large containers		Rolling road	
	Nb units	tonnage (mill. t)	Nb units	tonnage (mill. t)	Nb units	tonnage (mill. t)
1992	28	0.000	141 500	1.701		
1993	123	0.001	101 000	1.213	1 945	0.074
1994	1 910	0.017	118 000	1.425	4 515	0.172

Czech Rep	Containers (Nb)	Swap bodies (Nb)	Rolling road (units)	Total CT (million t)
1989	678 360			3.953
1990	587 150			3.542
1991	308 120			1.902
1992	208 840			1.506
1993	113 960		940	1.040
1994	131 170	3 233	23 567	1.540

Hungary	TEU containers	TEU swap bodies	Rolling road (units)	Ro-Ro (units)
1990	191 400	0	0	0
1991	115 900	1 500	0	0
1992	96 600	42 400	16 200	1 800
1993	98 900	81 200	28 700	4 900
1994	112 000	105 700	25 600	6 200

Source: National statistics.

With regard to national markets, the positions in Poland and Romania are quite different. In Poland, Polkombi, a combined carrier affiliated to the UIRR, was created in 1993. The flows are still limited (1 700 swap bodies and 25 000 containers in 1995 for Polkombi, 35 000 TEU for ICF), but Poland is setting up legislative provisions which should make access to the network easier for operators. Intercontainer also has a correspondent in that country. Romania, however, has a longer tradition of combined transport, which is mainly based on the port of Constanta. Until 1992, there was a substantial volume of large container traffic, which gradually declined. Traffic decreased until 1993 and then started to rise again in 1994 when new rolling road and swap body services were introduced[32]. In 1994, traffic amounted to 124 500 units (1.6 million tonnes), 90 per cent of which consisted of containers. In 1995, four regular daily services were operated from Bucharest to the main Romanian urban centres[33].

Routes involving the European Union are a new, fast-growing market in which combined transport should be able to make its mark. The UIRR[34] already has several members in central Europe. In 1995, these included Adria-Kombi (Slovenia and Croatia), Hungarokombi (Hungary), Polkombi (Poland), plus an agency in Prague and partners in other countries. The same applies to Intercontainer[35], which has stakes in Hungarian and Polish companies, an agency in Prague and agreements with other operators. These two groups of companies, which account for the bulk of inland combined transport in western Europe, are therefore investing in central Europe and their traffic is increasing. In 1994, Intercontainer traffic totalled 90 000 TEU in Hungary, 150 000 in Slovenia, 35 000 in Poland and 5 000 to 10 000 in Bulgaria, the Czech Republic, Croatia, Romania and Slovakia. In 1994, the UIRR's non-accompanied traffic mainly consisted of 35 000 TEU in Hungary, 25 000 in the Czech Republic and almost 10 000 in Slovenia and Poland (see Annex 4).

A market is therefore emerging, even if the volumes are still low compared with the major users of international combined transport, such as Italy and Germany [500 000 TEU via Intercontainer and 140 000 (Germany 300 000) via UIRR]. Accompanied combined transport shipments (mainly rolling road traffic), making it possible to cross the EU frontiers, also account for a substantial part of this market. For instance, in 1994, the rolling road system carried 25 000 lorries in Hungary, 23 000 in the Czech Republic and 12 000 in Slovenia.

In 1995, this push into the CECs was stepped up with the continued introduction of regular combined transport services. Kombiverkehr is running regular daily trains to Zagreb and Ljubljana, Hungary (Sopron, Budapest, Debrecen, Szeged), the Czech and Slovak Republics (twelve destinations) and Poland (a much slower service). Similarly, Intercontainer is operating regular through services to Slovenia and Hungary and using the Sopron terminal in Hungary as a hub for flows to the East and South-East (Greece, Turkey).

The main rolling road services are between Germany and Austria in the West and the Czech Republic, Slovenia and Hungary in the East. These services are mainly intended to facilitate frontier crossings (by avoiding queues) and transit through Austria (which imposes quotas).

Sea container traffic is also developing, particularly between the port of Hamburg and the Hungarian, Czech, Slovak and Slovene economic centres. The other northern ports seem to be much less involved in this trend.

3.4.2. *Success based on external factors (constraints on road transport)*

Although combined transport seems to be developing satisfactorily in central Europe, its success stems mainly from the constraints affecting road transport. These constraints, some of which are structurally inherent in road haulage, while others are "artificial" in that they are the result of transport policy, may be removed at a future date, which would affect the development of combined transport in its present form.

The first constraint on road haulage includes the poor quality of the road network, the length of hauls and, sometimes, the lack of safety. Road operating conditions are, therefore, critical. In comparison, the rail network is, admittedly, obsolete and sometimes in a poor state, but it is underutilised and service standards are more or less acceptable (the design and age of the networks often rule out speeds exceeding 100 km/h, but this is much more of a drawback for passengers than for freight).

The weakness of the local transport market (particularly as regards forwarders and the local vehicle fleet) is another aspect which may be in favour of combined transport.

But frontier crossings and all the obstacles to market access are a decisive factor[36]. As these obstacles (for example, waitings times of perhaps up to several days) are much less of a problem for rail, this mode is automatically

138

more advantageous. Another basic obstacle to road transport to and from the CECs is transit via Austria, which imposes quotas on the basis of Eco-credits. Owing to their poor characteristics, vehicles from central Europe are particularly concerned by these measures, which are aimed more at limiting pollution than reducing the total number of lorries. While in 1995, therefore, it seemed that the quotas for South-North transport (Italy-Germany) had not been exhausted, despite a marked increase in traffic, the rolling road services available in Hungary for transit via Austria were used much more at the end of the year (quotas exhausted) than at the beginning[37].

An alternative is also provided by Ro-Ro transport on the Danube to connect Budapest with Germany. This route, which was opened in 1993, provides good service and is used mainly by Hungarocamion, as well as by the Bulgarians and Romanians[38]. In 1994, this Ro-Ro traffic was up 25 per cent to 31 800 lorries. After the end of the war in the former Yugoslavia, it should be possible, in time, to develop this route for longer-haul combined transport -- whether accompanied or not -- whereas the Rhine-Main-Danube canal still has to prove its suitability for combined transport, given the number of locks on it.

3.4.3. Outlook uncertain for combined transport

This brief analysis of factors in the success of combined transport in central Europe shows that its foundations are shaky. Certain factors suggest that, in the long run, road haulage could be much more competitive. The problems relating to market access, frontier crossings and quota restrictions will be attenuated as the CECs form closer ties with the European Union and are in a much better position to use the road network. Also, road haulage costs (in particular wage costs) are still low in central Europe, whereas rail costs are much less flexible. Road haulage may therefore become even more competitive.

Infrastructure improvement will also be a major asset for road transport. The international organisations are, in fact, focusing on the improvement of the road network, which is undersized and particularly on the links between the capitals of the CEFTA and EU countries (and therefore on the main combined transport markets). For example, the first new piece of infrastructure introduced since 1989 was the missing western segment of the Budapest-Vienna road. Nonetheless, rail projects have accounted for 30 per cent of the total loans provided by the international financial institutions for transport in central Europe, and road projects for 50 per cent[39], which shows that rail has not been forgotten, despite the emphasis on improvements to the road system and their more obvious impact.

The lorry fleet should also be gradually adapted to EU standards (in any case, for international transport) for both economic and ecological reasons. These adjustments to the fleet will have two conflicting effects on combined transport. On the one hand, road haulage will be able to develop as vehicles that are more efficient and more acceptable to the countries in the heart of the EU become available. But, on the other hand, central European carriers will be able to use equipment that is suitable for combined transport, which is not the case at present, a fact that largely explains why accompanied combined transport has developed more quickly than non-accompanied. The present fleet includes few semi-trailers, road tractors and swap bodies. The vehicles often consist of medium-sized lorries (28 tonnes maximum) with or without trailers, for which only the rolling road can be used. Kombiverkehr's[40] managing director has therefore stressed that the rolling road must be seen as an initial step until rolling stock becomes suitable for more cost-effective types of operation.

Combined transport therefore provides a real opportunity for the CECs. Its development, however, has largely benefited from external constraints on road transport. If this development is to be sustained, it seems important that an appropriate institutional and legislative framework be put in place to present an advantage for rail (*inter alia,* by internalising external costs) but also that combined transport provide more reliable and efficient services based on a network of high-performance facilities. The CECs have certain specific assets (transit potential, long distances, a highly developed rail network, rail's high modal share) for the development of combined transport. But an all-round effort will be required and there is nothing to prove that it will succeed.

3.5. A large road vehicle fleet undergoing radical change

As we have already frequently stressed, one of the specific characteristics of central Europe is the make-up of its transport equipment. Despite all the railway rolling stock available, it cannot meet a declining demand satisfactorily, for its structure is unsuitable, with a very small number of specialised wagons, particularly for combined or rapid passenger transport. Traction is also often inadequate. In addition, the average age of stock is very high and, to a large extent, it is close on or has exceeded the decommissioning

140

age (the average age of Hungary's wagon stock is about 22 years, while over twelve per cent is more than 30 years old)[41]. In the case of road transport, the transition countries have inherited from the former system quite a large fleet, although its age and capacity characteristics (in the case of lorries) are quite different from those in the European Union. In the meantime, this fleet has grown further and older, whereas the structure of the utility vehicle fleet is gradually becoming more similar to that in the EU and therefore more adapted to demand.

3.5.1. An expanding and ageing vehicle fleet

The increase in the private car fleet in central Europe since 1989 has been quite spectacular. Between 1989 and 1994, the number of cars increased greatly (by 25 to 50 per cent in most countries). But this reflects the fact that progress started from a very low level of car ownership in the early 1980s. At the same time, the average age of vehicles is very high and is rising with the increase in car ownership. But it is necessary to look carefully at the figures provided, as shown by the examples of Hungary and Latvia. In the latter case, a new system of calculating the fleet in 1994, based on the figures for vehicles re-registered as from 1993, gives figures 30 per cent lower than those for the previous year[42] (Table 10). Similarly, in Hungary, official statistics appear in two documents describing the fleet[43]. One of them gives the data for the "total" Hungarian fleet, while the other gives data for the same fleet "without vehicles withdrawn from service". The "total" fleet is then 22 per cent higher for private cars and 37 per cent higher for buses and road tractors. Fleets are therefore obviously overestimated in certain national statistics, which do not take into account the withdrawal of older vehicles. The distortion introduced by this practice is quite frequent but it is particularly accentuated by the sudden changes in living standards and in the cost of using vehicles which have occurred during the transition period, as some of the population have stopped using their cars but have not parted with them.

Table 10. **Comparison of statistics for the Hungarian vehicle fleet: data with and without vehicles withdrawn from service (1994) -- thousands**

	Cars	Lorries	Buses	Road tractors	Trailers
Total vehicles recorded	2 884	386	32.0	51.8	300
Total vehicles minus those not in service	2 245	292	20.1	32.6	268
Difference (% vehicles not in service)	22%	24%	37%	37%	11%

Source: Hungarian Ministry of Transport.

Nonetheless, the average age of the private car fleet is still very high, even if vehicles not in service are subtracted. For example, the average age of Hungarian vehicles is 11.2 years, while 54 per cent of the fleet is more than ten years old. In Estonia, 65 per cent of the vehicle fleet is over ten years old[44]. The increase in the fleet size and the age of vehicles are due to two factors[45]. Owing to the scarcity of cars at the time (waiting period of over eight years for a new car in certain countries), the inhabitants of central Europe kept their cars for many years. In a period of crisis, they will still tend to hang on to them -- even if the running costs are too high and they have to reduce their mileage or not drive at all -- until the outlook is brighter. At the same time, the opening-up of frontiers has given them access to a market which is not regulated by scarcity but by prices. As they usually could not afford new cars, people in the CECs have opted for quite old second-hand cars at more reasonable prices. There has, accordingly, been a massive spending spree, but on already old vehicles, while the market for new vehicles was still sluggish (as seen in the difficulties encountered by Suzuki, whose output in Hungary is much lower than initially planned) (Table 11 and Annex 5).

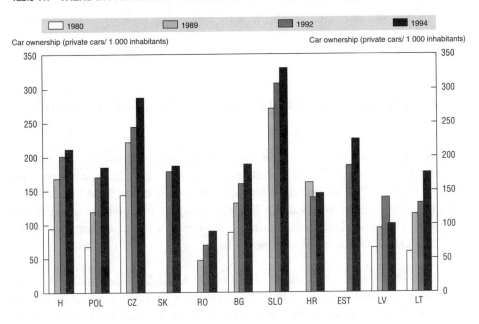

3.5.2. *Utility vehicles not adapted to demand*

The utility vehicle fleet is also very old (9.3 years on average, or about twice the figure for France). But, in addition, it is not adapted closely enough to market needs. Based as it is on the fleet from the socialist era, it still consists mainly of medium-sized lorries of about ten tonnes, with very few large road tractors, very few light utility vehicles (with a total permissible laden weight of less than five tonnes) and especially very light vehicles (less than 1.5 tonnes). The number of tractors with semi-trailers is also quite low. As already pointed out, there is a particular lack of vehicles suitable for non-accompanied combined transport and part of the fleet does not fully comply with the EU vehicle regulations (especially as regards pollution).

These characteristics of the central European fleet could gradually change as vehicles are replaced to meet new demands. However, given that household and company budgets are very tight, it would seem likely that, in the medium term, the second-hand market will continue to predominate and that average vehicle age will remain high, (the fleet is extremely large in relation to national wealth, compared to other countries with similar incomes, as in Latin America). If, however, the economies of the East really catch up with those of the EU, the differences between the fleets should be considerably reduced (as in the case of Prague's car fleet which has become very similar to those in some parts of the EU, with a car ownership of over 400 vehicles per 1 000 inhabitants).

4. CONCLUSION: EMERGENCE OF TRANSPORT POLICIES

Although not exhaustive, this analysis has nevertheless shown that the central European and Baltic countries have seen revolutionary economic changes since 1990. The initial macroeconomic transition phase has ended or is ending, while the transport sector has adapted quite independently to the new situation. The general macroeconomic framework for the transition now seems well established, as does the institutional basis.

A second stage, which must be aimed at setting up the microeconomic structures that will complete the transition to a modern economy, is now underway. The resulting system will have to be economically efficient so that private entreprise can develop; it will also have to lay down its major options concerning the management of public goods and services on the basis of sustainable development.

These requirements also apply to the transport sector, which is a vital part of the economic system. This sector must serve the economy as efficiently as possible by supporting domestic and foreign trade (competitiveness) and meet the social demand for mobility (cohesion), while safeguarding the future by implementing an appropriate policy (sustainable development). Accordingly, coherent and comprehensive transport policies will have to be drawn up and adjusted progressively by each country.

The challenges which are therefore emerging for this second transition phase will be to maintain and strengthen an integrated multimodal approach, in order to optimise the use of the transport system by permitting the most advantageous combinations of transport modes.

A balance will have to be found between the necessary increase in mobility, the economic advantage of promoting traffic, particularly in the case of transit for countries like the Baltic States and the impact of traffic growth on the natural and human environment.

If the transcript system is to be competitive in an open economic environment, the road sector and, in particular, the downstream forwarding and transport organisation functions, will have to be strengthened. The road haulage fleet and railway rolling stock will also have to be replaced in order to meet demand more effectively.

The restructuring of railway entreprises is also an imperative if rail is to retain its high modal share. It should also be stressed that rail will not be able to keep some of the heavy flows and a substantial volume of freight unless combined transport techniques are modernised in response to the inevitable challenge from improved road services.

Finally, although the situations of the CECs differ greatly from one another and include quite specific features compared with the European Union, the major issues facing them differ little from those at the centre of EU transport policies.

NOTES

1. W. Andreff (1993), *La Crise des Economies Socialistes : la rupture d'un système*, PUG.

2. B. Chavance (1992*), Les réformes économiques à l'est, de 1950 aux années 1990*, Nathan.

3. G. Chatelus (1996a), "La situation économique et politique en Europe Centrale en 94-95", dans Ch. Reynaud, M. Poincelet (eds.), *Quel rôle des institutions locales, nationales, internationales en Europe Centrale et Orientale ?*, Paradigme/INRETS-DEST.

4. J. Burnewicz (1995), "Les effets frontières et intégration internationale. La mesure des effets dans un scénario", dans Ch. Reynaud, M. Poincelet (eds.), *De la transition à l'intégration : quelles conditions pour les transports ?*, Paradigme/INRETS-DEST.

5. Ch. Reynaud, G. Chatelus, M. Poincelet (1996), "Economic and social change: Central and Eastern European countries", *13th International Symposium on Theory and Practice in Transport Economics: Transport: New Problems, New Solutions*, ECMT.

6. M. Lavigne (1995*), The economics of transition: from socialist economy to market economy*, Macmillan Press Ltd.

7. M. Lavigne (1995), *op. cit.*

8. UN Economic Commission for Europe, *Economic Bulletin for Europe*, United Nations.

9. Ch. Reynaud (1990), "Road Transport", in: *Prospects for East-West European Transport*, ECMT.

10. Ch. Reynaud (1991), "Un réseau de collecte d'informations dans les transports", Réunion des 8-9 novembre 1991, PNUD-INRETS.

11. ECMT (1995), *Trends in the Transport Sector, 1970-1994* (annual publication).

12. World Bank (1995), *World Development Report*.

13. UN Economic Commission for Europe (1995), *Economic Bulletin for Europe,* United Nations.

14. Nordic Project Fund/Nordic Investment Bank, EBRD, Ministry of Transport & Communication of Finland, Viatek, SweRoad (1993), *Via Baltica, Feasibility Study*, August.

15. G. Chatelus (1993), *Les transports en Europe Centrale: Inadéquation de l'offre face à une demande restructurée* - Paradigme/INRETS - DEST.

16. Ch. Reynaud, G. Chatelus, M. Poincelet (1996), *op. cit.*

17. C. Thouvenin (1993), *L'évolution des chemins de fer tchecoslovaques et hongrois*, Paradigme/INRETS-DEST.

18. ECMT (1995), *Trends in the Transport Sector, 1970-1994, op. cit.*.

19. G. Chatelus (1993), *op. cit.*

20. Ministry of Transport of the Czech Republic (1995), *Mobility in the Czech Republic: Development until now and forecast.*

21. Ministry of Transport, Hungary (1995a), *Transport Data Infrabooks* 15, 1985-1994.

22. Republic of Latvia, Ministry of Transport (1995), National Transport Development Program 1996-2010.

23. F. Lemoine, C. Leroy (1992), "Les échanges des pays d'Europe Centrale et Orientale: l'écueil d'une double concurrence", *Economie et Statistiques*, No.°260.

24. UN Economic Commission for Europe: *op. cit.*

25. UN Economic Commission for Europe (1992), *Economic Bulletin for Europe*, United Nations.

26. G. Chatelus (1993), *op. cit.*

27. M. Jelaska (1995), "The Slovenian view on the transport system during and after transition", in: Ch. Reynaud, M. Poincelet (eds.), *De la transition à l'intégration : quelles conditions pour les transports ?*, Paradigme/INRETS-DEST.

28. Republic of Latvia, Ministry of Transport (1995), National Transport Development Program 1996-2010.

29. Ministry of Transport, Estonia (1995), Reply to the ECMT questionnaire on traffic flows, forecasts and infrastructure needs.

30. Ministry of Transport, Lithuania (1995), Reply to the ECMT questionnaire on traffic flows, forecasts and infrastructure needs.

31. Intercontainer-Interfrigo (1995), *Rapport annuel 1994.*

32. Ministry of Transport, Romania (1995), Reply to the ECMT questionnaire on traffic flows, forecasts and infrastructure needs.

33. G. Chatelus (1996), Synthèse des débats, in: Ch. Reynaud, M. Poincelet (eds.), *Quel role des institutions locales, nationales, internationales en Europe Centrale et Orientale ?*, Paradigme/INRETS-DEST.

34. UIRR (1995), *Annual Statistics 1994.*

35. INTERCONTAINER (1995), *Rapport annuel 1995.*

36. ECMT (1996), *Access to European Transport Markets.*

37. G. Chatelus (1996b), *op. cit.*

38. Hungarian Ministry of Transport (1995), *The situation and probable development trends of combined transport in Hungary.*

39. M. Gaspard (1996), "Transport infrastructure financing in Central and Eastern Europe: Current developments and outlook", Draft working paper, European Commission DG7.

40. W. Maywald (1995), *La coopération est-ouest*, UIRR Report, 1994.

41. Ministry of Transport, Hungary (1995b), *Transport Data Infrabooks* 12, 1991-1992-1993-1994.

42. Republic of Latvia, Ministry of Transport (1995), *op. cit.*

43. Ministry of Transport, Hungary (1995c), Summary of the national vehicle fleet statistical data 1995: *Infrabooks* 16/I et 16/II.

44. Inseneribüroo Stratum (1996), *Roads and traffic in Estonia, 1995*.

45. G. Chatelus (1993), *op. cit.*

ANNEXES

Annex 1.   **PER CAPITA GDP IN 1993**

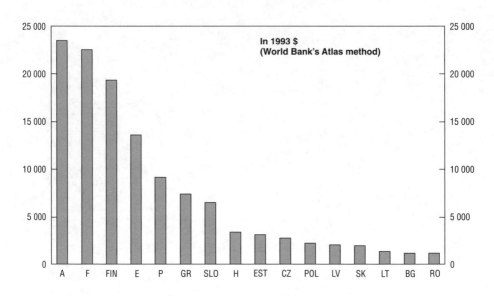

In 1993 $
(World Bank's Atlas method)

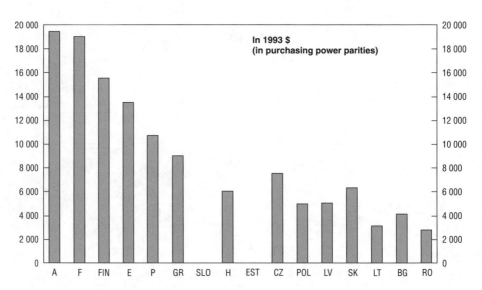

In 1993 $
(in purchasing power parities)

Source: World Bank (PPPs subject to wide margin of error).

Annex 1. **MAIN ECONOMIC INDICATORS FOR CENTRAL EUROPEAN COUNTRIES (FORECASTS FOR 1995 AND 1996)**

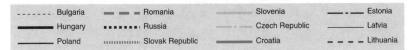

------- Bulgaria	=== Romania	Slovenia	--- Estonia
Hungary	.... Russia	Czech Republic	Latvia
Poland	.... Slovak Republic	Croatia	--- Lithuania

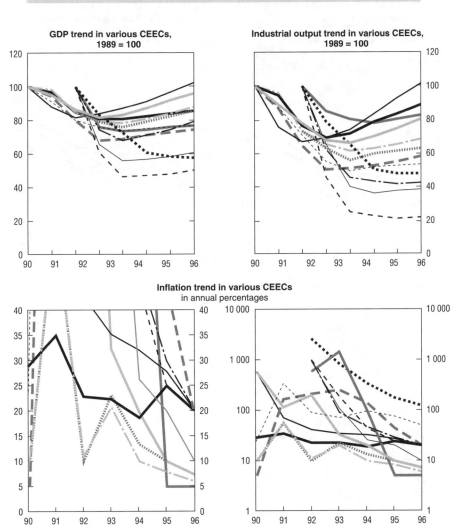

GDP trend in various CEECs, 1989 = 100

Industrial output trend in various CEECs, 1989 = 100

Inflation trend in various CEECs
in annual percentages

Source: Deutsche Bank Research Review.

153

**MAIN ECONOMIC INDICATORS FOR CENTRAL EUROPEAN COUNTRIES
(FORECASTS FOR 1995 AND 1996)**

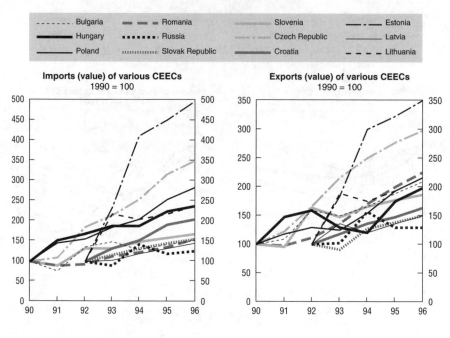

Imports (value) of various CEECs
1990 = 100

Exports (value) of various CEECs
1990 = 100

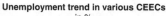

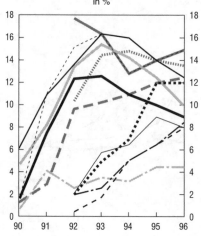

Unemployment trend in various CEECs
in %

Source: Deutsche Bank Research Review, INRETS-DEST.

Annex 2. **TREND IN TRAFFIC CARRIED IN CENTRAL EUROPE**

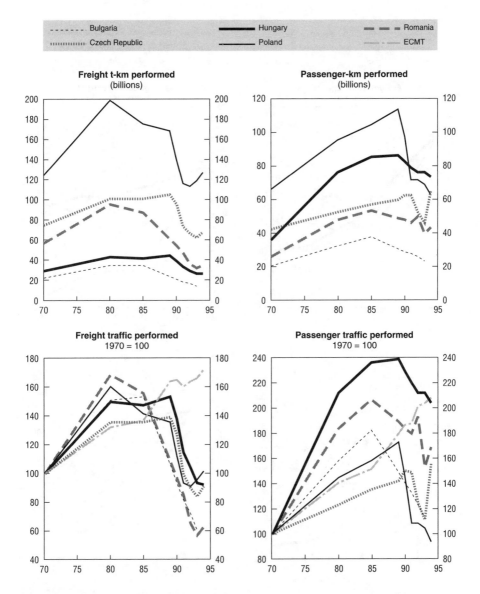

Notes: Czechoslovakia = Czech Rep. + Slovak Rep. as from 1993. Change in series in 1994.
         Passenger traffic: excluding private cars (except Hungary and Bulgaria).
Source: ECMT – INRETS-DEST graphs, 1996.

155

Annex 2. TREND IN TRAFFIC CARRIED IN CENTRAL EUROPE

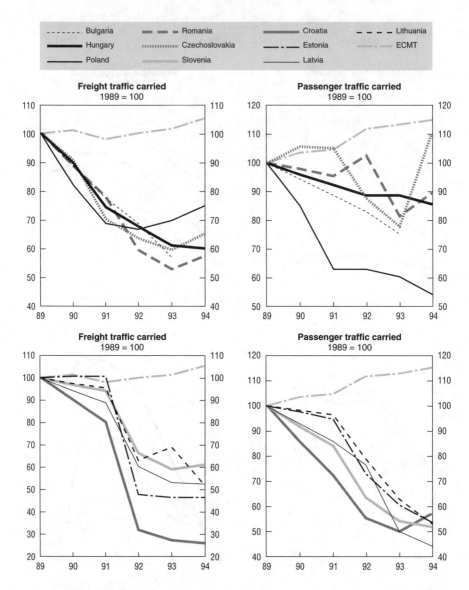

Notes: Passenger traffic: excluding private cars (except Hungary and Bulgaria).
Czechoslovakia = Czech Rep. + Slovak Rep. as from 1993. Change in series in 1994.
Source: ECMT – INRETS-DEST graphs, 1996.

T-KM CARRIED PER $ OF GNP, FRANCE = 1

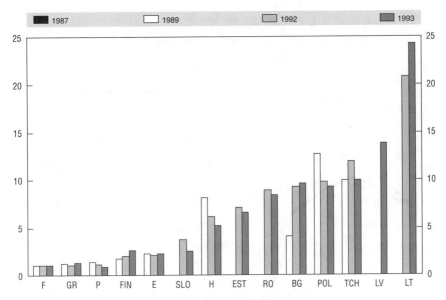

T-KM CARRIED PER $ OF GNP, FRANCE = 1
IN PURCHASING POWER PARITY TERMS

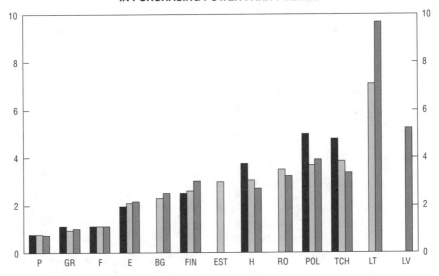

Source: ECMT, World Bank.

Annex 2. TREND IN RAIL TRANSPORT IN CENTRAL EUROPE

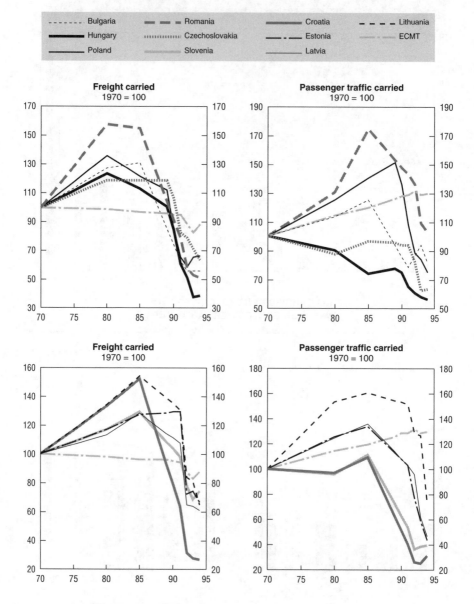

Source: ECMT – INRETS-DEST graphs, 1996.

Annex 2. **TREND IN RAIL TRANSPORT IN CENTRAL EUROPE**

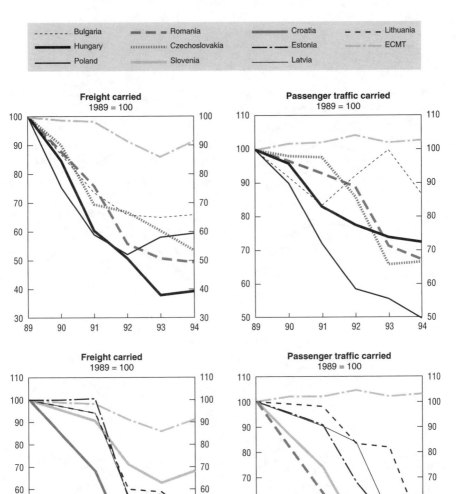

Source: ECMT – INRETS-DEST graphs, 1996.

159

Annex 2. **TREND IN ROAD TRANSPORT IN CENTRAL EUROPE**

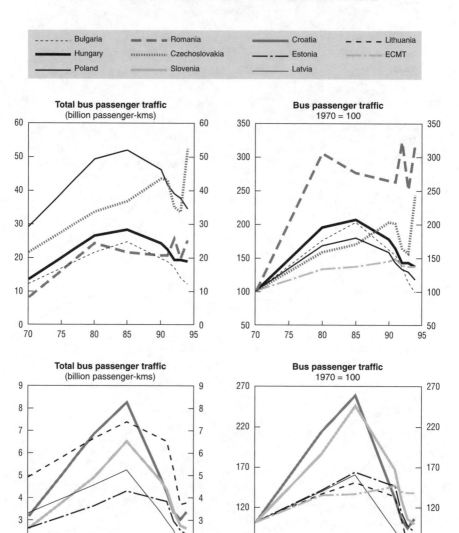

Source: ECMT – INRETS-DEST graphs, 1996.

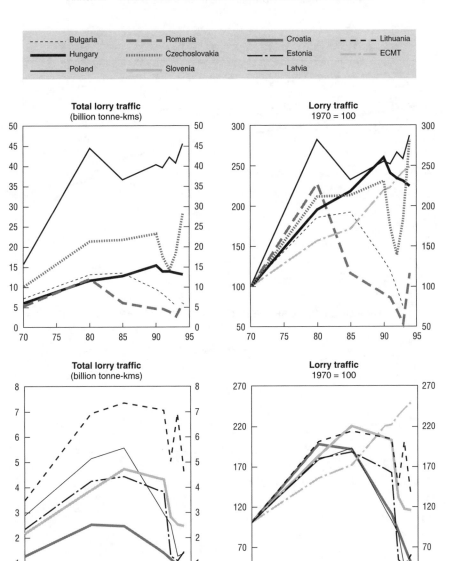

Source: ECMT – INRETS-DEST graphs, 1996.

TREND IN RAIL'S MODAL SHARE IN CENTRAL EUROPE (T-KM)

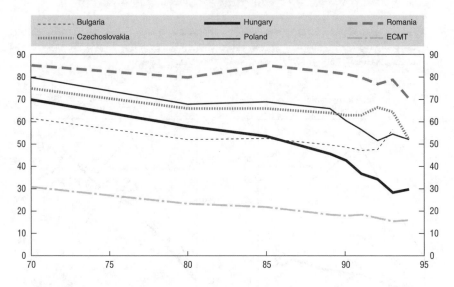

TREND IN RAIL'S MODAL SHARE IN THE BALTIC STATES AND EX-YUGOSLAVIA (T-KM)

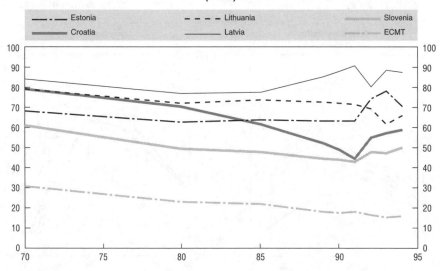

Source: ECMT.

Annex 3. **TREND IN THE GEOGRAPHICAL BREAKDOWN OF
CENTRAL EUROPEAN COUNTRIES' FOREIGN TRADE: IMPORTS**

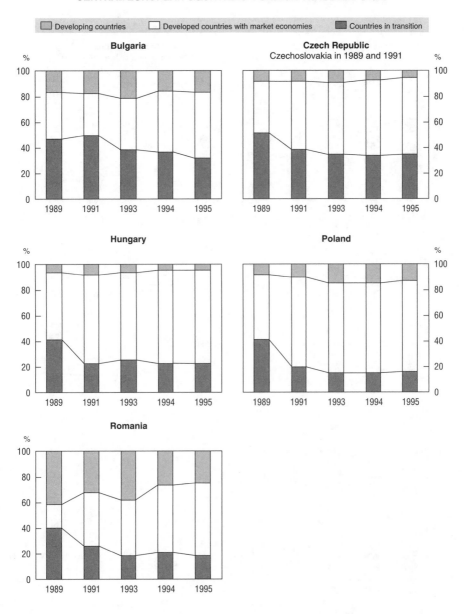

Source: UN/ECE – INRET-DEST graphs, 1996.

163

Annex 3.   **TREND IN THE GEOGRAPHICAL BREAKDOWN OF
CENTRAL EUROPEAN COUNTRIES' FOREIGN TRADE: EXPORTS**

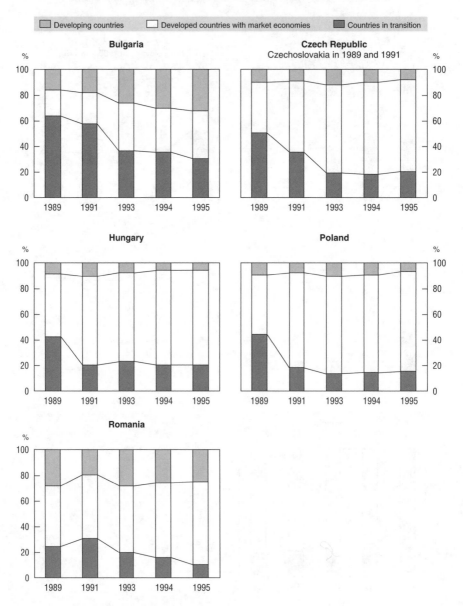

Source: UN/ECE – INRET-DEST graphs, 1996.

164

TREND IN THE GEOGRAPHICAL BREAKDOWN OF THE BALTIC COUNTRIES' FOREIGN TRADE: (VALUE, CURRENT $)

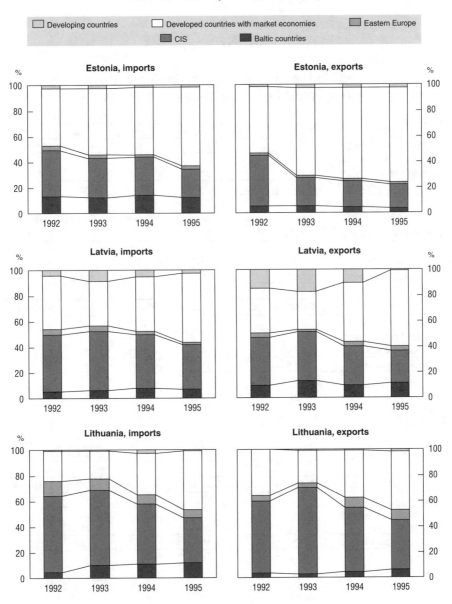

Source: UN/ECE – INRET-DEST graphs, 1996.

ANNEX 3

Trend in the geographical breakdown of trade
by Central European Country: Exports

1989	Bulgaria	Czechoslovakia	Hungary	Poland	Romania
Countries in transition	64%	51%	42%	44%	25%
Developed countries with market economies	20%	39%	49%	46%	47%
Developing countries	16%	10%	9%	10%	28%

1991	Bulgaria	Czechoslovakia	Hungary	Poland	Romania
Countries in transition	57%	35%	20%	18%	31%
Developed countries with market economies	24%	56%	70%	74%	49%
Developing countries	18%	9%	10%	8%	20%

1993	Bulgaria	Czech Republic	Hungary	Poland	Romania
Countries in transition	37%	19%	23%	14%	20%
Developed countries with market economies	37%	69%	69%	76%	52%
Developing countries	26%	12%	8%	11%	28%

1994	Bulgaria	Czech Republic	Hungary	Poland	Romania
Countries in transition	35%	19%	20%	14%	15%
Developed countries with market economies	35%	71%	74%	76%	58%
Developing countries	30%	10%	6%	10%	26%

1995	Bulgaria	Czech Republic	Hungary	Poland	Romania
Countries in transition	31%	20%	20%	15%	10%
Developed countries with market economies	38%	73%	74%	78%	65%
Developing countries	32%	8%	5%	6%	25%

Source: UN/ECE, INRETS-DEST Tables, 1996.

Trend in the geographical breakdown of trade
by central European country: Imports

1989	Bulgaria	Czechoslovakia	Hungary	Poland	Romania
Countries in transition	47%	51%	41%	41%	40%
Developed countries with market economies	36%	40%	52%	50%	18%
Developing countries	17%	9%	7%	9%	42%

1991	Bulgaria	Czechoslovakia	Hungary	Poland	Romania
Countries in transition	50%	39%	23%	20%	26%
Developed countries with market economies	32%	53%	69%	70%	42%
Developing countries	18%	8%	8%	11%	32%

1993	Bulgaria	Czech Republic	Hungary	Poland	Romania
Countries in transition	38%	34%	25%	15%	18%
Developed countries with market economies	41%	57%	68%	70%	44%
Developing countries	21%	9%	6%	15%	38%

1994	Bulgaria	Czech Republic	Hungary	Poland	Romania
Countries in transition	37%	33%	22%	15%	21%
Developed countries with market economies	47%	59%	73%	70%	53%
Developing countries	16%	8%	5%	15%	26%

1995	Bulgaria	Czech Republic	Hungary	Poland	Romania
Countries in transition	32%	35%	22%	16%	19%
Developed countries with market economies	51%	59%	73%	71%	56%
Developing countries	17%	6%	4%	13%	25%

Source: UN/ECE, INRETS-DEST Tables, 1996.

Structure of the Czech Republic's and Hungary's international traffic

		Hungary		
	1991	**1992**	**1993**	**1994**
Total tonnage ('000 tonnes)				
imports	18 397	14 964	16 504	18 253
exports	13 749	15 186	11 316	13 421
transit	13 392	13 618	8 764	9 822
total	45 538	43 768	36 584	41 496
Road share (%)				
imports	14	22	20	22
exports	29	29	37	37
transit	41	52	62	59
total	26	34	35	36
Transit share (%)				
imports	40	34	45	44
exports	30	35	31	32
transit	29	31	24	24
total	100	100	100	100
Total No. lorries				
imports	194	241	247	306
exports	263	290	282	351
transit	450	591	482	544
total	907	1 122	1 011	1 201
Share of foreign road hauliers (% total lorries)				
imports	41	50	55	55
exports	44	47	49	52
transit	97	96	94	96
total	70	73	72	73

Structure of the Czech Republic's and Hungary's
international traffic (continued)

Czech Republic				
	1991	1992	1993	1994
Total tonnage rail + road ('000 tonnes)				
imports			23 710	22 720
exports			36 600	38 450
transit			19 230	18 900
total			79 540	80 070
Transit share (%)				
imports			30	28
exports			46	48
transit			24	24
total			100	100
Road share (%)				
imports			21	20
exports			26	34
transit			59	70
total			32	39

Source: Czech and Hungarian Ministries of Transport.

ANNEX 4

UIRR and Intercontainer traffic from and to CECs

Inter-container	Bulgaria		Czech Rep.		Croatia		Hungary		Poland		Romania		Slovenia		Slovakia	
TEU	imp.	exp.	imp.	exp.	imp.	exp.	imp.	exp.	imp.	exp.	imp.	exp.	imp.	exp.	imp.	exp.
Total 90	786	712	10 990	6 662		*	15 211	22 479	5 314	4 960		*		*		*
Total 91	780	911	10 136	8 630		*	23 366	32 957	10 375	14 992	0	0		*		*
Total 92	1 358	1 258	8 315	6 563		*	33 430	38 796	9 968	14 884	607	568		*		*
Total 93																
Total 94	2 436	2 175	6 122	4 466	6 326	4 764	44 922	45 420	24 585	10 738	4 145	4 432	66 197	69 176	3 763	6 995
Transit 90	2 410		18 069		*		526		0	0	0	0	*		*	
Transit 91	3 430		21 334		*		5 676		2		30		*		*	
Transit 92	7 278		18 909		*		17 851		4		343		*		*	
Transit 93																
Transit 94	13 470		8 003		29 947		21 485		*		17 770		21 819		4 164	

170

UIRR and Intercontainer traffic from and to CECs (continued)

UIRR Shipments	Bulgaria		Czech Republic		Croatia		Hungary		Poland		Romania		Slovenia		Slovakia	
	imp.	exp.	imp.	exp.	imp.	exp.	imp.	exp.	imp.	exp.	imp.	exp.	imp.	exp.	imp.	exp.
Total 90																
Total 91	129	126					572	614					7 008	7 985		
Total 92			598	902			10 528	10 032					4 577	5 357		
Total 93								18 025	114	249				8 509		
Total 94	0	0	14 580	19 199	1 966	0	22 186	18 377	1 784	1 496	0	0	6 828	10 313	55	38

UIRR RR Shipments	Bulgaria		Czech Republic		Croatia		Hungary		Poland		Romania		Slovenia		Slovakia	
	imp.	exp.	imp.	exp.	imp.	exp.	imp.	exp.	imp.	exp.	imp.	exp.	imp.	exp.	imp.	exp.
Total 90																
Total 91	0	0	0	0			0	0		0			6 138	7 117		
Total 92	0	0	0	0			8 555	7 747	0	0			3 784	4 473		
Total 93																
Total	0	0	9 976	12 966	0	0	13 269	11 761	0	117	0	0	5 619	6 080	0	0

UIRR and Intercontainer traffic from and to CECs (continued)

UIRR TEU exc. RR	Bulgaria		Czech Republic		Croatia		Hungary		Poland		Romania		Slovenia		Slovakia	
	imp.	exp	imp.	exp.	imp.	exp.	imp.	exp.	imp.	exp.	imp.	exp.	imp.	exp.	imp.	exp.
Total 90	0	.	0	0	0	0	0	0	0	0	0	0	0	0	0	0
Total 91	297	290	0	0	0	0	1 316	1 412	0	0	0	0	2 001	1 996	0	0
Total 92	0	0	1 375	2 075	0	0	4 538	5 254	0	0	0	0	1 824	2 033	0	0
Total 93																
Total 94	**0**	**0**	**10 590**	**14 337**	**4 522**	**0**	**20 509**	**15 216**	**4 103**	**3 173**	**0**	**0**	**2 780**	**9 735**	**127**	**87**

Sources: UIRR and ICF.

Data used by INRETS-DEST Tables, November 1995.

ANNEX 5

Car ownership in central Europe and the Baltic countries

Total private cars per 1 000 inhabitants	1980	1985	1989	1990	1991	1992	1993	1994
Hungary	95	139	168	189	196	200	203	212
Poland	67	92	120	138	160	169	176	185
Czech Republic	144		221	229	236	244	261	288
Slovak Republic					171	179	186	186
Romania			47	56	60	69	78	91
Bulgaria	88	109	132	142	147	161	171	188
Slovenia			270	289	301	307	320	330
Croatia			162	170	154	140	135	146
Estonia					167	186	211	226
Latvia*	66	85	94	112	131	139	146	100
Lithuania	60	91	114	121	133	132	159	176

Growth in car ownership (%)	1989-92	1989-94	1991-94
Hungary	19	26	8
Poland	41	55	16
Czech Republic	10	30	22
Slovak Republic			9
Romania	46	92	50
Bulgaria	22	43	28
Slovenia	14	22	10
Croatia	-13	-10	-5
Estonia			35
Latvia*	48	6	-23
Lithuania	16	55	32

*   Change of series in 1994 (vehicles recorded electronically).

Sources: National statistics, national replies to the ECMT TIT Group's 1995 questionnaire, IRF.
Romania: Petreanu, Barbizon 95.

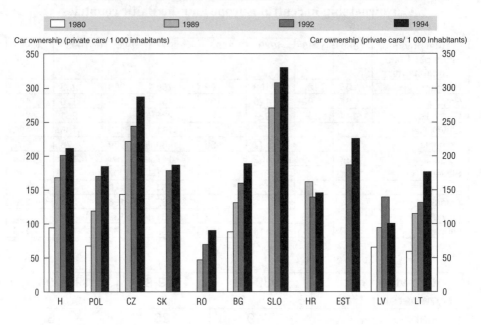

BIBLIOGRAPHY

Economic works and digests

W. Andreff (1993), *La Crise des Economies Socialistes : la rupture d'un système*, PUG.

B. Chavance (1992), *Les réformes économiques à l'est de 1950 aux années 1990*, Nathan.

M. Lavigne (1995), *The Economics of transition: from socialist economy to market economy*, Macmillan Press Ltd.

F. Lemoine, C. Leroy (1992), "Les échanges des pays d'Europe Centrale et Orientale : l'écueil d'une double concurrence", *Economie et Statistiques*, No.°260.

Ch. Reynaud (1990), "Road Transport", in: *Prospects for East-West European Transport*, ECMT.

Ch. Reynaud, G. Chatelus, M. Poincelet (1996), "Economic and social change: Central and Eastern European countries" in: *13th International Symposium on Theory and Practice in Transport Economics: Transport: New Problems, New Solutions*, ECMT.

UN Economic Commission for Europe, Economic Bulletin for Europe, United Nations.

World Bank (1995), *World Development Report 1995*.

Works on transport economics published by INRETS-DEST

Ch. Reynaud, M. Poincelet (1996) ed.: *Quel rôle des institutions locales, nationales, internationales en Europe centrale et orientale*, Paradigme/INRETS-DEST.

Ch. Reynaud, M. Poincelet (1995) ed.: *De la transition à l'intégration : quelles conditions pour les transports?*, Paradigme/INRETS-DEST.

G. Chatelus (1993), *Les transports en Europe Centrale: Inadéquation de l'offre face à une demande restructurée*, Paradigme/INRETS-DEST.

C. Thouvenin (1993), *L'évolution des chemins de fer tchéchoslovaques et hongrois*, Paradigme/INRETS-DEST.

Ch. Reynaud (1991), "Un réseau de collecte d'informations dans les transports", Réunion des 8-9 novembre 1991, PNUD-INRETS.

Other works on transport economics

ECMT (1996), *Access to European Transport Markets*.

M. Gaspard (1996), "Transport infrastructure financing in Central and Eastern Europe: Current developments and outlook", Draft working paper, European Commission, DG7.

W. Maywald (1995), *La coopération est-ouest* , UIRR Report, 1994.

Statistical digests and official national publications

ECMT (1995), *Trends in the Transport Sector 1970-1994*.

Nordic Project Fund/Nordic Investment Bank, EBRD, Ministry of Transport & Communication of Finland, Viatek , SweRoad (1993), *Via Baltica, Feasibility Study*, August.

Ministry of Transport of the Czech Republic (1995), *Mobility in the Czech Republic*.

Ministry of Transport, Hungary (1995a), *Transport Data Infrabooks* Nos.°12 to 16, 1985-1994.

Republic of Latvia, Ministry of Transport (1995), *National transport development program 1996-2010.*

Intercontainer-Interfrigo (1995), *Rapport annuel, 1994.*

UIRR (1995), *Statistiques annuelles, 1994.*

Inseneribüroo Stratum (1996), *Roads and traffic in Estonia, 1995.*

International Road Federation (1995), *Statistiques routières mondiales 1990-1994.*

HUNGARY

Katalin TANCZOS
Department of Transport Economics
Faculty of Transportation Engineering
Technical University of Budapest
Hungary

SUMMARY

Budapest, April 1996

1. CHANGES IN THE ECONOMIES OF THE CENTRAL AND EASTERN EUROPEAN COUNTRIES

1.1. Main characteristics of the central and eastern European economies prior to the transition

It is impossible to discuss the situation of transport in central and eastern Europe in isolation from the economic and political restructuring which has been sweeping the region since the dramatic social changes that began in 1989. These changes have been the most significant developments in the region since the end of the Second World War. The political, economic and social reforms are aimed at creating western-style market economies and achieving technical and social standards equivalent to those found in the European Union. The demise of the Council for Mutual Economic Assistance (CMEA), the collapse of the Soviet Union, the adoption of hard-currency accounting, inflows of western capital and technology, combined with political instability in the Balkans, have combined to exert profound effects on the region's trading relations and transport flows over the past few years.

Until 1989, the countries of central and eastern Europe were, to varying degrees, committed to inflexible economic and political objectives, with five-year plans and large-scale public ownership dictating economic development. Full employment was largely guaranteed and personal mobility severely constrained, while in industry, including the transport sector, state ownership of the means of production was characterised by overmanning, poor quality of service, outdated technology and low productivity. central plans emphasized investment in capital-intensive heavy industries, such as iron and steel or military equipment, to the detriment of consumer goods and "non-productive" service sectors, including transport. In practice, therefore, full employment and social protection were achieved at the price of economic backwardness and the absence of political freedom, and consistently lower economic performance and wealth creation than in the West.

Transport was no exception to the inefficiencies of the centrally-planned economy. Transport enterprises were primarily concerned with plan fulfilment rather than with profitability, and the whole sector was distorted by pervasive production, price and trade controls which in turn severely distorted input and output prices, divorcing resource use from resource costs. Consequently, investment in the transport sector lagged behind demand, and little attention was given to the quality of services provided. Arbitrary wage structures, job security and extensive benefits resulted in low productivity, and managers and workers had few incentives to innovate. The absence of any significant private sector severely inhibited individual entrepreneurship and initiative, with the result that these economies lacked the "creative destruction" characteristic of market economies.

These countries did not evolve independently; their development was shaped to a large extent at the regional level by the CMEA. With its stated objectives of promoting industrialisation and economic growth, whilst boosting regional trade and national production specialisation, the CMEA provided the Soviet Union with an instrument of political and economic hegemony over the central and eastern European countries. This organisation was able to harness intra- and interregional trade relations to the advantage of the Soviet Union. In the post-World War Two period, therefore, national interests were subordinated, through the CMEA, to those of the USSR and historic trade links with western Europe were shifted towards the East. The geographical distribution of the foreign trade of the socialist countries obeyed the so-called "one-third rule": one-third of trade went to the USSR, another third went to the CMEA States, and the remaining third to the rest of the World. The share of trade with hard currency countries was kept low for ideological reasons, but also due to lack of hard currency. Moreover, intra-CMEA prices failed to reflect world prices for raw materials and energy, leading to an extremely energy-intensive form of industrial production and further emphasizing the production of capital goods most suited for rail transportation. Flows consisted primarily of raw materials from the Soviet Union, headed by oil, iron, ore, coal, coke and potassium salts, and an important traffic of manufactured products and Polish coal from central and eastern Europe moving in the reverse direction. Intra-CMEA trade flows were predominantly in an East-West direction, with cross-border North-South linkages comparatively weak by comparison, as were also flows to and from western Europe.

Under the CMEA, transport was handicapped, like other sectors, by outmoded equipment and organisational practices based on the Soviet model, disincentives to improve quality, reduce costs and adopt innovations and a lack of sufficiently effective incentives to ensure efficient allocation of factors of production. Locomotive and other vehicle (bus, truck, car) design, for example, lagged behind western standards in terms of speed, performance and environmental protection, whilst track was in bad condition due to a combination of poor maintenance and heavy freight use. Moreover, the lack of realistic cost accounting coupled with ideological considerations had led, over the years, to chronic undercharging for passenger and freight services.

Basic data (1991) for some central and eastern European regions are shown in Table 1.

Table 1. **Basic data for some central and eastern European countries in 1991**

Country	Area sq. km	Population ('000s)	Population density/ sq. km	GNP per capita US$	Cars/1000 inhabitants
Bulgaria	110 910	8 974	81.2	4 425	161
Croatia	56 540	4 660	82.4	3 150	177
Czech Republic*	76 000	10 300	135.5	6 800	247
Hungary	93 030	10 584	113.7	5 311	197
Poland	312 685	37 811	120.9	2 854	151
Slovakia*	51 000	5 300	103.9	4 084	180
Slovenia	20 250	1 930	95.3	6 600	243
Romania	237 500	23 050	97.1	2 382	91

* Officially came into being on 1 January 1993.

1.2. Economic transformation

In 1990, the year in which social and economic change began, the GDP per capita of the central and eastern European countries barely exceeded 30-40 per cent of the European Community average. In 1992, the average economic performance of the countries in this area was 30 per cent below the 1989 level. The decline in GDP varied between 0.5 and 7.1 per cent in 1992. The establishment of a capital market accelerated or was started after the institutions of a market economy, a commodity market and a labour market appeared in the region. As a result of these developments, as well as the impact of reforms, production fell year by year. In a few transition countries (Poland, the Czech Republic, Hungary), the recession ended and the decline in output halted in 1994 following the implementation of privatisation programmes and reforms.

It would, of course, be a mistake to characterise the process of reform as being uniform across the region, or to argue that change can be accomplished smoothly and with equal effectiveness in every country. The goals of the new democracies are broadly similar but they are pursuing them at differing speeds, from different starting points and with varying degrees of upheaval.

Poland, Hungary and the Czech Republic are well on the way to transforming their command economies, despite significant transitional problems. In south-eastern Europe, reform has been slower and more hesitant where former communists have retained more influence (the Slovak Republic, Romania, Bulgaria); elsewhere, the collapse of Soviet hegemony has been followed by serious economic problems (Estonia, Latvia and Lithuania) or by political disintegration and civil war (Croatia). The exception is Slovenia, which boasts the highest GDP and strongest currency in the region, and which has an Association Agreement with the European Union similar to that already adopted by its four northern neighbours.

Within the region-wide process of change, therefore, a distinct core-periphery structure has already emerged, with increasing polarisation in terms of growth, foreign investment and prosperity between a unified Germany and the central and eastern European countries (Hungary, the Czech and Slovak Republics, Poland and Slovenia) on the one hand, and the stagnant, conflict-ridden economies of the Balkans on the other.

The main characteristics of the economic transformation underway in the region are described below.

The transition period in the **Czech Republic** can be summarised as follows: a radical reform programme with a relatively low level of inflation and unemployment rate; the Czech Republic is the second largest recipient, after Hungary, of foreign investment in central and eastern Europe. After a severe short-term recession, economic reforms are taking effect, old industries are closing down and the private sector is rapidly expanding.

The transition period in **Poland** has the following characteristics: successful handling of a high debt service, a strong recovery with privatisation and industrial restructuring well underway. The Polish privatisation process encompasses almost every form of privatisation being used in central and eastern Europe: spontaneous, mass, competitive and capital-inclusive privatisation, but there have also been cases where privatisation shares have been distributed, free of charge, among workers. GDP and industrial production grew 5 per cent in 1993 and by even more in 1994. The steep increase in investment, which had plummeted at the start of the transition period, resulted in substantial purchases of machinery and capital goods.

Slovenia has the highest GDP and strongest currency in the region. Market reforms are taking place smoothly. There was a steep increase in investment in 1994 and government spending on infrastructure has also played a significant part in the economic revival.

In **Hungary,** as a result of the privatisation and restructuring process which started at the beginning of the decade, the average annual decrease in real GDP exceeded 5 per cent during the three-year period between 1990 and 1992. The decrease slowed in 1993. Even if the market share of Hungarian products and services exported to western Europe increased considerably, it could not compensate for the loss of the CMEA market. As the economy has continued to decline, less and less financial resources have been allocated to investment. Instead of a desirable 22 to 24 per cent, the share of GDP allocated to investment has been only 17 to 18 per cent. It is regrettable that, even within this low rate, the share of infrastructure investment, and implicitly investment in transport infrastructure, has been falling steadily. The backlog of transport investment in 1992 exceeded 30 per cent of the country's GDP. Due to the delay in the structural transformation of the economy, and to the impact of the world-wide recession, Hungarian industrial production in 1992 was 35 per cent lower than its level in 1985. However, in 1994, there were already some promising signs. Industrial production stopped falling, and it actually rose in 1995. The situation in the real economy seems to confirm forecasts that the economy will stabilize:

-- The inflation rate is being contained between 20-30 per cent;
-- The unemployment rate is oscillating at around 11 to 12 per cent;
-- Although the rate of inflow of foreign capital has slowed down, it is still the highest in the region;
-- Privatisation and economic restructuring are underway, and the private sector's share in GDP is already estimated at about 70 per cent.

In the **Slovak Republic,** reforms have been paralysed by political infighting. The initial prospects were already poor and at first production fell steeply, but in the second half of 1994 real GDP growth was recorded.

In the Baltic States, **Estonia, Latvia and Lithuania**, the severance of traditional trade links with the former Soviet republics (CIS countries), the implementation of reforms and the development of market mechanisms have been strongly promoted. This led to a slump in production of between one-half and two-thirds over the period 1989-93. The deeper recession -- compared with the other central and eastern European countries -- which accompanied the transition process in the Baltic countries seemed to have bottomed out in 1994. The fall in GDP was halted in Estonia and slowed sharply in Latvia (a decrease of 2.2 per cent) and to a lesser extent in Lithuania (where the decrease was 6.5 per cent). These countries are controlling their public debt quite well and have been able to stabilize their newly convertible currencies; last but not least, the unemployment rate is still surprisingly low (2-6 per cent), taking into account the fall in their production. Although it has fallen considerably, the inflation rate was still very high in 1994 (30-50 per cent) and the trade balance deteriorated sharply owing to a steep increase in imports.

In **Bulgaria and Romania**, economic recovery was delayed by weak government and the effects of international sanctions against Serbia. Reforms have been watered down to a large extent by political divisions. Little foreign capital has gone to these countries and the privatisation process has not made enough headway. These countries have a very high rate of inflation (125 per cent in Bulgaria and 137 per cent in Romania). In 1994, the improvement in the economic situation was appreciable: output grew by 3.4 per cent in Romania though by only 0.2 per cent in Bulgaria.

Up to now, **Croatia** has suffered from the civil war. Future economic development hinges on a political solution being found to the war in the region. Once there is political stabilization, the country will be able to attract significant foreign investment. In 1994, the economy grew by only 0.8 per cent.

The transport sector being a service sector, it must be able to respond rapidly to socioeconomic changes and to any new demand. Under-developed transport infrastructure is an impediment to the economic development of the central and eastern European region. Rapid development of infrastructure, based on real demand, gives an impetus to the economy, and promotes the international division of labour and trade. Through the multiplier effect, transport investment is an efficient means of reviving the economy.

2. TRANSPORT IN THE CENTRAL AND EASTERN EUROPEAN COUNTRIES

2.1. Consequences of the previous economic structure

2.1.1. Evaluation of the influence of the demand side

The previous regimes were centrally-planned command economies: property relations remained unchanged even in those countries (Hungary, for example) where market mechanisms played a considerable role. Low prices and a concomitant disregard for market factors meant that companies and sectors sought to implement new investments regardless of their cost, at the same time neglecting the maintenance of existing infrastructure and plant.

Transport demand was directed by the centre; traffic was forced to use only main corridors, in line with the centralised planning structure, and the development of radial corridors was promoted. Low passenger and freight tariffs created excessive transport demand, revenue from which did not cover actual transport costs, and low tariffs were not offset by revenue from any other resource.

A few figures give an idea of the intensity of transport use in the central and eastern European countries in 1992 (measured in tonne-km per dollar of GDP, adjusted for purchasing power parities): Bulgaria 0.72; Czechoslovakia 0.82; Hungary 0.59; Poland 0.88; in comparison, in Austria, the figure was 0.21). This transport intensity can be explained by the fact that commodities and construction materials and most of the heavy, low-value commodities which generate transport activities were produced in much greater quantities in these countries than in the West.

2.1.2. Evaluation of the supply side

The transport systems of the central and eastern European countries were very different from those in western countries. The overall accessibility of transport services was generally lower although they generated higher volumes of freight per dollar of national income. The central and eastern European countries as a whole relied to a greater extent than most other countries on railways, and to a far lesser extent on roads, for both freight and passenger transport. The network configuration in these countries reflects the previous trade patterns among CMEA countries, dominated by the former Soviet Union. Border crossings with western Europe constituted major bottlenecks and there were missing road links, especially along East-West corridors.

Transport contributed about 6-8 percentage points to GDP on average. The development, operation and maintenance of the transport sector represented a valuable market for several economic sectors: the building industry, the vehicle manufacturing industry, including mechanical engineering, the chemical industry and the glass industry, etc. One in ten jobs in these countries was connected to transport.

There were, however, significant differences between the central and eastern European countries.

In 1989, the modal split for passenger and freight traffic varied between individual countries. The share of cars and taxis ranged from 36 per cent in Bulgaria to 58 per cent in the former Yugoslavia. Conversely, rail's share in passenger transport varied from 11 per cent in Yugoslavia to 24.2 per cent in Poland. Overall, rail's share of transport in the central and eastern European countries was 3-5 times that in western countries.

In freight transportation, modal shares partially reflected specific geographical circumstances (for instance, the relatively high share of waterways in Hungary), but railways were the chief mode, accounting for over 50 per cent of tonne-kms in Bulgaria (50.1 per cent), the Czech and Slovak Republics (66.5 per cent) and Poland (67.6 per cent), and 40.2 per cent in Hungary. Road, by contrast, was a secondary mode, accounting for only 20-25 per cent of the market in the centrally-positioned countries (Hungary, the Czech Republic and Poland), and exceeding 40 per cent only in Bulgaria and the former Yugoslavia (reflecting the more rural nature of their geography, more suited to road transport).

The high priority given to rail transport under the old regime was the upshot of a combination of economic and ideological factors, reinforced by direct state planning principles which emphasized railway accessibility for all major population centres and enterprises and restricted road transport to little more than a feeder role. As for passenger transport, private car ownership was considered a symbol of excessive western consumerism and a manifestation of cultural decadence, whilst the lack of necessary resources, technology and know-how inhibited the development of the domestic car industry. This resulted in car ownership levels of between one-quarter and one-half of those found in the West, with a regional mean in 1992 of 188 cars per thousand of population.

Public transport (including rail) was heavily subsidised. Consumer choice of private cars was limited to East German Trabants and Wartburgs, Russian Ladas, Czech Skodas and Polish Fiats, with little chance of obtaining imports from the West. Even the best "eastern" cars were far inferior to western models, being slow, uncomfortable and unreliable. In Hungary, where a degree of economic liberalisation had been introduced during the 1980s, the waiting list in 1989 was about five years for a Lada and three to four years for a Skoda. High fuel prices resulted in very high running costs compared to the low fares for public transport.

Average passenger journey distances were broadly similar to those in western European countries but freight shipment distances were a little shorter. Passenger train loading was similar to that in western Europe but freight loading was significantly higher. Traffic density per kilometre was generally lower than in the West, indicating that large parts of the networks of the central and eastern European countries were lightly used, and reflecting limited capacity in terms of double tracking and signalling technology. Indicators of motorway route density reflect the relative neglect of the road network during the planned- economy period (for example, in Hungary, 41.34 km/million of population compared with 140 km in the Netherlands).

These figures need to be set alongside data relating to the quality and efficiency of the rail and road networks. The proportion of public investment allocated to rail infrastructure has generally been below the levels required to maintain technical, economic and commercial standards; as a result, the state of the network has deteriorated to a point where it imposes significant costs on operators and users, and constitutes a major impediment to economic growth. The Polish rail network, for example, though the seventh largest in the world in terms of length, has long experienced backlogs in maintenance and repair. Deliveries of new rolling stock have lagged well behind requirements. Similarly, whilst the modernisation of marshalling yards and extension of electrification have been pushed ahead, the latter has not been accompanied by parallel improvements in the signalling system, resulting in only limited increases in carrying capacity.

The European Bank for Reconstruction and Development estimated that, overall, some US$ 30-40 billion would be required to bring the region's conventional railways up to western standards, excluding any investments that may be planned in high-speed lines; a sum required to upgrade the road networks in the region would be almost double this amount.

The size and quality of the networks can be illustrated by a few examples. In terms of size, the Polish railway network is clearly the largest, exceeded in Europe only by the SNCF and DB. The size of the railway networks in the other central and eastern European countries is closer to the European average. As for quality, the central and eastern European rail networks generally have less double tracking than in the West. The levels of electrification are below western levels too.

The overall labour productivity of the railways (taking into account the different mix of passenger and freight services) in the central and eastern European countries was only about 30-40 per cent of that of the western European railways.

2.2. Changes in demand connected with the new market economy

The political and economic events of the past five years have resulted in dramatic changes within the transport sector. While the changes in passenger and freight transport demand have been broadly similar in all the transition countries, it is necessary to distinguish trends within the different groups of central and eastern European countries. Because the amount of data available is limited, the analysis will be restricted to a few countries in transition (mainly the central European ones). Consistent and reliable data, showing the linkages between changing intercity transport demand and the restructuring underway in this sector, was provided only for Hungary; the analysis will therefore be based on the data of this country.

2.2.1. Passenger transport

The sweeping changes which have taken place in the last six years have had an impact on passenger transport. The changes that took place in the 1980s caused public passenger transport to decline still further. In addition, the number of individual vehicles has been steadily increasing, although rising car use costs have greatly reduced annual vehicle use. The demand for long-distance bus transport has also fallen significantly.

Generally speaking, the decrease in the demand for public transport is closely correlated with the economic situation of these countries, taking into account the restructuring of the institutional system and fare increases in recent years.

The pattern of rush-hour traffic has changed somewhat because there has been an increase in daytime journeys due to the growth of private business, changes in the distribution of traffic, and travel by unemployed people. Passenger transport, mainly by road, increased in more developed areas and declined in areas hit by the recession.

The domestic economic and social changes taking place in the central and eastern European countries were accompanied by a shift in the trend and volume of international trade and tourism. International trade was diverted from eastern countries to western ones. As for tourism, the emphasis also shifted to the West and -- further to the easing of travel restrictions and other economic changes in all the central and eastern European countries -- the number of foreigners visiting individual countries and the reasons for their visits also changed.

It is estimated that passenger transport (in terms of passenger-km) will evolve in line with the increase in GDP until the end of century. At the end of century, the level of passenger transport will be similar to that in the early 1980s, but the structural and qualitative breakdown will be different. The economic upswing expected after 2000 may generate a higher rate of increase in transport. On preliminary estimates, passenger transport will increase at a slightly higher rate than the rate of increase in GDP.

Concerning the modal split of passenger transport, it is realistic to expect a further decrease in the share of rail and public transport by road, though this decrease can be offset to some extent by a fare and price policy that meets the needs of the national economy. For environmental, energy-saving, sectoral and social reasons, it is reasonable to subsidise public transport. The growth of private transport should comply with the principle of "sustainable development".

Table 2 gives aggregated data (including local and intercity traffic) for passenger transport (expressed in billion passenger-kilometres) in the countries in transition between 1980 and 1994. The data are grouped into three categories -- Core countries: Poland, Hungary, the Czech Republic and the

Slovak Republic (previously the Czechoslovak Republic) and Slovenia; Baltic countries: Estonia, Lithuania, Latvia; Balkan countries: Romania, Bulgaria, and Croatia.

Table 2. **Passenger transport (billion passenger-km)**
in 1980, 1985, 1993 and 1994

a) **Rail**

COUNTRY	1980	1985	1993	1994
CS	18.04	19.84		
CZ			8.29	8.49
H	13.71	11.21	8.77	8.57
PL	46.33	1.67	30.87	27.61
SK			4.57	4.55
SLO	1.44		0.57	0.59
EST	1.55	1.65	0.72	0.54
LT	3.26	3.42	2.70	1.57
LV	4.77	5.21	2.36	1.79
RO	23.22	31.08	19.40	18.31
BG	7.06	7.77	5.84	5.06
HR	3.62	4.06	0.95	1.18

b) **Private cars**
(data available only for two countries)

COUNTRY	1980	1985	1993	1994
H	36.00	45.80	48.00	46.20
BG	3.73	4.73	3.04	n.a.

c) Buses and coaches

COUNTRY	1980	1985	1993	1994
CS	33.75	36.62		
CZ			21.91	41.29**
H	26.42	28.02	19.03	18.64
PL	49.22	52.09	37.81	34.26
SK			11.45	10.89
SLO	4.99	3.51	2.78	2.50
EST	3.66	1.28	2.54	2.35
LT	6.67	7.39	3.67	3.75
LV	4.55	5.27	1.72	1.8
RO	24.02	21.69	19.82	25.02
BG	21.61	24.72	13.98	12.12
HR	6.82	8.25	3.01	3.35

**/break in the series

d) Total road transport and total passenger transport

Country	Total road transport				Total passenger transport			
	1980	1985	1993	1994	1980	1985	1993	1994
CS	33.75*	36.62*			51.80*	56.46*		
CZ			21.91	41.29**,*			30.20*	49.78**,*
H	62.42	73.82	67.23	64.84	76.14	85.03	76.00	73.41
PL	49.22*	52.09*	37.81*	34.26*	49.22*	52.09*	37.81*	34.26*
SK			11.45*	10.89*			16.01*	15.44*
SLO	4.93*	6.51*	2.78*	2.60*	6.36*	8.17*	3.25*	3..13
EST	3.66*	4.28*	2.54*	2.35*	5.21*	5.93*	3.26*	2.89*
LT	6.67*	7.39*	3.67*	3.75*	9.93*	10.80*	6.37*	5.32*
LV	4.55*	5.27*	1.72*	1.80*	9.32*	10.48*	4.08*	3.59*
RO	24.02*	21.69*	19.82*	25.02*	47.24*	52.77*	39.22*	43.33*
BG	74.45	76.33	91.97	94.77	81.41	82.90	98.67	101.41
HR	6.82*	8.25*	3.01*	3.35*	10.44*	12.31*	3.96*	4.53*

*   Excluding private cars.
**   Break in the series.

On the basis of these data, it is possible to analyse trends country by country.

The average decrease in rail passenger traffic in 1994 was 8 per cent; in comparison with 1989, however, traffic was down dramatically, by more than 46.5 per cent. This decline was largely attributable to the decline in personal mobility as a result of falling incomes and often substantial increases in rail fares, coupled with greater competition from private cars.

It is clear from the time series for rail passenger traffic that, in the first group of countries, after a significant decline in demand before 1993, the slope of the trend changed and that in some countries there was even a small increase (e.g. the Czech Republic and Croatia); in the Baltic States, the dramatic decline in traffic occurred slightly later, after 1993.

Analysis of bus and coach traffic in 1994 shows a significant increase in Romania, where the number of passenger-kms was already higher than in 1985 or in 1980. A similar, but less significant increase, was recorded in Croatia (11 per cent) and in two Baltic States (Lithuania 2 per cent, Latvia 4 per cent). The remaining countries experienced a further decline in bus and coach traffic in 1994.

It is impossible to give a complete picture of the passenger transport situation because of the lack of information concerning private car use. In **Hungary**, for example, there was a significant decrease in mileage in 1993 and 1994, which can be explained by higher running costs and especially by the steep increase in petrol prices. The growth in private transport was due to an increase in the passenger car fleet, on the one hand, and to the appearance of private taxis on the other.

The reasons for the changes in the modal split of passenger transport were very similar in all the central and eastern European countries. This can be illustrated by the Hungarian case.

The modal split under the former regime -- and in the other socialist countries as well -- was characterised by distorted costs and cross-subsidisation. In 1993, 87.1 per cent of passenger transport (in terms of passenger-kms went by road, 10.6 per cent by rail, 2.2 per cent by air and 0.1 per cent by inland waterway). Rail's share of interurban public transport decreased by 6.5 per cent over 13 years. Road's share of public transport increased by 1.5 per cent from 1980 to 1993, while the number of passengers transported fell considerably. The share of inland waterways and air transport in total passenger transport is small; however, the share of inland waterways hardly changed, while that of air transport doubled.

2.2.2. Freight transport

A direct effect of the economic changes -- the emergence of market and property relations, inflation, unemployment running at over 10 per cent, industrial production down by one-third, the breakdown of co-ordination between production plants, a slump in agricultural production -- has been that transport demand has been rationalised but has fallen. The growth of domestic small businesses has been quite rapid, but privatisation has taken place more slowly than expected. The big, state-owned companies are on the verge of bankruptcy, while activities like building, assembling, mining or metallurgy, which typically have a high transport content, have declined sharply.

The population has new needs and new businesses have sprung up which involve less transport. Demand for local and short-distance hauls is growing, eroding still further the position of the railways and transforming the structure of road haulage. A large number of up-to-date small trucks have appeared on the roads and domestic HGV traffic has fallen perceptibly. Demand for inland water transport has fallen simultaneously.

Freight transport demand -- in terms of tonne-kilometres -- has fallen by a much lower rate than GDP. In line with the modernisation of the economy and the growth of less bulky but higher-value goods, freight transport is unlikely to increase until the end of century, while its long-term rate of increase will be somewhat lower than the rate of increase in GDP.

Table 3 gives aggregated data for freight transport (expressed in billion tonne-kilometres) for the countries in transition between 1980 and 1994. The data have been grouped as in Table 2.

Table 3. **Freight transport (billion tonne-kilometres) by rail and road**

COUNTRY	RAIL				ROAD			
	1980	1985	1993	1994	1980	1985	1993	1994
CS	66.21	66.20			21.34	21.46		
CZ			25.61	23.16			13.1	22.66**
H	24.40	22.31	7.46	7.43	11.40	12.72	13.38	13.01
PL	134.74	120.64	64.36	65.79	44.55	36.59	40.74	45.37
SK			14.30	12.30			5.46	5.87
SLO	3.85	4.29	2.26	2.45	3.91	4.69	2.50	2.44
EST	5.92	6.45	3.74	3.38	4.22	4.44	1.06	1.42
LT	18.24	20.93	11.03	8.85	6.92	7.37	6.91	4.57
LV	17.59	19.93	9.85	9.52	5.13	5.55	1.25	1.40
RO	75.54	74.22	25.17	24.70	11.76	5.96	2.78	5.97
BG	17.68	18.17	7.70	7.77	13.07	13.47	5.21	
HR	7.56	8.68	1.59	1.53	2.51*	2.43*	0.88*	0.62*

*   Transport for hire and reward only.
**   Excluding own-account road transport.

The average rate of change in freight transport (the detailed analysis is confined to the surface transport modes, rail and road), expressed in terms of tonne-kilometres, can be calculated from the time series in the above table. The difficulties associated with the transformation of the economic and political system, coupled with the steep fall in production and the problems resulting from the break-up of the former Yugoslavia, inevitably affected freight transport in these countries. In terms of tonne-kilometres, it fell by over 47 per cent between 1988 and 1993. The decline accelerated in the first two years of this period, gradually slowed in 1992, and in 1993 there were the first signs of an upturn in some countries. As the upturn continued and spread to most of the other countries, there was a positive impact on freight traffic in the region. 1994 was the first year since 1988 that the annual growth was positive, averaging 4 per cent.

The detailed time series show that performance varied across countries. In 1994, total freight traffic increased substantially in Romania (+9.5 per cent) and Poland (+7 per cent), but fell sharply in Lithuania (-25.2 per cent), the Slovak Republic (-7.3 per cent) and Croatia (-6.5 per cent).

Not all modes were affected to the same extent by the generally negative trend in freight traffic from 1989 to 1993 in the transition countries. Nor did they all benefit to the same extent from the turnaround in 1994. In 1993, road hauliers managed to halt the decline in their business.

Rail and inland waterway freight traffic was again down in 1994. Rail freight traffic declined dramatically in the Czech Republic (-10 per cent), in the Baltic region (Estonia, -10 per cent, Lithuania, -20 per cent and Latvia, -3 per cent) and a moderate decline was also recorded in Romania (-2 per cent) and Croatia (-4 per cent). The average rate of decline in rail freight traffic in the central and eastern European countries was 3.7 per cent. The main cause of the decline was a sharp fall in domestic traffic (-11.7 per cent). International rail traffic increased by 8.2 per cent. The overall fall in rail freight traffic since 1989 was 55 per cent. The only countries in which rail traffic increased in 1994 were Slovenia (+8.2 per cent), Hungary (+3.6 per cent) and Poland (+2.2 per cent).

The changes in road freight traffic reflected the process of privatisation of major enterprises. The road haulage market is increasingly fragmented, with a much greater number of operators. It is important to emphasize the flexibility of the road sector, which has responded to the changes in road haulage demand that have accompanied the economic reforms. In 1994, road freight traffic increased significantly in Romania, Estonia, Poland and Latvia (in each of these countries the increase was more than 10 per cent). Only Lithuania and Croatia registered a small decrease in demand in this sector.

To illustrate the changes taking place in freight transport demand, we shall look at Hungary.

The main economic parameters for Hungary are as follows:

- In 1995, GDP is forecast to increase by 1.5 per cent compared to the previous year. Output and exports are growing, there has been an improvement in productivity, and new projects are being started. However, the 6-8 per cent increase in production during the first half of the year showed signs of easing off in the second half. In some sectors and services, activity was flat throughout the year;
- Nationwide employment fell by 1 per cent on the previous year, while the number of jobs in businesses employing more than ten people fell by 4.5 per cent;
- Employees' gross average earnings increased by an average of 17 per cent;
- Overall, borrowing by businesses increased by nearly 100 billion HUF (0.5 billion ECU) in 1995. In addition, the amount of direct foreign credit increased by more than 50 per cent.

The privatisation of Hungary's blue-chip state enterprises dragged on until the end of last year, although eventually the proceeds of the sell-offs exceeded expectations. The 1995 budget envisaged privatisation receipts of 150 billion HUF (0.75 billion ECU) for the Hungarian Privatisation and State Holding Company; however, the actual proceeds exceeded 455 billion HUF (2.3 billion ECU). In one year, the company received more income than had been generated in the whole history of Hungarian privatisation from 1990-94. In 1995, not only was income substantially greater, but there was a change in the quality of Hungarian privatisation. The sale of shares in the electricity and gas utilities will stabilize the country's energy supplies, because the new owners have undertaken contractually to inject 400 billion HUF (2 billion ECU) into the utilities for urgent renovation and modernisation. The gas companies, for instance, have undertaken the construction of new pipelines and the connection of several hundred localities to the gas supply. Local authorities will receive about 20 billion HUF (0.1 billion ECU) from the sale of assets.

To date, about two-thirds of state property slated for privatisation has been sold, while that still to be sold is valued at more than 800 billion HUF (4 billion ECU). The process will be finished in the next few years.

Transport trends, and especially the modal split, need to be set in relation to the economic changes taking place.

The previous production structure was out of date, resulting in a high demand for freight haulage. Hungarian freight haulage as a percentage of GNP was several times that in developed European countries.

In 1990, before the economic and social changes took place, the modal split of freight transport, expressed in tonne-kilometres, was as follows: road, 29.21 per cent; rail, 32.33 per cent; inland waterways, 28.24 per cent; pipelines, 10.19 per cent; and air transport, 0.03 per cent.

The slow structural changes that have taken place in the modal split can be gauged from the data series. By 1995, the split had changed as follows: the share of road transport was 48.67 per cent (of this figure, small enterprises accounted for 27.34 per cent), rail had dropped to 30.42 per cent, inland waterway transport was down to 4.55 per cent, pipelines were up to 16.35 per cent, and air transport was less than 0.1 per cent.

Rail's share of freight transport is higher than in West European countries due to an outdated production structure and the former pattern of foreign trade. The tonne-km/per capita index of the railways in the mid-1980s was more than two-thirds higher than in Austria, and nearly double the figure for Germany. However, rail's share of freight transport has fallen considerably since then, in respect of both performance and share.

Road's share of freight transport has increased considerably in the last decade. The bulk of road haulage is carried out by big organisations, and private hauliers started to make an impact only from the second half of the decade.

The share of shipping (comprising both sea and inland waterway transport) grew between 1980 and 1990, though it was sea transport that accounted for the increase.. The share of inland waterways fell sharply. Though transport via the Danube is cheap and environmentally-friendly, it is less and less exploited. During the period 1990-93, shipping also fell in absolute terms, due to general economic restructuring and the recession, though this does not show up in the performance ratio because of an even larger recession in overall transport.

The negative impacts of the transport modal split on energy use and the environment, which are characteristic of the West European transport system, were also felt in Hungary. The developed countries are now seeking to co-ordinate policies with a view to influencing the modal split, one of the main aims being to increase the attractiveness of more environmentally-friendly transport by means of market-oriented tax policies and state subsidies.

2.3. Future trends in the modal split

2.3.1. *Passenger transport*

The existing level of car ownership warrants maintaining public transport at a level higher than that prevailing in western Europe. In addition, public transport reduces traffic congestion, is less harmful to the environment, saves space and promotes urban development -- all social reasons for maintaining it and improving its quality.

Improving the quality of passenger transport means upgrading roads, tracks, vehicles, servicing facilities and information services.

Besides improving quality, there is a public service obligation:

-- to provide long-distance transport to every part of the country;
-- to provide local transport services in residential areas, at a reasonable cost and with a frequency warranted by mobility patterns, with support from local or central government. Where necessary, it should be provided jointly by central and local government.

International air, rail, bus and inland waterway services should be operated on a commercial basis.

With a view to promoting environmental protection and energy conservation, support should be given to the use of:

-- intercity rail transport;
-- underground, tram, trolley and environment-friendly rail and bus services, if possible in urban transport.

Financing can be used as a means of regulation. Passenger transport should be divided into:

-- basic transport provided by central and local government;
-- other passenger services run on commercial lines.

2.3.2. Freight transport

Freight transport should aim to provide the best possible service to the economy, to meet European standards, to protect the environment and to promote energy saving and efficiency.

Freight transport is subject to restrictions and regulations introduced in some countries for the purpose of protecting the local market and preserving the modal split.

In the field of international freight transport, increasing use will be made of telematics and logistical systems, and greater importance will be attached to environment protection.

In addition to transportation proper, activities like forwarding, storage, packing and customs processing should be expanded. Waste disposal facilities should be developed. Freight transport should become an integral part of the production, supply and distribution chain, and logistic centres should be established. In addition to shipping, loading, storage and packing, logistic centres should provide all the necessary support for the manufacture and marketing of goods. Combined transport should likewise be promoted.

For reasons of environmental protection and energy saving, the State should promote rail, inland waterway and combined transport via regulation, subsidies and other direct and indirect means. In particular, a proper framework of tariffs, taxes, organisational and technical measures should be put in place for transit freight.

The transport of hazardous materials needs to be regulated and co-ordinated at both national and international level. Technical, legal and environmental measures related to the transport of hazardous materials, implemented by the European Union and neighbouring countries, should be monitored closely. The countries in transition should participate in the framing of international regulations on hazardous materials. They should seek to harmonize their regulations with European regulations and practice. Rail and inland waterways are particularly suited to the safe transport of hazardous goods.

3. CHANGES IN THE TRANSPORT INFRASTRUCTURE OF THE COUNTRIES IN TRANSITION IN RESPONSE TO CHANGES IN DEMAND

The transport system comprises several vertically-organised sub-sectors: road, rail, inland waterway, air and pipelines. It may be public (provided by central or local government) or commercial. The public provision of transport presupposes decisionmaking authority and accountability. It can be differentiated by national, regional or local level. The construction and development of public transport networks, together with transport regulation, is the responsibility of central government, while local transport is the responsibility of local government.

The scope of state competence varies according to the sub-sector, and the laws, standards, international treaties, etc., relating to the given sub-sector. The latter constitute the framework within which transport operates.

The State, within its statutory sphere of activity, exercises direct or indirect control over the construction and operation of infrastructure and transport networks. Its role is very similar in both inland transport sectors (road and rail). The role of the State with regard to inland waterways, and especially air transport, is very different. Irrespective of the sub-sector, it has a basic obligation to meet certain requirements relating to national and civil defence and to exercise surveillance.

After discussing the changes required in the transport infrastructure of central and eastern European countries in general, we shall look at the Hungarian case again by way of example.

3.1. Road network

The central government is responsible for about one-third of the road network, the remaining two-thirds being the responsibility of local governments. These responsibilities cover development, maintenance and operation.

The road network is owned first and foremost by the Ministry of Transport, Telecommunications and Water Management (MTTWM), though local governments also own roads. The Ministry is responsible for national issues, and the local governments for local ones. Regional responsibilities are divided between county governments and local organisations of the MTTWM, i.e. the road directorates. Other Ministries and authorities may also put their viewpoints on any issue, amounting to a further measure of state control. Social and voluntary organisations, local assemblies and governments, together with the Parliament, also debate road transport issues.

Within the above framework, the State is responsible for:

-- Preparation of a development strategy (to ensure that the transport sector meets the needs of the economy, long-term definition of the aims of road transport within overall transportation, assessment of demand, setting priorities, project financing and implementation);
-- Technical and procedural regulation (professional standards, legal frameworks, licensing rules, quality and safety standards);
-- Financing (management of road funds, calculating the costs of development, maintenance and operation, preparation of loan applications, concession contracts, general financial control);

- General managerial functions (purchase of land for infrastructure development, sale of land that is not needed, ensuring that maintenance is carried out properly).
- Project development (design, implementation and construction, financing, conclusion of commercial contracts, technical and financial supervision of investors, quality and financial control);
- Operation and maintenance (organisation, materials and personnel, safety requirements, leasing and commercial contracts, maintenance and operation requirements, emergency measures, on-going monitoring);
- Overseeing of R&D activity (setting strategic priorities, organisation and financial conditions, application of R&D findings);
- Authorisation and certification (appointing chief designer, licensing of legal and other experts, other qualifications).

To develop the motorway network, it is necessary to provide the necessary land, to plan long-term use and to prevent land speculation.

Alongside the posts of city and county chief architect, the posts of city and county chief engineer should be created. (Though most infrastructure investment consists of civil engineering, decisions are frequently taken by people who are not properly qualified.)

3.2. Rail network

The 1993 Railway Act seeks to promote environmentally-friendly rail transport and ensure that it meets public service obligations and objectives of transport policy. It distinguishes between:

- infrastructure (construction, upgrading and maintenance, use of railway tracks and facilities); and
- commercial services, i.e. the carriage of passengers and goods by rail.

In the longer term, the infrastructure operator is committed to leasing railway tracks and facilities to domestic or (on the basis of reciprocity) foreign railway companies.

National rail infrastructure and facilities are, and will remain, in exclusive state ownership; local public railways and facilities belong to local urban governments, while the rail system in the capital belongs to the city government. The State's main responsibilities are the following:

Central government:

-- Promoting rail transport policies that take account of the need to protect the built and natural environment;
-- Supervision;
-- Implementation of undertakings and commitments in international rail transport;
-- Establishment and operation of a national railway company;
-- Operation of rail infrastructure;
-- Topping up rail transport revenue from the central budget;
-- Organising calls for bids, bid appraisal, conclusion of concession contracts;
-- Organisation of rail transport for the purposes of national and civil defence.

Local government:

-- Promoting the development of local public railways; operation of railway infrastructure;
-- Local government subsidies for the local lines;
-- Topping up revenue from local rail services with subsidies from local government budgets;
-- Issuing calls for bids, bid assessment and conclusion of concession contracts.

The scale of rail infrastructure projects over the next few years, for example, for electrification, will be determined by the amount of central funding available.

Joint projects (between central government and local government, and between local government and companies) may also be implemented.

3.3. The inland waterway network

The opening of the Danube-Maine-Rhine waterway in the autumn of 1992 created a direct inland waterway link to western Europe; inland waterway transport thus has an important role to play in European transport. The new waterway offers a non-polluting means of transport for the Rhine area and especially for the Danube region, and will enable the Hungarian import-export trade to be conducted more efficiently. At the same time, the elimination of bottlenecks in networks and ports will restore to this traditionally low-cost and environmentally-friendly transport mode the competitive edge it lost in previous decades.

A prerequisite for inland waterway transport is a suitable waterway, a network of ports and an entrepreneurial environment. Transport policy aims to meet these three conditions. Comparison of the costs of the various modes shows that, in an efficient transport system, inland waterways have both economic and environmental advantages. They have an important role to play in combined transport in Hungary, and can help to divert traffic from polluting road transport to the railways or waterways, both of which are safer and less polluting, at least as far as bulk cargoes are concerned.

The State oversees the construction of infrastructure (waterways and public ports). A primary goal is to develop the Danube waterway, as well as the network of national public ports, since these decide the degree to which Hungary can participate in international waterway transport. The development of regional and local ports will depend on local market conditions.

State supervision is warranted even at less important levels of infrastructure in order to ensure compliance with European standards. The present and future classifications of domestic waterways should comply with these standards.

3.4. Air transport

The Hungarian Republic participates in international air transport in a dual capacity. On the one hand, it must fulfil its commitments under international agreements: it is liable for the maintenance and operation of airports and services for international air transport. On the other hand, it is a contracting party to nearly sixty bilateral international aviation agreements. The Hungarian national carrier operates international scheduled air connection services between Budapest and several capitals and cities throughout the world. Hungarian carriers fly over the air-space of the contracting states and uses their airports.

Airports

Airports comprise both civil airports and military or other types of aerodrome (for recreational flying, business aviation, etc.). The State is responsible for running them.

Air services

Given Hungary's geographical situation and international commitments, it would need air transport even if it had no carriers or aircraft of its own. Transport statistics show a strong increase in air transit, several times greater than traffic to and from Budapest or making stopovers in Budapest.

Following the Soviet withdrawal, air-space capacity has been increased. A new Aviation Act has been passed which complies with European rules for civil and military aviation.

The Transport Ministers of the European Civil Aviation Commission (ECAC) member countries have approved the programme of harmonization and integration of European air traffic control. It is essential to implement a uniform European air traffic control system before the end of the decade. The development programme for domestic air traffic has been drawn up with an eye to the implementation of an integrated European air traffic control system.

In the EUROCONTROL member countries, airport operation is separated from air traffic control services. Airports, whether with or without a state guarantee, are run on commercial lines, while air traffic control services -- except for services supplied in certain airports -- are not, although they are being privatised in some countries (Switzerland, Austria, etc.). The maintenance and development costs of such services are covered by navigation fees, and EUROCONTROL carries out the relevant accounting and other duties.

4. ADJUSTMENTS REQUIRED TO EXISTING ROAD AND RAIL INFRASTRUCTURE

4.1. Modernisation of road infrastructure

The Hungarian road network development plan involves the construction of motorways to the country's borders, from Budapest to Vienna and Bratislava, Budapest to Belgrade, and thence to Ukraine-Slovenia and Croatia. They will then be connected to international Trans-European trunk networks. It is also planned to develop the present radial structure of the Hungarian network, and in particular an orbital motorway around Budapest.

In addition to the construction of motorways within the master plan of the Trans-European motorways network, the following investments are planned:

-- Enlargement of the capacity of three sections of the trunk road network where there are bottlenecks; construction of by-passes to improve safety at accident black spots;
-- Enlargement of the capacity of roads and bridges;
-- Construction of bridges and ring roads.

The M1 motorway between Budapest and the Austrian border was completed in 1995, and it is planned to complete the M15 section to the Slovakian border by 1997. The transport administration would like to conclude concession contracts in 1995 for the extension of the M5 motorway to Belgrade. The M3 motorway to Ukraine will be funded by the State. Tenders for the extension to and operation of the M7 motorway to the Adriatic area will be launched in 1996.

Modernisation of the road network is seen as being crucial to economic growth and an important step towards accession to the European Union. Innovative financing techniques have pushed the country ahead in central and eastern Europe. Hungary's use of Build-Operate-Transfer (BOT) techniques is seen as pioneering in the region. By granting concessions to construct roads and then to operate them as toll-roads for a period of 35 years, taxpayers' pockets are spared.

The country needed around US$ 3.5 billion to build 500-600 kilometres of motorway, and it was obvious there was not going to be enough public money available. Traditionally, infrastructure was considered to be a public service and was financed out of taxpayers' money, but in the past century the pay-as-you-go principle has become widely accepted. Tolls will be set according to market demand, with those of the M1-M15 being relatively high because of the large volume of international traffic with the ability to pay them which they will carry, while those of the M5 will be only half as much. Sixty to seventy per cent of the traffic on the former is international, but only 30 per cent of the traffic on the latter is international, although that proportion is expected to increase if peace is reached in the former Yugoslavia. Those drivers who do not want to pay tolls will be free to use other roads, which will continue to be maintained as until now.

The low ability-to-pay of users may threaten the viability of the M3 motorway extension. Western traffic is negligible, and toll rates will need to reflect this. The State therefore ended up establishing its own concession company to take on the project.

Upgrading of border crossing points and related facilities is also required because of the increase in international (especially truck) traffic.

It is also essential to modernise the domestic road vehicle fleet and to replace outdated vehicles. The number of passenger cars is set to increase to 2.4 million by the end of the century. The number of buses does not need to be increased, but their quality should be improved. A slight increase in the number of trucks can be expected, and the increase in the number of smaller-capacity vehicles will continue under the influence of economic restructuring.

4.2. Modernisation of the railways

The development of the rail network should comply with EU directives and practice. Preference should be given to this transport mode on safety, environmental and energy-saving grounds.

State resources should be made available for the maintenance and development of rail infrastructure. Support for railway modernisation should not be seen as a drain on the budget but as the prerequisite for ensuring that the rail system meets the needs of the economy.

Market conditions require that long-term spare capacity be shed. Various criteria can be identified for adapting operation to effective demand:

-- Reasonable distances for freight handling facilities, frequency of servicing according to traffic;
-- Passenger transport and freight haulage requirements.

Suitable levels of service should be identified in conjunction with the economic organisations and local governments concerned.

The necessary resources are not available in the short term to halt the decline in the railways, but they should be supported by the State on environmental, energy-saving and other grounds. Even to stabilize its share of transport at a lower level than the present one, but higher than that in western Europe, will require a major effort. As flexible a policy as possible should be put in place for the "commercial railway" to allow it to compete with road haulage markets. In calculating the state subsidy for the railways, the social benefits of rail transport should be taken into account.

Objectives until the turn of century:

-- A major restructuring of the railways, optimisation of costs, improved safety, quality and competitiveness;
-- Adequate investments for maintenance and development.

Priority will be given to the following:

-- Infrastructure developments to preserve the transit competitiveness of the Hungarian network and to increase its role within the European trunk network (e.g. reconstruction of the Hegyeshalom-Budapest line);
-- Upgrading of any sections of the trunk network warranted by market demand;
-- Investments to reduce operating costs, improve safety and connect the network to international information systems;
-- Selective upgrading of passenger rolling stock, especially for international, intercity and suburban traffic ;
-- Purchase of railway wagons suitable for combined transport (these wagons will not necessarily have to be the property of railway companies);
-- Upgrading of feeder lines after lifting of speed restrictions;
-- Rationalisation of the operation of local lines; require local authorities to contribute to the operating costs of by-lines with little traffic;

-- Further to a review of regional development, environmental protection, economic and policy considerations, final or temporary closure of lines on which there is a chronic shortage of demand;
-- In the long term, construction of a new "VO" railway line to the south of Budapest is also conceivable.

5. CHANGES IN THE OPERATION OF INTERCITY TRANSPORT

The pace of transformation and restructuring varies across the central and eastern European countries but the direction of the changes is very similar. Some countries are at a more advanced stage of transition than others. The transformation has gone furthest in the Czech Republic, Poland and Hungary. Since March of this year, the first two countries have been Members of the OECD. Their accession was the acknowledgement by western governments of the efforts their governments have been making to reform the economic and social structures of their countries.

After describing general trends, we shall illustrate some important features of the transition process from the Hungarian example.

5.1. Changes in the legal and organisational framework

5.1.1.   Changes in the legal framework and rules regulating business activity

The primary purpose of the legal framework is to regulate property and contractual relationships between transport carriers. The regulatory framework pertaining to sub-sectors has been partially completed.

National roads, railways, waterways, national ports and international airports are all the exclusive property of the State. Local roads are likewise owned by local governments.

The Act on Concessions allows the right to use or operate assets owned by the State or local governments to be ceded to third parties in return for payment.

Act XCIV of 1993 on the railways distinguishes between "track" (infrastructure) and "commercial services".

The "Railway Act" came into force on 1 January 1994. In the same year, the Ministry of Transport, Telecommunications and Water Management signed a contract with MAV Rt (the Railway Company of Hungary). The railways were divided into "infrastructure" and "commercial services", but the same company may manage both.

This division is in line with the trend in western Europe, the aim being to make railways more commercially-minded and to ease the burden on the state budget.

Act I of 1988 on Road Transport states that the road network consists of public roads and private roads. Public roads are of national or local interest.

The Act regulates the rights of road owners and the activity of economic organisations participating in road passenger and freight transport. The public service obligations of central and local government need to be specified more clearly, and market requirements should be identified.

Although the Act was modelled on regulatory developments in Europe, from 1990 some restrictions had to be introduced on international freight shipping in order to avoid market disruption; legal harmonization is still required at European level.

5.1.2. *Organisational changes*

The transformation of state-owned companies belonging to the Ministry of Transport, Telecommunications and Water Management was completed by 30 June 1993.

Firstly, the non-passenger business of the VOLAN companies was hived off and the companies now carry only passengers.

In 1994, the VOLAN Group carried 450 million intercity passengers and chalked up 7.3 billion passenger-kilometres.

The VOLAN Group has 29 divisions and own equity of about 24.7 billion HUF (0.122 billion ECU) and a registered capital of 12.5 billion HUF (62.5 million ECU). In 1994, it had a revenue of 33.8 billion HUF

(170 million ECU), while profits totalled 312 million HUF (1.56 million ECU). Net revenue for 1995 was 46 billion HUF (0.23 ECU). Equity in 1995 amounted to 26 billion HUF (0.13 billion ECU) while pre-tax profits for the same year were 350 million HUF (1.75 million ECU).

In 1989, the 27 companies in the VOLAN Group established the VOLAN Union, which today comprises 60 companies. Each company in the Union operates independently. Thirty-one are engaged in passenger transport, 18 in domestic and international goods forwarding, and 11 in other service activities, including computer technology, tourism, education, etc.

The Hungarian Privatisation and State Holding Company takes the view that the VOLAN companies have to be privatised. But as bus transport is of strategic significance in the country's transport system, the Government must take this into account.

Over 43 per cent of the bus fleet is more than ten years old and six hundred new buses per year will need to be acquired in the coming years.

Another company stated for privatisation is Hungarocamion, which used to be the largest road haulage company. Since August 1995, Hungarocamion has been under new management. The majority owner, the Hungarian Privatisation and State Holding Company, is relying on the new management to wipe out the company's vast accumulated deficit. This will be the only way to ensure the successful privatisation of the company and to obtain fresh capital investment. It is planned that, by the end of the year, the company will break even, and that by 1997 it will be profitable.

In 1995, the new management revamped the entire structure of the company; *inter alia*, it introduced telecommunication links between the head office and vehicles on the road. Under ever-increasing competition from other hauliers, Hungarocamion has been forced to accept a much smaller slice of the forwarding market than it had in 1992, one reason for this being that more than 50 per cent of Hungarian export-import turnover is carried by foreign road haulage companies. The only way that Hungarocamion can strengthen its market position is to adopt more aggressive marketing. However, this requires the modernisation of the vehicle fleet.

Cost-cutting has been a priority of the company for some time, involving a reduction in staff numbers. In the second part of 1995, it laid off 150 workers, and more will have to go. By the end of the current year, Hungarocamion will have a workforce of 2 900. The company intends to use part of its revenue for the purchase of new vehicles and repayment of loans. It also wishes to develop an advanced computerised information network.

At present, the Hungarian Privatisation and State Holding Company holds 96.6 per cent of the shares, with the rest owned by local authorities. At the end of 1994, the company had a registered capital of 5.2 billion HUF (26 million ECU). It closed 1993 with a deficit of 527 million HUF (2.6 million ECU), which by end-1994 had grown to 1.4 billion HUF (7 million ECU). At present, it has short-term debts amounting to 447 million HUF (2.2 million ECU) and a long-term debt of 2 million HUF (0.01 million ECU).

In the case of MAV, the first step in transforming the company was, likewise, to sell off non-core activities. MAV became a 100 per cent state-owned joint-stock company as of June 30 1993. By the end of this year, the partial restructuring of MAV will have been completed. The structural reorganisation and modernisation of the company has been started. Non-core activities (e.g. design, construction, production, maintenance, etc.) are being privatised step-by-step, extending the market sphere. Management has been reorganised. Various MAV properties have already been sold off. This process began in 1995 and is expected to gather momentum in 1996.

The company will sell off more assets, including its vehicle repair workshops, seven in all. MAV employees and managers have already expressed considerable interest in the purchase of MAV assets, partly due to the fact that MAV-owned investments generated 400 million HUF (2 million ECU) in dividends last year. This initiative is supported by MAV's own management, and local leaders and workers are keen to acquire shares. In 1996, MAV is expected to collect 7 billion HUF (35 million ECU) from the various sales.

The role of state monopolies continues to decline, while that of small and medium-sized ventures is growing. Private ventures already play an important role in road haulage, non-scheduled passenger transport, taxi transport and the car repair business. In all, there are 2 859 companies in the transport sector, 138 of which employ more than fifty people. There are about 1 000 forwarding organisations, and 68 000 private shipping ventures providing employment for about 450 000 people.

5.2. Prices and fares

Official regulation of transport prices is very extensive. Because of the declining performance of the transport sector, the high share of fixed costs in total costs and increasing specific expenses, average transport price increases have outstripped inflation.

Because the necessary budgetary funding was not forthcoming, passenger fares had to be raised. Despite the relatively high increase, however, official prices still do not allow an adequate profit, including that necessary to cover development costs, to be earned. Losses on passenger rail transport are thus increasing every year.

Despite the increase in intercity bus fares, revenue is still inadequate to cover vehicle replacement and repairs.

Planned cut-backs in government spending will necessitate further increases in transport prices. But any increases should be kept within the narrowest possible range, given the inevitable social-political impact. In the long term, price regulation will be reduced.

6. PRIORITIES FOR THE REFORM OF INTERCITY TRANSPORT IN THE CENTRALAND EASTERN EUROPEAN COUNTRIES

The majority of the countries in transition are restructuring their transport systems in a similar way to Hungary, with some differences that reflect the different phases of transition.

Poland is concentrating on upgrading existing infrastructure: reconstruction of the Wroclaw-Warsaw line (on the Rome-Vienna-Warsaw-St. Petersburg route) and the Cracow-Muszyna line (for the international passenger service from Cracow to southern Europe). It has formulated its position as regards the siting of the North-South motorway and the envisaged Via Baltic route. The liberalisation of access to the market and the creation of competitive conditions have already created a consumer market in transport services. The number of newly-established private transportation enterprises (including taxis) exceeded 45 000 by the end of 1989, and it is estimated that at present there are approximately 70 000 transportation enterprises operating in Poland. Some of these firms have already gone bankrupt but many more new ones are being set up.

The role of the private sector is continuing to grow. Most freight operators are one-lorry businesses. There are only a few private firms with over 100 vehicles. Structural changes in the sector are envisaged in the near future which will affect the size of firms. Competition will result in concentration. In the case of enterprises providing subsidised intercity passenger services, state intervention is still considerable.

Privatisation of bus undertakings is being done on a case-by-case basis. Financially-sound enterprises will be privatised directly, with the creation of companies in which the Treasury is the sole shareholder. However, this method necessitates finding both the necessary capital resources and bidders interested in operating bus services. In the case of ailing enterprises, the possibility of allowing them to go bankrupt is not ruled out.

With regard to rail transport, a contract between the State and the railway company has not yet been signed but is due to be finalised in the near future.

To sum up, it can be said that Poland's transport policy is encountering numerous obstacles on the path towards the country's integration into the European Union, but that they can be overcome if comprehensive economic, technical, organisational and legal measures are undertaken in good time.

The **Czech Republic** is promoting intercity transport. Priority is being given to the following areas: road construction and modernisation, upgrading of rail connections with European networks. Special emphasis is being given to the connections with Germany, the Slovak Republic and the Polish and Austrian railways.

The introduction of a market economy has already had a positive impact on the transportation sector. The process of privatisation is practically finished. Newly established transportation enterprises, especially road haulage firms, have adjusted very well to market conditions in terms of speed and reliability. There are nearly 40 000 registered road haulage firms in the Czech Republic, 10 000 of which operate in the international market.

As regards rail transport, the first step has been taken towards establishing an efficient intercity transportation system. Operation and infrastructure maintenance and development have been separated. Much of the infrastructure is outdated, preventing rail from competing effectively with road transport.

In **Hungary**, the privatisation process underway in the bus transport sector (VOLAN) will increase competition and, by the same token, the efficiency of intercity road transport. Private car use, especially for business travel, is rising rapidly.

The rail undertaking (MAV) has also drawn up a strategic plan in which intercity passenger transport is assigned a very important role. Priority is being given to the following: increasing the frequency of intercity (IC) services as demanded by the passenger market; the introduction of a diagonal connection of existing IC services through Budapest's Eastern Railway Station, and the development of new IC links. An efficient IC system, connecting the regions to the capital and to one another, will be implemented by the turn of the century.

Comfortable, air-conditioned IC trains will run, on average, every two hours at speeds of 80-140 km/h depending on the line. Scheduled waiting times at connections throughout the country will not exceed ten minutes, and fares will be tailored to demand.

Expansion of freight transport services is another priority.

7. CONCLUSION

The dramatic changes that have taken place in the social and economic structures of the central and eastern European countries have generated radical changes in passenger and freight traffic in the region. The countries in transition will have to adapt to the European transportation system by exploiting the opportunities opened up by the market economy.

Detailed analysis of the restructuring underway in the various countries in the region has shown that there is no one "best solution" applicable to all of them. The speed of transformation, the different methods of privatisation being used, and many other factors which are not discussed here, will all have an impact on the results and effectiveness of the newly-established systems. By providing a forum for exchanges of experiences and information, the Round Table offers a unique opportunity to learn from each other and to devise solutions to the problems besetting each country in the region.

BIBLIOGRAPHY

Bennathan, E., J. Fraser and L.S. Thompson (1992), *Freight transport demand, determinants and intensity*, World Bank, INUTD.

Michalak, W. and R. Gibb (1993), *Development of the transport system. Prospects for East-West integration.*

Spear, H.J. (1994), "European railway comparisons. The case of eastern and central Europe in the post-communist era", MSc Thesis, University of Leeds, ITS.

Ministry of Transport, Telecommunications and Water Management (1994), *The concept of Hungarian transport policy*, Budapest.

Ministry of Transport and Maritime Economy (1994), *Transport Policy*, Warsaw.

Volek, J. (1995), *Transportation politics of Czech Republics in the context of European transportation politics*, Sopot.

Tanczos, K. (1995), "Harmonisation of competition in Hungarian transport", *TRANS '95, Common Europe -- Opportunities and risks for transport*, Warsaw.

Tanczos, K. (1995), "Hungarian transport policy in the process of integration with the European Union", *Transport and Logistics*, Sopot, 4/1995.

Tanczos, K. (1996), "Railways of Central and Eastern Europe: facing new challenges", *The World's Railways.*

ECMT (1996), *Trends in the Transport Sector 1970-1994*, Paris.

Statistical Yearbooks of Hungary.

POLAND

Jan BURNEWICZ
Chair of Comparative analysis of Transportation Systems
University of Gdansk
Poland

SUMMARY

Gdansk, March 1996

INTRODUCTION

This report sets out to analyse developments in the intercity transport market in the CECs[1] since 1989. Following the collapse of the old economic regime, the CECs went into a very deep economic recession, as attested by a decline in GDP and a very sharp drop in transport demand. The resulting shortage of finance led to spending cuts in the transport sector. One of the casualties was official statistics. The lack of data, or readily verifiable and comparable data, posed a number of problems for researchers working on the analysis of transport trends in the CECs. Quite soon after the collapse of Communism, the exchange of ideas between the East and West stepped up and some preliminary analyses and comparisons have emerged from conferences, seminars and joint projects since that time.

As a concept, countries in transition is rather vague. It can be understood in the wider sense as covering quite a large group comprising the former Communist bloc countries (i.e. the CECs, the CIS[2] and the countries of the former Yugoslavia). Strictly speaking, it refers only to the first four associate members of the European Union (under the 1991 Agreements): i.e. Hungary, Poland, the Czech Republic and the Slovak Republic. In this report, "countries in transition" refers to the 11 countries which joined the ECMT in 1991 and 1992, i.e. Bulgaria (BG), Croatia (HR), Estonia (EST), Hungary (H), Latvia (LV), Lithuania (LT), Poland (PL), Romania (RO), the Slovak Republic (SK), Slovenia (SLO) and the Czech Republic (CZ).

More data on Poland than on other countries were available to the author of this report. The situation in Hungary is well documented and adequate data were available on Bulgaria, Romania, the Czech Republic, the Slovak Republic and Slovenia. Fewer data were available on the Baltic States and Croatia, however. Consequently, a comparative analysis of transport trends has proved possible only for the first seven countries; the data and opinions given on the other four are, at best, sketchy.

Analysing the structural changes in the transport sector in the CECs in quantitative terms was quite straightforward, despite some gaps in the official statistics. However, it proved much more difficult to try to generalise about the trends and solutions adopted without an in-depth study analysis of new legislation and expert opinion. The author is well aware of the shortcomings of this report, and the opinions and conclusions expressed in it are purely his own.

1. COUNTRIES IN TRANSITION -- SEEKING THEIR PLACE IN THE EUROPEAN ECONOMY

The economic transition of the CECs is proceeding on three fronts: functional, structural and spatial. Functional change, i.e. replacing the centrally-planned economy by a market economy, is the most fundamental aspect of the transition process. Liberalisation is the first step towards a market economy: companies are beginning to make their own production decisions, prices are dictated only by demand and supply in the free market, the State is no longer subsidising products, etc. However, more market competition is impossible without the type of structural change that is needed to encourage new firms to set up, to dismantle production and distribution monopolies, privatise companies and infrastructure, modernise technology and organisational structures and change sectoral and modal structures. As economic activity does not take place in a vacuum, the transition to a market economy will not happen without spatial change: international integration, the redirection of trade flows, decentralisation of decisionmaking.

Transport is both the object and agent of the changes outlined above[3]. Just as in industry, trade and other areas of economic activity, the transport sector and transport undertakings are going through a (fairly slow) liberalisation process and both privatisation and structural change are urgently needed. The pace of change in economic spatial patterns will be determined by transport capacity and performance. Often, transport can be a barrier to change in the economies of the CECs.

1.1. The need for structural reforms in the economies of the CECs

Since 1990, the determination of the countries and governments of Europe to create a genuine European Community has been a highly positive historical development, after so many centuries of war and conflict. The creation of such a community is a long-term process, the scenario for which has not been laid down in advance. Already it seems clear that the goal is to bring the peoples and economies of Europe into closer convergence while at the same time respecting cultural differences and consumer choice. The CECs will probably become members of the European Union in 2000-2005, providing that they manage to make essential structural changes before then.

In order to enter the Single Market, each of the new Member States must satisfy minimum economic convergence criteria. The criteria that the CECs have to meet were set out in the EU's 1995 White Paper[4]. It goes without saying that firms will not be able to compete on equal terms in the transport market if they are of very different sizes, if the costs of the factors of production differ by a ratio of more than 1 to 5, etc.

However, the White Paper of 3 May 1995, on preparing the countries of central and eastern Europe for integration into the internal market, makes no mention of the need for structural reform of the transport sector in the CECs. The Commission of the European Communities stipulates the Community transport legislation that the associate countries must incorporate in their national legislation -- legislation on fair competition, technical standards, employment, safety, etc. -- but omits all mention of restructuring the transport sector in central and eastern Europe.

One may be forgiven for wondering whether the EU considers the current structures to be satisfactory and in the interests of Community transport operators. Objections might arise where such structures seem to give large, state-owned transport enterprises in eastern Europe an artificial competitive advantage over EU firms. Size too could well give an unfair advantage in the road and waterway sectors and in ancillary activities. On the other hand, the nature of rail and air transport is such that there is no vast difference in size between western and central European operators.

Restructuring of the transport sector in the CECs is necessary to avoid harming the operation of the European market and, just as importantly, to improve the profitability and efficiency of large, state-owned enterprises. Wasteful and non-profitable structures are a burden on both individual countries and the whole of Europe.

1.2. The political, economic and social background to the reforms

There is now little distinction between the political systems currently operating in the CECs. All have accepted (representative) parliamentary democracy, have free elections, have abolished one-party rule and defend the right to form political parties, trades unions, etc. Democracy is nowhere at risk, despite widespread political in-fighting. The return to power of the new-style communists in several countries may have an impact on the privatisation drive but will not halt it.

Restructuring was accompanied by a decline in economic growth, at its lowest over the period 1989-93[5]. By 1994, the CECs had returned to growth, though at different rates: Bulgaria, 1.4 per cent; Poland, 5.2 per cent. Other factors that had an impact on structural change were unemployment and population growth rates. In 1994, rates of unemployment varied from as little as 3.3 per cent in the Czech Republic to 16.3 and 16.5 per cent in Bulgaria and Poland, respectively[6]. Figure 1 compares the rates for each of these three indicators in six of the CECs and four EU Member States.

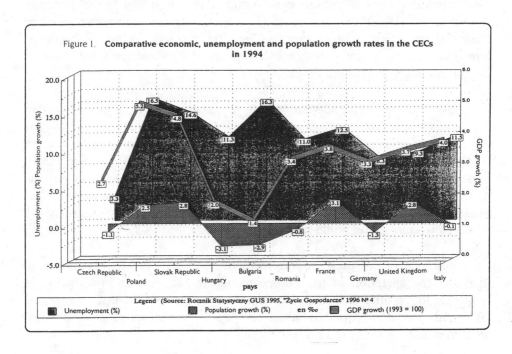

Figure 1. **Comparative economic, unemployment and population growth rates in the CECs in 1994**

Legend (Source: Rocznik Statystyczny GUS 1995, "Życie Gospodarcze" 1996 Nº 4)

Unemployment (%)   Population growth (%)   en ‰   GDP growth (1993 = 100)

228

Figure 1 suggests that there was a positive correlation between population growth rate and GDP growth rate in 1994. Unemployment rates in the CECs to a large extent reflected the stage reached in restructuring enterprises the rate was lower in countries where restructuring was less advanced. Unemployment rates in general are exaggeratedly high as the black economy -- sometimes extremely large -- provides a great deal of undeclared employment. The fall in unemployment rates can therefore be attributed to the declaration of previously undeclared employment[7].

Other factors which had a positive impact on economic restructuring in the CECs were: rising exports, falling inflation[8], the injection of foreign capital and financial aid under the PHARE programme.

1.3. The impact of integration with the European Union on structural reforms in the CECs

From the outset, association with the EU had a major impact on the CECs' foreign trade flows and soon became the key factor in economic growth. The dissolution of the CMEA meant the immediate disappearance of a market for rather shoddy products, both because there was a degree of reluctance to maintain normal relations with former members of the CMEA and because consumers began to shun products from the former socialist bloc countries. However, the growth in trade between the CECs and the EU was hindered by quotas and "special" restrictions (agriculture and steel industries) that were designed to protect vulnerable Community industries[9]. These restrictions will be lifted in or around 2000 to 2002.

In all of the CECs (except Bulgaria), trade with the EU exceeded trade with the CIS. Currently, more than 40 per cent of the CECs' exports go to the EU, which also accounts for over 30 per cent of their imports. In Poland, EU trade accounted for over 62 per cent of exports and more than 57 per cent of imports in 1994[10]. In addition to the redirection of trade flows there was a change in flow structure, i.e. in the types of product exported. Under the pressure of competition, CEC exports of manufactured goods (with the exception of textiles) began to fall and exports of semi-finished goods (wood, paper, steel, etc.) rose. This has had a major impact on modal split in the international transport sector, where maritime and rail transport are losing out to road haulage.

The Schengen Agreement, which opened up the borders between the CECs and the EU, has resulted in a massive increase in international passenger transport. However, queuing times at border crossing-points in central Europe (sometimes over 24 hours) mean that the number of people making international trips by car is still far short of potential demand. The fact that it is so easy to buy used cars in EU Member States has been a decisive factor in the rapid spread of car ownership in the CECs and in the subsequent increase in the use of cars for domestic and international trips.

1.4. The transport sector in the economic reform process

In the CECs, the pace of reforms in the transport sector has been much slower than in the rest of the economy. This can be ascribed to technical and economic factors specific to the sector: an extensive infrastructure which is difficult to privatise or change; the management system; the need for state subsidies for loss-making road or rail passenger transport operators; large state-owned enterprises whose employees are resistant to the idea of restructuring, etc.

Within the transport sector, the scope for structural change varies widely depending on the mode. On the face of it, road transport would seem to be the most easy to reorganise but, paradoxically, LSOEs[11] in the road transport sector are often more conservative than those in the air, waterway and maritime transport sectors, which have more experience of the stiff competition on international markets and whose staff are more aware of the need for change and the impossibility of continuing to rely on state subsidies. The hardest case is the railways, which are used to subsidies and to having a monopoly. In this, the railways in the CECs are not so very different to those in the EU (apart from their technical condition).

To pave the way for structural change, the CECs have made several amendments to their legislation in order to abolish certain rights and privileges: toll-free motorways, free entry into the industry, the right to subsidised travel, etc. are recognised principles. Provision for private funding for infrastructure and a substantial reduction in the number of sectors protected by the State (air transport, airports and sea ports) have been steps in the right direction.

The road transport sector, by its very nature, is well suited to the rapid development of new private enterprises. It is the sector that has witnessed the most noticeable changes in the CECs: in terms of the number of firms, it is beginning to outstrip western Europe, where entry into the industry has traditionally been easier. As an idea, "small is beautiful" is losing support; the CECs are beginning to realise that securing a suitable mix of small, medium and large enterprises is the more rational course.

1.5. Role of SMEs and large enterprises in the eastern European transport sector

Up to 1989, the CECs were considered as countries dominated by LSOEs. In the international road transport sector, western European experts and journalists used to point out the difficulties involved in standing up to unfair competition from large enterprises such as Hungarocamion in Hungary (over 1 800 vehicles), PEKAES-Auto-Transport in Poland (over 1 200 HGVs), Somat in Bulgaria (4 500 road vehicles), Sovtransavto in Russia and Romtrans in Romania[12]. The European Commission had monitored the operations of eastern European transport undertakings and issued three reports[13]. The observations and analyses conducted at the time (over the period 1981-86) showed no market distortion and no undue dominance of the market by East European operators (see Figure 2). It may well be that, after 1989, the situation gave East European operators more of an advantage -- they now hold over 60 per cent of the CEC-EU transport market -- but no statistics are available.

Figure 2. **Share of international road freight transport markets eastern European and western European operators**

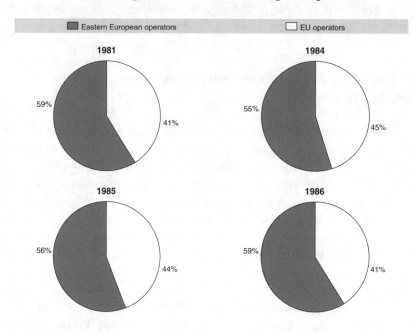

Source: COM(89)78 final, p. 19.

Despite this, since 1989, it is the CECs that have been afraid of the large, western road freight forwarding and haulage groups, such as: Danzas (turnover FF 30 billion, 15 300 employees), Ziegler (turnover FF 12 billion, 4 500 employees), Schenker (turnover upwards of DM 2.6 billion), NFC (turnover FF 14 billion), LEP (turnover FF 13 billion), Kühne & Nagel and Panalpina[14]. As yet, these groups do not have a very high profile on CEC markets but, with borders set to open up in the near future, they are perceived as a threat to SMEs.

SMEs dominate the road sector in the CECs. In 1994, 96.5 per cent of enterprises in the sector (82 000 in all) were privately owned. Private firms had an average of only 1.5 employees and usually operated 1 or 2 HGVs[15]. In Hungary in 1993, 97 per cent of all firms in the transport sector were SMEs[16]. Some 80 per cent of Hungarian road haulage firms operated only 1-5 vehicles, as opposed to 87.7 per cent in the Czech Republic[17]. The average EU road haulage firm is much larger: Belgium (1988) 5.9 vehicles, Netherlands (1985) 5.3 vehicles, Spain (1986) 3.2 vehicles, Italy (1985) 2.1 vehicles[18]. In 1992, the average number of employees per firm in the road sector (state-owned + private firms) was 3.9^{19} in Poland and 7.3 per cent in France[20]. Bulgaria and Romania aside, the road sector in the CECs appears to be much more fragmented than in the EU.

1.6. Privatisation: methods, progress and barriers

Privatisation is the key to transition from a centrally-planned economy to a free market economy. The transport market in the CECs, dominated by the state sector until 1989, presents plenty of opportunities for privatisation. All of the CECs embraced the concept of privatisation and began to implement it fairly quickly. Changes of this sort in the form of ownership can be implemented either by setting up new, privately-owned firms or by transferring existing, state-owned firms to private sector ownership. The first of these methods is easier to manage than the second. Privatising an LSOE often calls for consensus between management, the owner (in this case, the State) and employees. In practice, it has often meant scaling down LSOEs, since the proceeds from the sale of part of their vehicle fleets can be used to set up new private firms which then buy back the vehicles.

The approach to privatisation is not exactly the same in all the CECs. They have all liberalised market entry for new firms but there have been marked differences in the approach to the privatisation of state-owned enterprises. Each country is trying to feel its own way, offering some opportunities for investment to those who have capital and some opportunities for employees. Generally, special legislation was introduced to pave the way for privatising LSOEs (particularly in the case of airlines and railways), whereas the basis for privatisation of the road sector was often the legislation generally applicable to industry and business. The State may equally well opt to sell off enterprises to domestic investors or foreign investors, employees of state-owned enterprises or to local authorities.

Since the road sector has not suffered from a decline in production, it offers the best prospects for rapid privatisation and, hence, for the creation of new enterprises. In all of the CECs, privatisation of the freight sector has proved much easier than privatisation of the passenger transport sector, where the huge losses of the public service providers have frightened off private investors and imposed a number of constraints. Privatisation of the road transport sector has meant the entry into the market of tens of thousands of firms in all of the CECs. State-owned enterprises in the air, maritime and waterway sectors, as well as in the freight forwarding sector, have also been privatised but with less dramatic results than in the road transport sector, where the grip of the old monopolies and oligopolies has been completely broken, despite the opposition of the LSOEs. However, in the air and maritime sectors, privatisation has not dismantled the old monopolistic structures.

Privatisation of the domestic road transport sector in central Europe has either been completed or is well advanced. The situation is rather different in the international transport sector, where the old monopolies are intact although their ancillary businesses (particularly repair shops)[21] are seeking to be hived off and privatised. Despite international competition and the continued presence of the old state-owned giants on the market, many new, private firms are electing to set up in the international sector in preference to the domestic market.

Foreign investment has been a major feature of privatisations in the freight forwarding sector, which is much less developed in the CECs than in western Europe and has remained highly fragmented throughout the 1990s. In order to block the entry of foreign freight forwarders, the CECs are encouraging SMEs to merge or to form groups. In this market, there is wide support for the idea that an oligopolistic market -- one carved up between two to three operators -- would be the best solution (unarguably the best solution for the combined transport sector).

1.7. Different strategies for restructuring the transport sector in the countries in transition

The CECs have tackled the problem of restructuring their transport sectors on several different levels and from different angles. To survive in a market economy and to facilitate integration with the EU, the transport sector must implement technical, economic, structural, spatial and social reforms. On the technical side, the reforms will usually entail the introduction of new technologies (to reduce energy consumption, air pollution, increase speed, etc.), new types of fleets and rolling stock and the construction of new generation infrastructure. Economic reforms are aimed at ensuring that transport enterprises are commercially and financially self-sufficient and at separating them from the public sector. They will change the transport sector's impact on general economic indicators. Structural reforms encompass privatisation (described briefly above), restructuring the LSOEs and changing the share of the modal split and the market share of operators. Spatial changes (changes in network coverage) are essential to ensure equitable infrastructure provision (especially roads) in the different regions and standardization of national transport systems. Social reforms in the transport sector relate to changes in the structure of employment.

Added to all of the above are changes in the role of the central, regional, local and international authorities in the management of transport in the CECs.

A summary of the main reforms is given in Table 1.

Given the lack of information, only a limited number of transport reforms in the CECs could be analysed for this report. It is extremely difficult to find comprehensive data on technical and technological changes and on economic, spatial and social reforms. However, using official and semi-official statistics, it was possible to analyse structural changes in ownership, transport modes and, to a lesser extent, the split between domestic and international transport. Some interference between different types of change was observed. Reforms in the system of ownership dictate what technical, technological and social changes will follow. The dominance of private ownership has not resulted in the development of advanced transport technology (purpose-built equipment, computerized traffic management systems, combined transport). The changes that have been observed are due not to the numbers of privatised firms but to initiatives by government and by the largest private firms. The larger part played by international transport and stiffer competition on the market could slow the privatisation process and, with it, the creation of small companies which are not capable of holding out against the major internationals. Some changes are not feasible without a change in policy (subsidies, employment structure, etc.).

Table 1. **Types of changes observed in the CEC transport sector since 1989**

Types of change	Field		Examples	
			Before	After
Technical or technology	All modes	T1	conventional transport	→ combined transport
		T2	standard equipment	→ purpose-built equipment
		T3	dispersed traffic	→ centralised traffic management
	Road	T4	separate services	→ integrated services
		T5	conventional equipment	→ environmentally-friendly equipment
		T6	ordinary roads	→ motorways
	Rail	T7	non-electrified lines	→ electrified lines
		T8	traditional services	→ high-speed services
		T9	basic transport services	→ complex services (transport+ancillary services)
	Waterway	T10	cargo vessel + tug	→ more motorbarges and tugs
Economic	All modes	E1	subsidised firms	→ self-financing firms predominant
		E2	publicly-financed infrastructure	→ public and private infrastructure finance
Structural	All modes	R1	predominantly public ownership	→ predominantly private ownership
		R2	rail predominant	→ stiff competition between rail and other modes
		R3	monopolistic markets	→ competitive markets
	Freight transport	R4	heavy bulk freight predominant	→ more manufactured goods
		R5	mainly hire or reward	→ own-account transport has a slight edge
	Passenger	R6	public transport predominant	→ transport by private car predominant
		R7	rail and bus evenly balanced	→ more transport by bus
Spatial	All modes	S1	domestic transport predominant	→ more international transport
		S2	intra-CEEC traffic predominant	→ international CEC-EU predominant
Social	All modes	C1	overmanning	→ job cuts
		C2	jobs in transport only	→ jobs in ancillary businesses

Source: J. Burnewicz, 1996.

Macroeconomic and transport policy goals differ from one CEC to the next, regardless of the stage of economic development they have reached. Paradoxically, it is the least-developed countries, which do not have the financial resources to meet them, that have set technical and technology-related goals. The more advanced countries tend to set goals for economic, structural and social reforms with a view to integration with the EU. As regards the shift in the pattern of their trade, there are many similarities between the CECs: since 1990, the redirection of trade and international transport towards the EU has become more marked with each passing year, although from 1996 one can expect to see an increase in trade within the CEFTA[22].

Progress in transport sector reforms in the CECs is dictated by the role the sector plays in the macroeconomic strategy of the country concerned and by its impact on basic economic indicators: GDP, employment, fixed capital formation (capital investment), government spending (see Figure 3).

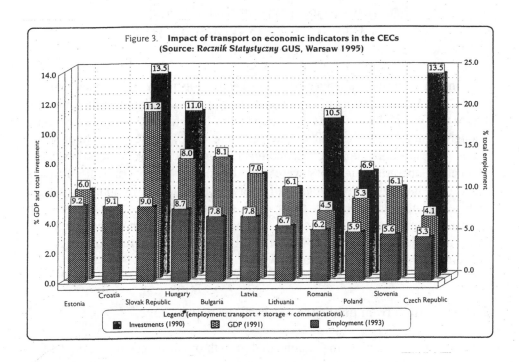

Figure 3. **Impact of transport on economic indicators in the CECs**
(Source: *Rocznik Statystyczny* GUS, Warsaw 1995)

237

Figure 3 indicates that social changes in the transport sector were more significant in Estonia, Croatia, the Slovak Republic and Hungary (approximately 9 per cent of total jobs) and less so in the Czech Republic, Slovenia, Poland and Romania. It should be noted that, in all of the CECs, there is quite a strong correlation between the impact of transport on total employment and on GDP. However, the extent of investment in transport in the CECs (as a percentage of GDP) depends largely on financial policy. In the Czech Republic, where transport's share in both employment and GDP was low (4-5 per cent), investment was relatively high (13.5 per cent), opening up the possibility of technical change as well as structural and spatial reforms. The situation was the reverse in Poland, where transport is not considered a priority investment area (in 1994, transport received 3.5 per cent of total funding, whereas post and telecommunications received 5.1 per cent[23]).

2. DEVELOPMENTS IN THE INTERCITY PASSENGER TRANSPORT SECTOR

In the intercity passenger transport sector, the main development in the CECs was stiffer competition between the private car and public transport. Given the financial constraints, the period from 1989 to 1995 did not prove long enough to implement technical changes (new types of services, high-speed trains, etc. in short supply). Economic reforms were also blocked because companies operating at a loss were still dependent on government subsidies (especially bus and conventional rail operators). Other developments were a change in modal split (rail transport's share decreased) and progress in dismantling monopolies (bus and air transport). Further to the liberalisation of movement between the CECs and the EU, international transport began to account for a greater share of travel overall.

2.1. The switch from public transport to the private car

Four factors explain the exponential growth of car ownership in the CECs: every household desperately wanted a car, since few had been able to own one in the past; it was easy to buy second-hand cars imported from the West; people were free to set up businesses which needed cars and vans; access to public transport in less populated areas was limited.

As the numbers increased, private cars began to account for a greater share of intercity travel but it is difficult to analyse such trends in the CECs due to the lack of full official statistics and estimates. Table 2 gives data for four CECs which bear out the above statement and highlight differences between the countries concerned.

Table 2. **Passenger transport (1990-92) in four Central European Countries in billion passenger-kilometres**

Mode	Year	Bulgaria	Czech Republic	Hungary	Poland
Rail	1990	7.80	13.36	11.40	54.20
	1992	5.39	11.76	9.18	32.57
	1993	5.84	8.54	8.77	30.87
Private car	1990	15.10	39.90	47.00	70.00
	1992	16.20	44.30	47.50	101.70
	1993	17.10	47.20	48.00	115.90
Bus	1990	31.60	28.18	21.85	46.60
	1992	20.80	42.95	19.37	39.00
	1993	20.10	31.81	19.23	37.81
TOTAL	1990	54.50	81.44	80.25	170.80
	1992	42.39	99.01	76.05	173.27
	1993	43.04	87.55	76.00	184.58

Sources: *Trends in the Transport Sector, 1970-1993*, ECMT, Paris, 1995; *Polityka transportowa*, Warsaw, 1995; "The Concept of Hungarian Transport Policy", Budapest, 1994; *Mobility in the Czech Republic*, IRU, Geneva, 1995, *Rocznik Statystyczny GUS*, Warsaw, 1995.

In Hungary, the rate of increase in travel by private car (+2.1 per cent) from 1990 to 1993 was lower than the rate of increase in ownership (+7.6 per cent). The situation in Bulgaria was similar. In Poland the reverse was true: travel increased by 65.6 per cent for a 28.7 per cent increase in the number of private cars. The reason for this was that Poland saw a larger increase in the average distance travelled per year (up from 6 653 to 8 558 km) than did the other CECs (Bulgaria from 5 728 to 5 777 km, Hungary from 10 257 to 11 472 km). This trend is explained by Poland's policy of keeping fuel prices relatively low so as not to push up inflation and by an increase in real terms in household income.

Changes in modal split in the passenger transport sector (excluding air, waterway and maritime transport) in the four CECs over the period 1990-93 are illustrated in Figure 4.

Figure 4. **Modal split in the passenger transport sector**
Bulgaria, Czech Republic, Hungary, Poland, 1990-93

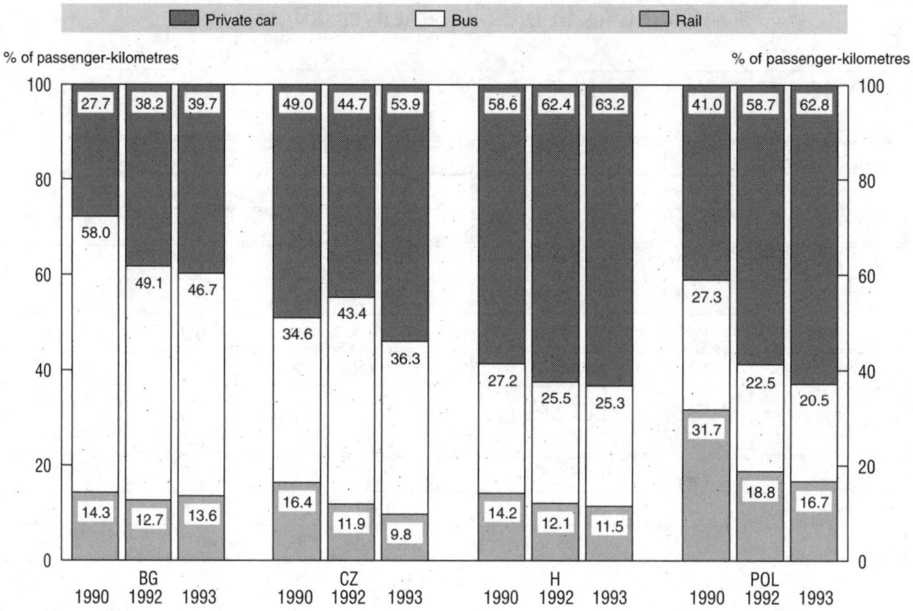

Legend: Private car, Bus, Rail

% of passenger-kilometres (left and right axes, 0–100)

	BG			CZ			H			POL		
	1990	1992	1993	1990	1992	1993	1990	1992	1993	1990	1992	1993
Private car	27.7	38.2	39.7	49.0	44.7	53.9	58.6	62.4	63.2	41.0	58.7	62.8
Bus	58.0	49.1	46.7	34.6	43.4	36.3	27.2	25.5	25.3	27.3	22.5	20.5
Rail	14.3	12.7	13.6	16.4	11.9	9.8	14.2	12.1	11.5	31.7	18.8	16.7

Source: ECMT statistics, 1995 and national statistics.

The changes in the modal split illustrated in Figure 4 are quite dramatic: rarely has the structure of such a sector changed so radically in a period of only three years.

Of the four countries analysed, only Poland recorded an increase in both private car ownership (from 41.0 to 62.8 per cent) and passenger-kilometres (from 170.8 to 180.6 billion). In the three others, car ownership increased but the total number of trips declined steadily. Rail and bus travel was down in all four countries, particularly rail travel in Poland (-43 per cent) and the Czech Republic (-36.1). Bulgaria also registered a sharp decline in the number of passenger-kilometres for bus travel (-36.4 per cent).

The picture would not be complete without mentioning trends in air passenger transport for the period 1990-93 in the CECs. This mode saw its share decline in Poland (-17.5 per cent) and in Hungary (-24.8 per cent) but increase in Romania (+2.6 per cent) and the Czech Republic (+18 per cent). Air passenger transport still plays a much smaller role in the CECs than in EU Member States.

2.2. The economic climate in the public transport sector

In the CECs, the economic situation of passenger transport operators is less favourable than that of freight transport firms. In the rail sector, passenger transport services are subsidised by profitable freight transport operations and by government. Reforms in this sector are taking the form of cuts in government subsidies with the result that traffic is falling. In Poland, for instance, which has the highest rail passenger figures of all the CECs, subsidies as a percentage of revenue per passenger-kilometre (subsidies + revenues from fares) were cut as follows from 1989 to 1994: 1989, 72.8 per cent; 1990, 67.3 per cent; 1991, 53.7 per cent; 1992, 48.8 per cent; 1993, 48.2 per cent; 1994, 46.2 per cent[24]. Railways seem to be faring better in the Czech Republic where subsidies amounted to 62.4 per cent of total revenues in 1992, and worse in Hungary where government subsidies covered only 19 per cent of costs in 1991[25]. In none of the three countries did government subsidies plus fare revenues cover the railway's operating costs and since much of the profits from freight traffic go to make up the operating loss, the amounts available for investment are substantially reduced.

Bus passenger transport services are also government-subsidised but to a lesser extent than rail services. In Poland, subsidies (as a percentage of value of services provided) were as follows: 1989, 24 per cent; 1990, 34.2 per cent; 1991, 15.2 per cent; 1992, 16 per cent; 1993, 13.7 per cent; 1994, 11.2 per cent[26]. The position of road transport operators is not at all comparable with that of the railways. Road transport undertakings are increasingly numerous and they do not have to provide passenger services, unlike the railways, which are constrained by a "public service" obligation.

Other public passenger transport services in the CECs have to operate just as strictly as financially self-sufficient firms. Even inland waterway transport can no longer depend on subsidies, except for small local ferry services.

2.3. The search for more efficient and more effective structures

Reforms in the intercity transport sector have not meant the end of the LSOEs, which frequently still have a natural monopoly. SMEs cannot take the place of the regular national bus service, they can only supplement it. Since that is the case, transforming the LSOEs in the road passenger transport sector into more efficient, more effective operations is crucial. It is equally crucial for the railways and the airlines.

In the rail passenger transport sector in Poland, there have been few radical changes. Under the system introduced by the new Law of 1995[27] on Polish national railways, PKP may transfer some of its assets to a company or lend them to other bodies. Where justified on social or economic grounds, the railway undertaking may transfer assets that the State Treasury wishes to dispose of, free of charge, to a local authority or other government body. In practice, only one attempt was made (in 1992) to set up a regional rail passenger transport company (Lubuska Kolej Regionalna S.A.) but the experiment failed in 1995[28]. Studies on a full-scale restructuring of PKP (four reports from 1992 to 1995) have not yet decided on the final model. PKP will probably be kept and three new independent infrastructure, passenger service and freight units set up[29]. The rationalisation of its passenger transport services is one plank in PKP's corporate strategy, which aims to set up new train systems (EC, IC) operating alongside express and local services. PKP is also planning to withdraw from regional transport and to continue its urban services.

Following the dissolution of the Czech and Slovak Federal Republic, two national railway companies were set up: Czech Railways (CD) and Slovak Railways (ZSR). Since 1 July 1993, CD has comprised three sectors: track, commercial operations, assets management and privatisation. The attempt to privatise CD failed after strikes by the rail unions[30]. However, passenger transport services were rationalised and the number of little used or unprofitable lines was reduced.

In Hungary, the Law on railways of 1 January 1994 provides for the restructuring of the rail sector. The public transport obligation would be ensured jointly by "track" and "commercial operations" divisions which would take care of infrastructure and passenger services[31], respectively. The new Bulgarian Law on railways of 25 May 1995 provides for contracts between

BDZ and local authorities stipulating the conditions for local passenger transport services[32]. In Slovenia operations and infrastructure maintenance were split into separate profit and cost centres[33] in July 1993.

Restructuring of LSOEs in the road passenger transport sector has been more extensive, although it is not proceeding quickly enough, due to the economic climate. In Poland, from 1992-96, 22 of the 174 PKS Group subsidiaries operating in the passenger transport sector were placed under private management, although they are still part of the group[34]. In Hungary in 1992, 29 VOLÁN subsidiaries operating in the passenger transport sector were restructured. Restructuring of the Czech Republic's CSAD companies was carried out from 1994 to 1995[35].

Airlines in the CECs are most often joint stock-companies in which the State still holds the majority share (e.g. PLL, Lot in Poland, MALÉV in Hungary, and Czech Airlines). Strategic alliances with powerful foreign partners may help these companies to improve their market position.

2.4. Privatisation in the passenger transport sector

The CECs have not all taken the same approach to privatising their public transport services. The legal approaches taken, the strength of public support for the reforms and the pace and outcome of privatisation have all been very different.

Generally, privatisation has taken one of the following forms: mass privatisation (issues of share vouchers to the general public); sell-offs to employees and management; or sales by auction, usually to large foreign investors. Mass privatisation was used in the Czech Republic, is planned in Poland, and is under consideration in Romania, Bulgaria, Latvia and Estonia. The advantage of mass privatisation is its speed, but the drawback is that it does not provide any injection of new capital for firms that sorely need it. Sell-offs to employees have been most common in Slovenia, a country with long experience of workers' self-management, and in Poland and the other countries referred to above. Direct sell-offs have been widely used in Hungary to attract genuine buyers who are ready to inject capital into firms and modernise them[36].

The proliferation of new firms in the wake of privatisation is most noticeable in the road sector. In Poland, despite the presence of over 170 state-owned PKS enterprises, a number of private passenger transport operators are already running 7 000 to 8 000 buses and coaches. Statistics on these operators are not available; however, their share of the market is estimated at around six to seven per cent. These small operators have been accused of unfair competition (departures timed a few minutes before PKS bus departure times, dumping, using stops without contributing to maintenance costs, ignoring safety standards, etc.). The competition hit PKS's passenger transport business (profits down 4.9 per cent) and 35 of its enterprises reported a loss[37] in 1993.

In Hungary, privatisation of the intercity road passenger transport sector has been much slower than privatisation of the freight sector. The explanation is that small operators find it much more difficult to meet the technical standards required for regular services. Another constraint has been that the State still has its say in the decisionmaking process as it legally holds a controlling share in 29 VOLÁN companies (50 per cent + 1 vote)[38]. Despite these problems, private operators managed to increase their share of the market, in terms of passenger-kilometres, from 2.1 per cent to 15.6 per cent in the period 1990 to 1993[39]. The Czech Republic was planning to privatise the CSAD group by the end of 1995. In Latvia, the disappearance of the Soviet giant, Sovtransavto, in 1990 paved the way for privatisation, which is now fairly well advanced: in 1994, 500 private operators were already operating some 1 100 buses[40].

In the CECs, privatisation of the airlines will follow the reforms already in hand and will enable large foreign companies to purchase shares. However, in the case of PLL, Lot, MALÉV and Czech Airlines, the State will remain the majority shareholder.

Privatisation of the railways in the CECs is one of the ways forward but no constructive moves in that direction have yet been made. Poland is considering setting up an independent consortium to upgrade the E-20 (the Berlin-Poznan-Warsaw line) but PKP's management is understandably reluctant to cede the line which is the best in its network. The CECs are studying railway privatisation in Germany and the United Kingdom. Privatisation of inland waterway and maritime transport has a better chance of succeeding, providing that the profitable freight sector can be developed and that investors willing to inject capital into sectors that are in financial difficulty everywhere can be found. The emergence of private firms specialising in the carriage of passengers by waterway is unlikely.

2.5. Role of the State in creating and managing new structures

Privatisation of public passenger transport services does not seem to be the ideal solution for the CECs. The privatisation process must be viewed in the broader context of economic transition. It is not enough to create new firms, the management of existing LSOEs must also be changed. Economic restructuring in the CECs has been a two-speed process: liberalisation has proceeded quickly, but major impediments have slowed decentralisation. Liberalisation is having a major impact on restructuring in the freight transport sector while decentralisation frequently affects structural change in passenger transport services. In order to decentralise, the State must cede power to regional and local authorities. In practice, though, it has only done so to a limited extent to date. In Poland, central government spending on transport amounted to 20 504 billion Zlotys, while regional and local authorities spent Zl 1 106 billion and 2 881 billion (i.e. respectively 84 per cent, 4 per cent and 12 per cent of total spending). Central government subsidies for intercity bus and passenger train services totalled Zl 8 434 billion, or one-third of total transport spending. Subsidies were granted to both state-owned and private operators, but essentially served to prop up the LSOEs.

Government intervention will be needed to restructure the intercity passenger transport services provided by LSOEs. For bus operators, the key is to increase the role of the regional and local authorities and reduce the role of the Ministry of Transport and the Ministry of Ownership Changes. Often, the legal status of LSOEs operating in the road passenger transport sector, coupled with the state of their finances, rules out privatisation. In order to pave the way for privatisation and to enable such enterprises to stay on the market, their finances will have to be straightened out and a more efficient management system will have to be introduced (private sector management contracts).

In the case of the railways, restructuring has been extremely slow or only superficial (when left to change-resistant railway employees). Public pressure is one factor which will help ensure that the reforms go ahead. As far as passenger transport by rail is concerned, there is a limit to how much restructuring can be done. It is impossible to hive off non-profitable businesses in the passenger transport sector without state funding and adequate subsidies (higher than those given at present). EU Directive No. 440/91 provides for the creation of new rail freight companies in the future but it is unlikely that there will be a rush to set up new passenger transport companies. Two dilemmas which may well require state intervention are: how to help networks sell or transfer, free of charge, their secondary and regional lines; and how to counter regional railway managers' opposition to local government proposals that they should take over responsibility for rail infrastructure in major cities (e.g. Gdansk, in Poland).

3. DEVELOPMENTS IN INTERCITY FREIGHT TRANSPORT

Developments in the freight transport sector in the CECs have been much more radical than in the passenger transport sector. As a result, slightly more reliable statistical data, information and opinions are available. The most significant developments in the sector have been: a drop in traffic, the expanding role of road haulage, a dramatic increase in the number of firms, faster international than domestic traffic growth and stiffer international competition. Despite the vast numbers of new firms, the LSOEs have managed to survive, but have had to change to do so. The road freight market is already so fragmented that mergers have become the natural response to the organisational shortcomings of SMEs.

3.1. Trends in modal split

The state of the economies of the CECs explain the changes in the modal split of freight traffic which occurred from 1990 to 1993. From a policy point of view, this was a very significant period, marked by a steep drop in industrial output and a subsequent fall in transport demand. Table 3 shows the traffic statistics available for the period in tonne-kilometres.

Rail traffic declined in all of the CECs by 39.4 per cent on average; Hungary reported the largest drop (-55.6 per cent) and Poland the smallest (-22.9 per cent) thanks to renewed growth -- 19.6 per cent over the period 1992-95[41].

Table 3. Freight transport in the CECs (in billion tonne-kilometres 1990-93)

Mode	Year	BG	CZ	SK	EST	H	HR	LT	LV	PL	RO	SLO	TOTAL
Rail	1990	14.10	38.05	26.25	5.00	16.80	3.00	19.00	18.50	83.50	57.30	4.00	285.50
	1992	7.76	31.11	13.08	3.65	10.02	1.77	11.34	10.12	57.76	28.17	2.57	177.35
	1993	7.70	25.61	14.30	3.74	7.46	1.59	11.03	9.85	64.36	25.17	2.26	173.07
Road	1990	17.20	16.82	6.48	4.50	15.20	3.00	5.00	5.90	40.30	5.00	4.00	123.40
	1992	6.79	20.25	6.00	1.26	12.80	1.13	4.99	2.50	42.01	3.60	2.78	104.11
	1993	6.03	24.36	5.46	1.06	13.38	0.88	6.91	1.70	40.74	2.78	2.47	105.77
Waterway	1990	1.50	1.40	3.00	0.00	2.10	0.00	0.10	0.15	1.00	2.00		11.25
	1992	0.84	1.29	1.69	0.00	1.57	0.00	0.05	0.02	0.75	1.89		8.10
	1993	0.46	1.28	0.84	0.00	1.62	0.00	0.05	0.00	0.66	1.59		6.50
Pipeline	1990	1.00	2.70	4.81		5.29	2.90			13.89	4.00		34.59
	1992	0.26	1.92	3.41		4.33	0.31			11.93	2.56		24.72
	1993	0.31	1.98	3.52		4.33	0.31			12.20	2.47		25.12
TOTAL	1990	33.80	58.97	40.54	9.50	39.39	8.90	24.10	24.55	138.69	68.30	8.00	454.74
	1992	15.65	54.57	24.18	4.91	28.72	3.21	16.38	12.64	112.45	36.22	5.35	314.28
	1993	14.50	53.23	24.12	4.80	26.79	2.78	17.99	11.55	117.96	32.01	4.73	310.46

Sources: *Transport Trends 1970-1993*, ECMT, Paris, 1995; *Rocznik Statystyczny GUS*, Warsaw, 1995; *Concept of Hungarian Transport Policy*, Budapest, 1994; IRU Statistics Group, Geneva, 1995.

In the same period, the decline in road transport, less marked than that in rail transport, averaged 14.3 per cent across all eleven CECs. Road traffic increased in three countries (the Czech Republic, Lithuania, Poland), but showed a substantial decline in countries such as Bulgaria, Estonia, Latvia and Croatia (down 65-76 per cent).

The data on road freight transport should be interpreted with caution as the statistical methods used are not standard and are unreliable. For example, the figures for Romania for 1993 are variously reported as 2.78 billion t-km (according to ECMT statistics[42]) and 14.5 billion t-km (according to the Polish statistics office, GUS[43]). Roadside and border crossing-point surveys indicate strong growth in road freight traffic in all of the CECs.

Inland waterway traffic is not very significant in the CECs. It fell by an average of 42.2 per cent over the period 1990-93. The opening of the Rhine-Main-Danube link did not lead to a rise in traffic in countries bordering the Danube. Bulgaria and the Slovak Republic reported a substantial fall in traffic (70 per cent). In the Czech Republic, Hungary and Romania, the decline was not so marked (9-23 per cent).

Practically all of the CECs use oil pipeline transport but complete statistics on it are not available. Following the 1990-92 crisis, this mode of transport is again making a recovery, especially in Poland, which accounts for half of the total tonne-kilometres carried by this mode in the CECs. The increase in road traffic has been accompanied by higher fuel consumption and hence increased use of oil pipelines.

The trends outlined above have radically changed the modal split in freight traffic, as illustrated in Figure 5.

Figure 5. **Modal split in freight traffic in the CECs, 1990-93**

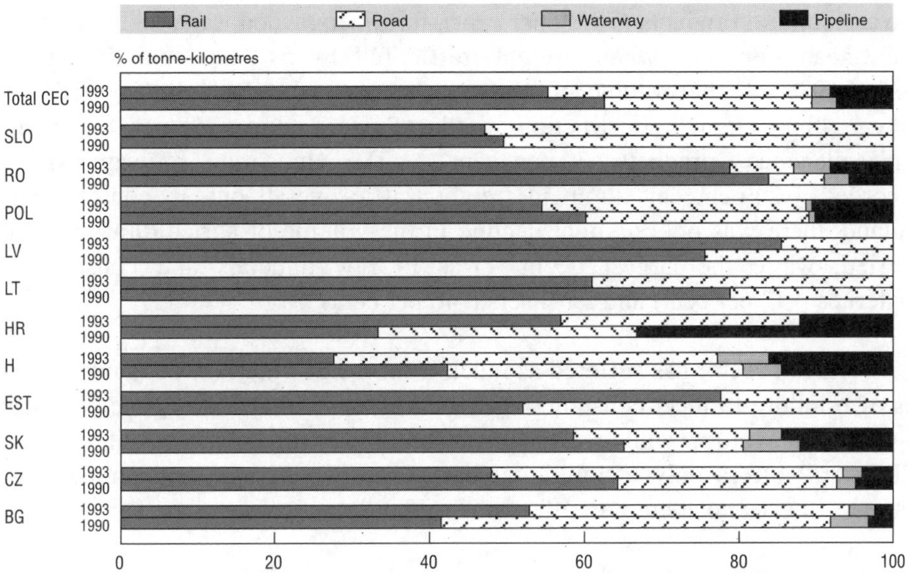

In three years (1990-93), rail transport in central Europe lost, on average, 7.1 per cent of its share of the freight market (down to 55.7 per cent from 62.8 per cent) while road increased its share by 7.0 per cent (from 27.1 to 34.1 per cent). Inland waterways and pipeline transport have maintained their shares (2.5 per cent and 8.0 per cent, respectively). Despite the increase in road's share, it still holds nowhere near the position on the CEC markets that it does in the EU. However, in those CEC countries that are returning to growth and are well on the way to integration with the EU (Poland, Hungary, the Czech Republic and the Slovak Republic), its share is still increasing. In the other CECs, the situation is the reverse and rail is even increasing its market share.

3.2. Rail traffic declining or flat

Paradoxically, the fall in demand for rail transport is not related to industrial restructuring or to the redirection of export trade flows. In Poland over the period 1989-94, production in the coal mining industry fell by 8 per cent while coal transport by rail fell by 44 per cent; steel production fell by 12 per cent but rail transport of minerals and metals fell by 41 per cent and 55 per cent, respectively[44]. The figures reflect the fierce competition from the

249

road mode which is beginning to carry products that were traditionally transported by rail. In PKP's case, the markets in which it has lost most ground are agricultural products (70-80 per cent), fertilizers, wood, sand and gravel. In the Czech Republic, where freight traffic fell by 51.9 per cent during the period 1989-94, the volume of minerals and steel products transported was down 48 per cent, construction products were down 68 per cent and "miscellaneous" products, 70 per cent[45]. The Hungarian railway (MAV) recorded a 24 per cent slump in freight traffic overall but, in contrast with Poland, there was only a slight decline in the volume of agricultural products carried, while the largest decline was in raw minerals and construction materials (-47 per cent) and fertilisers (-40 per cent)[46].

The rail sector has suffered as much from the downturn in demand as from its own failure to meet consumer's new requirements. Delivery time by rail is 3-4 days on average, while road hauliers can deliver in 10-15 hours. Rail in the CECs still offers only a traditional basic transport service and, unlike road hauliers, makes no attempt to offer enhanced or logistical services.

International traffic differs in scale and trends from country to country, depending on geographical location. In Hungary, where there is a lot of rail through-traffic, international traffic rose. In the Czech Republic during the period 1992-94, the decline in international traffic (-27 per cent) was greater than that in total traffic (-22 per cent), while in Poland the increase in international traffic (+28 per cent) was accompanied by a markedly smaller increase in total traffic (+7 per cent).

3.3. Dramatic rise in road traffic and environmental pollution

During the 1989-92 recession, there was little indication of the dramatic rise in road traffic that was to follow, especially in those countries in which the transition process was not so far advanced. From 1991, road freight traffic began to rise significantly in Poland and the Czech Republic but declined in Hungary. Figure 6 shows the trends in billion tonne-kilometres.

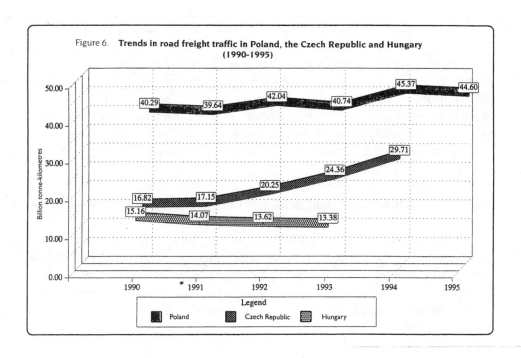

Figure 6. **Trends in road freight traffic in Poland, the Czech Republic and Hungary (1990-1995)**

The Czech Republic recorded the highest steady rise in road freight traffic (18-22 per cent per year from 1991 to 1994). In Poland, there was also a distinct, if less steady, increase. Statistics for Hungary showed a decline of 12 per cent during the period 1990-93, although the reported increase in the number of operators (29 500 to 60 373[47]) suggests that the traffic figures may not be very reliable. The likely explanation is limited access to data on private operators, whose activities are more extensive than the official statistics indicate.

Even with road freight traffic stagnating, the CECs are beginning to feel the effects on the environment. Obsolete vehicles -- in 1993, the average age was 9.5 years in Poland[48], 8.1 years in Hungary and 5.6 years in the Czech Republic[49] -- are causing increased air pollution. In the Czech Republic, the increase in road freight traffic during the period 1991-94 resulted in higher overall diesel consumption in the transport sector (up from 58.1 to 68.2 per cent), bringing total energy consumption by the sector up from 27.4 to 31.9 per cent. During the same period, CO emissions increased by 8.6 per cent and NO_x emissions by 13.1 per cent[50]. Over the period 1990-95 in Poland, diesel consumption rose by 26.4 per cent, increasing pollutant emissions by over 15 per cent.

251

The increase in road traffic has also been accompanied by an increase in noise pollution. In 1990 in the Czech Republic, it was estimated that 13.5 per cent of the population was exposed to road traffic noise levels higher than 65 dB(A)[51]. In the same period in Poland, it was estimated that 14.4 per cent of the population was exposed to levels of over 55 dB(A)[52]. The increasing number of HGVs of western manufacture in use is slowing the rise in noise pollution but already noise abatement measures, such as double-glazing, noise barriers and new types of tyres, are having to be introduced.

3.4. The structure of the road transport market: number and size of firms

The road sector in the CECs has perhaps undergone the most radical restructuring of the entire reform process. During the period 1990-95, the CECs noted a rapid increase in the number of private firms, all of them small enterprises (usually 1- or 2-vehicle operations). In most cases, these firms purchased second-hand vehicles from state-owned enterprises or from dealers importing from the West.

Unfortunately, we do not have comprehensive data on the number of road transport firms operating in the CECs. What is really needed is a breakdown of data on such firms by form of ownership, size, type of services provided (passenger, freight) and sector (domestic/international traffic). The data that are available, unreliable as they are (except for Poland, Hungary and the Czech Republic) are given in Table 4.

Table 4. **Number of private road transport firms operating in the CECs**
(passengers + freight)

Countries	1980	1990	1993	1994	1995
Czech Republic	n.a.	n.a.	40 461	36 706	36 461
Slovak Republic	n.a.	n.a.	370 (?)	n.a.	n.a.
Hungary	8	29 500	60 373	n.a.	n.a.
Poland	8 888	62 351	82 342	77 842	n.a.
Bulgaria	n.a.	n.a.	7 067	n.a.	n.a.
Romania	n.a.	n.a.	3 328	n.a.	n.a.
Slovenia	n.a.	n.a.	2 746	n.a.	n.a.
Lithuania	n.a.	n.a.	n.a.	n.a.	n.a.
Latvia	n.a.	n.a.	26 (?)	n.a.	n.a.
Estonia	n.a.	n.a.	n.a.	n.a.	n.a.
Croatia	n.a.	n.a.	n.a.	n.a.	n.a.

Note: n.a. -- not available; (?) -- data highly unreliable.

Source: Based on *Rocznik Statystyczny GUS*, Warsaw, 1991-1995; *The Concept of Hungarian Transport Policy, op. cit.*, p. I/12 ; *Conditions of European Integration of Central and Eastern European Hauliers, op. cit.*, p. 31; Room document, meeting of IRU Statistics Group, 10 October 1995; J. Burnewicz: "Privatisation and deregulation of road transport in Poland", *op. cit.*, pp. 7 and 24.

From Table 4, it can be seen that by far the largest increase in the number of private road transport firms in the period 1980-93 was in Hungary -- it was multiplied by 7 000(!). In Poland in the same period, the number of firms increased ninefold. In Poland and the Czech Republic, from 1993 (the turning point) onwards, the number of firms has been declining as a result of bankruptcies and mergers.

In Poland, which has the highest number of private operators, the break-up of the major state-owned enterprises has been in evidence since 1991. As a result of the privatisation of the LSOEs, since 1993 there have been no large firms operating more than 300 vehicles. From 1991 to 1994, the number of firms with over five employees operating more than 20 vehicles increased from 44.6 per cent to 79.9 per cent, while the number of those operating more than 150 vehicles fell from 4.4 per cent to 0.4 per cent.

Figure 7. **Structure of road transport firms in the CECs by number of employees**

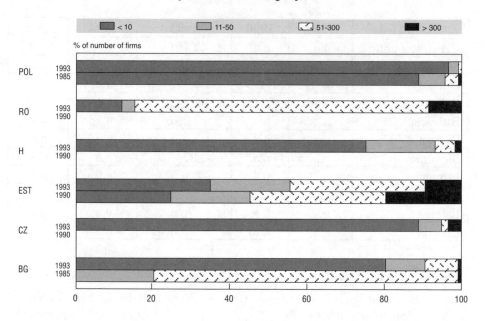

As Figure 7 shows, in terms of numbers employed, the structure of transport firms changed substantially over the period 1985-93. In Bulgaria's case, there were no SMEs operating in the road transport sector in 1985 but by 1993 they formed 80 per cent of the sector. In Estonia and Poland, there was little noticeable change over the period, but for different reasons. In Poland by 1985, almost 89 per cent of all firms in the sector were SMEs, while in Estonia, even now, the percentage is under 35 per cent.

In the road freight transport industry in the CECs, the private sector is expanding fastest in terms of numbers of firms. In terms of employment, vehicle capacity and share of the market, expansion has been much less dramatic. The numbers employed by private SMEs in the road sector in Poland in the period 1988-94 rose from 12.9 per cent to 44.1 per cent, the number of vehicles from 52.4 to 73.8 per cent, vehicle capacity (tonnage) from 39.2 to 61.0 per cent and volume of freight carried from under 40 to 84 per cent. In Hungary, the numbers employed in the private sector over the period 1990-93 rose from 10.4 per cent to 25 per cent and the volume carried (tonne-kilometres) increased from 17.7 per cent to 66.9 per cent[53]. In Bulgaria in 1993, private SMEs were providing 19.8 per cent of all jobs in the transport sector, mainly in the urban and road transport sectors and 15.8 per cent of the transport sector's turnover[54]. By 1995, their share in the volume of road traffic was estimated at 10-15 per cent[55]. The only data available for 1993 in Lithuania are the percentage of HGVs (54 per cent) and buses (39 per cent) owned by SMEs[56]. Such percentages indicate that the countries which are the furthest advanced in the transition process (Poland, Hungary, the Czech Republic) have a much higher percentage (60 per cent) of private SMEs in the transport sector than those which are just embarking on reform.

3.5. The impact of international competition on transport firms

The liberalisation of the economy in the CECs has led to fragmentation in the transport industry, while international competition (liberalisation of market access) is now beginning to prompt mergers and the formation of groups (holding groups). In theory at least, the threat of competition from western Europe is not a real one since the costs of firms in the CECs are typically quite low. In France in 1994, the prime cost of employing a driver for one hour's work (driving + other duties + time on call) was estimated at FF 103/h[57]. The equivalent in Poland should be Zl 46/h but is, in fact, only ZL 4.5/h (plus per diem travel costs of ZL 9.5/h[58]). The cost differentials between French and Bulgarian or Lithuanian companies give the latter countries even more of an advantage. This said, any cost advantage is largely cancelled out by the higher productivity of western road transport operators.

Central European firms are dependent for business on western freight forwarders, which offer a freight handling service to exporters and importers all over Europe. This has prompted firms in the CECs to set up joint ventures with western hauliers and forwarders. Western groups are also beginning to set up subsidiaries in the CECs, bypassing local firms. The number of joint-stock companies with foreign capital on the Polish transport market rose over the period 1989-94 as follows: from 14 in 1989 to 67 in 1990, 207 in 1991, 341 in 1992, 532 in 1993 and 511 in 1994. From 1991 to 1994, foreign-owned firms in the Polish private transport sector increased their share of turnover from 1.6 to 6.1 per cent[59]. The bulk of this (over 10 per cent) was from freight forwarding operations. Of the 2 819 joint ventures in the transport sector in Hungary in 1994 (over 2 700 in road transport and forwarding), 138 had more than 50 employees[60].

The largest foreign investment deal in the road transport sector in the CECs was the acquisition by Vili Betz (Germany) of a 55 per cent share in SOMAT-BULGARIA[61]. Foreign capital has also played a part in the reorganisation of PEKAES-AUTO-TRANSPORT in Poland and HUNGAROCAMION in Hungary, but in both cases the State has retained a substantial shareholding.

3.6. Privatisation in the freight transport sector

Privatisation has been achieved both through the emergence of new private operators in the sector and through the restructuring of LSOEs. The first of these methods of privatisation was covered in section 3.4. on the structure of the road transport market. Except for the road and freight forwarding sectors, privatisation has not resulted in vast numbers of new private firms entering the market. The railways have been largely untouched by privatisation, apart from the separation of non-transport activities (construction offices, maintenance shops, etc.). Some CECs are considering separating infrastructure management from commercial services.

Privatising LSOEs, on the basis of the specially introduced legislation that is now in place, has entailed converting them into semi-public companies or splitting them up between a number of private firms. The first of these approaches was the most commonly used in the maritime, inland waterway and air transport sectors. None of the major state-owned maritime and air transport enterprises have been split up between private owners, although they may have been split into smaller units. Airlines are a special case: governments have introduced special legislation covering their privatisation, and passenger operations are never separated from cargo operations. There have been two approaches to the privatisation of LSOEs in the road transport sector: sometimes they have been transferred intact to the private sector, sometimes they have been split into a number of smaller, privately-owned enterprises.

Statistics on progress in privatising the transport sector in the CECs are surprisingly scarce. By no means has every CEC a list of LSOEs in the road transport sector that are candidates for privatisation and it is impossible to evaluate the impact of every individual privatisation operation carried out. One can only cite the number of such operations and attempt to gauge their impact on the sector.

In Poland, current legislation[62] provides for two methods of privatisation: through the formation of companies wholly owned by the State Treasury or through liquidation. In practice, a number of privatisation procedures are used. In the period 1990-95, of the LSOEs that came under the Ministry of Transport and the Maritime Economy, 85 were privatised and the privatisation of 39 others had begun. Thirty-two major state-owned Polish transport enterprises were transferred to private ownership and the financial restructuring of ten others was completed. This quite high total (166 in all) covers two types of enterprise: those operating exclusively in the transport sector (34) and "others" (132)[63]. The status of most PKS firms (over 170) remained unchanged.

In Hungary, practically all major state-owned road haulage enterprises were converted (split up) into business corporations or limited companies with, in the case of HUNGAROCAMION, the State retaining a 25 per cent share. In the Czech Republic, privatisation of the road and inland waterway sectors was completed in 1995 and there are now 35 000 road transport operators and 36 new waterway transport companies on the market. In Latvia, some forty state-owned transport undertakings had been privatised by 1994. In Romania, around seventy have been earmarked as suitable for privatisation[64] and in 1993 approximately 14 per cent of Romania's state-owned operations were privatised. Lithuania has privatised 63 per cent (in terms of capital) of its road haulage industry and was planning to complete privatisation of the industry as early as 1993[65]. In 1995, 320 Bulgarian undertakings were being considered for privatisation and 100 of them were actually privatised[66].

By the same year, the privatisation of the road haulage industry in the CECs was already well underway in terms of numbers of LSOEs and SMEs, generally representing 70 per cent of all operators in the sector. In Poland, Hungary and the Czech Republic, the percentage was just under 99 per cent. In the other CECs, some 30-50 per cent of operators had been privatised by 1994. However, the percentage of vehicles and jobs in the private sector was still relatively low, 20-60 per cent and 10-60 per cent, respectively, of the total number of vehicles and jobs in the industry. This would suggest that, from the standpoint of ownership structure at any rate, the gap between central and western European road hauliers has narrowed substantially. However, the gap is still wide when it comes to the quality of vehicles and management skills.

3.7. Role of the State in encouraging structural change

Preparing the CECs for membership of the European Union is the role of government. Governments are aware that the restructuring of the transport sector is the *sine qua non* for integration of central European operators into the

Single Market. At the same time, the transport industry in the CECs is increasingly coming to realise that change is inevitable and that it has more to gain than to lose from membership[67].

Governments are formulating transport policy statements and pressing ahead with legislative and structural reforms. The Czech Republic and Hungary, followed by Poland, are at the forefront of this process. In all three countries, transport policy goals have been formulated and made public, legislation on privatisation has been in place since 1990-91 and the percentage of privatisations completed is high. Poland has been slower in privatising its LSOEs (PKS) than have Hungary and the Czech Republic. Poland's Ministry of Transport has come in for criticism from the Cabinet's Council for Economic and Social Strategy for its slowness in privatising the railways and the maritime transport industry and for its uninspired approach to the privatisation of LSOEs in the passenger transport sector[68].

The governments of the CECs will face greater difficulties when it comes to formulating and implementing a reasonable policy for restructuring the railways. For the moment, they are studying the United Kingdom's and Germany's privatisation programmes but are unlikely to commence any in-depth restructuring of the railways before 2000. The main problems are overmanning (in Poland, the railways employ over 100 000 people!) and difficulties in finding other jobs for railway employees. Quite clearly, governments need to do more in the area of reskilling in the transport sector. The Hungarian[69] and Polish[70] governments' transport policy statements both point to the differences between the structure of employment in the transport industry in the EU and in their respective countries. In the EU, railway workers occupy 16.1 per cent of all jobs in the transport sector; the figure is 42.6 per cent in Hungary and 51.4 per cent in Poland. In the CECs, it is essential to create a more modern transport system, based more extensively on ancillary services and logistics.

As competition has not led to an increase in the number of airlines operating in western Europe, the governments of the CECs are giving substantial financial backing to their own airlines. Following airline mergers in the EU, they are worried that small central European operators will be forced out of business without state support.

4. CONCLUSIONS

From 1990 to 1995, structural reforms in the intercity transport sector in the countries in transition (the CECs) went ahead much as expected before the process was launched. The aim was to bring all of these countries into line with the EU: the private sector has been expanded, statistics show an exponential increase in the number of SMEs, road transport is taking an increasingly larger share of the market, international traffic is growing more rapidly than domestic traffic, car ownership is diverting a significant portion of users from public transport with each year.

Nor is it surprising that the extent of reforms in the transport sector in central Europe is dependent on the success of the general economic transition. The figures and tables in this report confirm that the countries where the results of privatisation are most tangible are the Czech Republic, Hungary and Poland. A number of signs show that privatisation is also a transport policy priority in the rest of the CECs. Any differences in approach to the reforms reflect the specific social, technical and geographic circumstances of each country.

NOTES

1. CECs: Central European Countries. CEECs: Central and Eastern European Countries.

2. CIS: Commonwealth of Independent States (the former USSR).

3. A breakdown of the structural changes is given in Table 1.

4. White Paper, Preparation of the Associated Countries of Central and Eastern Europe for Integration into the Internal Market of the Union, Brussels, 3 May 1995.

5. In 1991, Bulgaria, Hungary, Czechoslovakia and Romania registered a drop in GDP of the order of 12-15 per cent compared with 1990. (*Source:* INRETS-DEST, November 1995.)

6. *Rocznik Statystyczny GUS* 1995, Warsaw, 1995, p. 576.

7. G. Chatelus (1995), *"Indicateurs économiques et transport dans les principaux pays d'Europe centrale"*, in: De la transition à l'intégration : quelles conditions pour les transports ?, INRETS-DEST, Paradigme, Paris, p.33.

8. In the Czech Republic, 8 per cent; 20 per cent in Poland and Hungary.

9. G. Chatelus (1993), *Les transports en Europe centrale. Inadéquation de l'offre face à une demande restructurée*, INRETS-DEST, Paradigme, Paris, pp. 29-30.

10. *Rocznik Statystyczny GUS* 1995, Warsaw, 1995, p. 454.

11. Large, state-owned enterprises.

12.   J. Mallet (1989), *"Le transport routier* made in *Europe de l'Est",* Camions Magazine, No. 68, pp. 154-157.

13.   COM(84) 349 final, COM(87) 32 final and COM(89) 78 final.

14.   A. Artous (1991), *"Grandes manoeuvres dans les grands groupes",* Camions Magazine, No. 89, pp. 62-71.

15.   J. Burnewicz (1996), *"Privatisation and Deregulation of Road Transport in Poland"*, ECMT, January.

16.   Ministry of Transport, Telecommunications and Water Management (1994), *"The Concept of Hungarian Transport Policy"*, Working Paper, Budapest, April, p. I/12.

17.   KTI (1995), *Conditions of European Integration of Central and Eastern European Hauliers*, Budapest, April, p. 81.

18.   *"Combien d'entreprises ?",* L'Officiel des Transporteurs, (1989), No. 1559, pp. 19-20.

19.   *Rocznik Statystyczny GUS* 1993, Warsaw, 1993, pp. LXIII and 113.

20.   *Mémento de statistiques des transports*, OEST, Paris, December 1994, p. 131.

21.   G. Chatelus (1993), *Les transports en Europe centrale. Inadéquation de l'offre face à une demande restructurée,* INRETS-DEST, Paradigme, Paris, p. 102.

22.   CEFTA, Central European Free Trade Area (Poland, Czech Republic, Slovak Republic and Hungary).

23.   *Rocznik Statystyczny GUS*, Warsaw, 1995, p.507.

24.   *Raport o stanie gospodarczym przedsies biorstwa "Polskie Koleje Pan-stwowe"* Warsaw, 1995.

25. Ch. Thouvenin (1992), *L'évolution des chemins de fer tchécoslovaques et hongrois*, INRETS-DEST, Paradigme, Paris, pp. 81-82 and 261.

26. *Rocznik Statystyczny GUS* 1990-1995, Warsaw.

27. *Ustawa z dnia 6 lipca 1995 r. o przedsiebiorstwie panstwowym "Polskie Koleje Panstwowe"*. Dziennik Ustaw 1995, No. 95, p. 474.

28. On 12th May 1995, the Minister of Transport withdrew the regulation conferring the status of a public service railway company on *"Lubuska Kolej Regionalna"*.

29. *Nasza kolej. Dlaczego i jak ja restrukturyzowac*. DG PKP, Warsaw, September 1994, pp. 44-49.

30. O. Prucha (1995), *"Les Chemins de Fer tchèques: qu'a t-on apporté dans le domaine du service public? Problèmes des privatisations"*. Quel rôle des institutions locales, nationales, internationales en Europe Centrale et Orientale?, INRETS Seminar, Barbizon, 13-15 November.

31. The Concept of Hungarian Transport Policy, *op. cit.*, p. II/19.

32. V. Rajkov (1995), *"Rôle des institutions locales, nationales et internationales pour le développement du transport en République de Bulgarie"*, Quel rôle des institutions locales, nationales, internationales en Europe Centrale et Orientale?, INRETS Seminar, Barbizon, 13-15 November .

33. M. Jelaska (1993), *"Railway Transport Restructuring and Problems of Transit in Slovenia"*, Comment définir des priorités en transport: quels critères et quelles procédures? INRETS Seminar, Barbizon, December, p. 184.

34. Data from the Ministry of Transport and the Maritime Economy, Poland, March 1996.

35. Unpublished data, Inland Transport Committee, United Nations Economic Commission for Europe, Geneva, July 1994.

36.   G. Chatelus, *Indicateurs économiques et transport dans les principaux pays d'Europe Centrale*, *op.cit.*, pp. 36-38.

37.   Cz. Piela: *Podstawowe problemy PKS.* *"Przeglad Komunikacyjny"* 1995, No. 2.

38.   *"The Concept of Hungarian Transport Policy"*, *op. cit.*, pp. II/21-II/22.

39.   Unpublished data from the Inland Transport Committee. United Nations Economic Commission for Europe, Geneva, July 1994.

40.   A. Olants (1995), *"International road carriage policy in Latvia and integration into the European Market"*. ECMT Seminar on the integration of Central and Eastern operators into the European transport market, Paris, 16-17 March.

41.   In 1995, rail freight traffic in Poland was estimated at 69.1 billion tonne-kilometres (according to GUS monthly statistics), equivalent to approximately 40 per cent of total traffic for the CECs.

42.   *Trends in the Transport Sector 1970-1993*, ECMT, Paris 1995.

43.   *Rocznik Statystyczny GUS*, Warsaw, 1995, p. 639.

44.   The total volume of freight transported by PKP fell by 44 per cent overall during the period 1989-94 (*Rocznik Statystyczny GUS*, Warsaw, 1995, p. 430).

45.   Mobility in the Czech Republic, CESMAD, Prague, 1995.

46.   Ch. Thouvenin, *L'évolution des chemins de fer tchécoslovaques et hongrois*, *op. cit.*, p. 257.

47.   The Concept of Hungarian Transport Policy, *op. cit.*, p. I/12.

48. T. Dorosiewicz: *Struktura marek i wieku samochodów osobowych, ciezarowych i autobusów w Polsce zarejestrowanych w koncu 1992 r. Instytut Transportu Samochodowego. "Prace Zeszyt 78*, Warsaw, 1994, pp. 98-100.

49. *Conditions of European Integration of Central and Eastern European Hauliers.* KTI, Budapest 1995, p. 157 (recalculated by J. Burnewicz).

50. *Environmental policy in the Czech Republic*, SRC International CS, Prague, 1995.

51. *Emissions of noise from transport in the Czech Republic.* SRC International CS, Prague, 1995, p. 6.

52. M. Bak, E. Adamowicz, J. Burnewicz (1996), *External cost of transport and internalisation -- Poland*, Sopot, February, p. 14.

53. Unpublished data, Inland Transport Committee, United Nations Economic Commission for Europe, Geneva, July 1994.

54. V. Rajkov (1995), *"Rôle des institutions locales, nationales et internationales pour le développement du transport en République de Bulgarie"*, Quel rôle des institutions locales, nationales, internationales en Europe Centrale et Orientale?, INRETS Seminar, Barbizon, 13-15 November.

55. Unpublished data, Inland Transport Committee, United Nations Economic Commission for Europe, Geneva, July 1995.

56. Unpublished data, Inland Transport Committee, United Nations Economic Commission for Europe, Geneva, July 1993.

57. *Prix de revient "route".* Bulletin des Transports et de la Logistique, 1994, No. 2585, p. 752.

58. Monitoring firm wykonujacych miedzynarodowy transport drogowy. University of Gdansk, Sopot, 1994, p. 21.

59. *Rocznik Statystyczny GUS*, Warsaw, 1992-1995.

60.   Unpublished data, Inland Transport Committee, United Nations Economic Commission for Europe, Geneva, July 1994.

61.   V. Rajkov, *op. cit.*, p.7.

62.   The Law of 13 July 1990 on the privatisation of state-owned enterprises;   the Law of 19 October 1991 on the restructuring of agricultural assets managed by the State Treasury;   the Law of 5 February 1993 on the transfer of ownership of state-owned enterprises of special importance to the national economy;   and the Law of 30 April 1993 on national investment funds and their privatisation.

63.   Unpublished data, Ministry of Transport and the Maritime Economy, Warsaw, March 1996.

64.   Unpublished data, Inland Transport Committee, United Nations Economic Commission for Europe, Geneva, July 1994.

65.   Transport policy trends. Lithuania's replies to the questionnaire issued by the Inland Transport Committee, United Nations Economic Commission for Europe, Geneva, 21 July 1993.

66.   Transport policy trends. Bulgaria's replies to the questionnaire issued by the Inland Transport Committee, United Nations Economic Commission for Europe, Geneva, 21 July 1995.

67.   Surveys on the prospects for Polish international transport enterprises, carried out by H. Brdulak.   TRANS '95 Conference, Warsaw, 19-20 October 1995.

68.   *Strategiczne problemy polityki transportowej.   Rada Strategii Spoleczno-Gospodarczej przy Radzie Ministrów*, Warsaw 1995, pp. 13-15.

69.   The Concept of Hungarian Transport Policy, *op. cit.,* p. II/33.

70.   *Polityka transportowa*, Warsaw, 1995, p. 83.

OTHER COMMUNICATION

During the Round Table, Mr. Petreanu provided a written contribution describing the situation in his country. This contribution is reproduced below, for information.

ROMANIA

Dominic PETREANU
General Directorate for Land Transport
Ministry of Transport
Bucarest

TRANSPORT TRENDS IN ROMANIA

1. Public passenger transport

	1989	1990	1994	1995
Rail				
Passengers (million)	481	408	207	210
Passenger-kms (million)	35 456	30 582	18 313	18 879
Average distance	73.7	74.9	88.46	89.6

In July 1996, the average length of journey was 102.9 kms. 66 per cent of the total volume of rail passenger transport was between adjoining regions.

Coaches and buses

	1989	1990	1994	1995
Passengers (million)	878	780	425	413
Passenger-kms (million)	23 077	24 007	14 058	21 438
Average distance	26.3	30.8	33.1	51.9

The decline in passenger traffic was due essentially to a reduction in short-distance (commuter) transport by rail, bus and coach.

The increase in the length of the average journey by road was due to an increase in inter-city transport (which was strictly limited before 1990) as compared with transport in rural areas.

2. Freight transport (for hire or reward and own-account)

Rail

	1989	1990	1994	1995
Tonnes (million)	306.3	218.8	99.1	105.1
Tonne-kms (million)	81 131	57 253	24 704	27 179
Average distance	265	262	249	...

Road (inter-city and local transport, dump truck only)

	1989	1990	1994	1995
Tonnes (million)	1 081	843	600	616
Tonne-kms (million)	22 751	25 281	25 560	...
Average distance	21	30.3	42.6	...

Because of privatisation, it is difficult to estimate the total volume of freight transport. The figures for 1994 and 1995 are thus given for guidance only.

The fall in rail traffic was not due, as it is often claimed, to competition from road haulage. The decline in freight transport by category of freight between 1989 and 1995 is shown in annex.

3. Road traffic trends (vehicles/24 hours)

The data were collected at seven different points on main roads outside towns so as to eliminate the influence of local traffic.

1985 = 100

		1985	1990	1995
cars		100	187.2	307.9
lorries				
	2 axles	100	116.1	204.6
	3 axles	100	141.2	176.2
	>3 axles	100	130.3	237.3
	total	100	123.2	209.8
buses and coaches		100	89.1	147.4

The trend of traffic is rigorously determined from the technical point of view, but the increase is not reflected in the statistics for transport volumes.

ANNEX

Main types of freight carried by rail, tonnage of which fell sharply between 1989 and 1995

	Tonnage (mill. tonnes) +/-	Average distance (km)
Timber	- 10	
Quarry products	- 57	126
Iron ore and scrap	- 20	214
Coal and coke	- 27	369
Petroleum products	- 18	247
Lime, cement, construction materials	- 18	219
Metal	- 16	
TOTAL	161	
Foodstuffs, beverages, tobacco	- 25	283
Manufactures, fabrics, clothing, footwear, furniture, etc.	- 2.5	329
Metal goods	+2.5	

Road haulage recorded an increase in tonnage of the following:

Grain	+4.5 mill. tonnes	50 km
Foodstuffs, beverages, tobacco	+45	55

It recorded a decrease in tonnage of the following:

Quarry products	- 1 300 mill. tonnes	11km
Timber	- 6	90
Iron ore and scrap	- 16	18
Coal and coke	- 13	15
Construction materials	- 200	21
Metal	- 60	42
Manufactures, fabrics, clothing, footwear, furniture	- 3	61

SUMMARY OF DISCUSSIONS

SUMMARY

1. INTRODUCTION

After the fall of the Berlin Wall and the demise of the former economic system, the Central and Eastern European countries had to cope with an extremely critical economic situation marked by falling GDP and a very sharp corresponding decline in their transport activity. Owing to the lack of budgetary resources, investment in transport was greatly reduced and the statistical system deteriorated. But quite soon there was an increase in East-West trade.

Like the economy as a whole, the transport sector has moved on from a supply-driven system to a demand-pull situation. Decisions are no longer dictated by planning requirements but by the market. After five or six years of reform, the Round Table therefore reviewed the situation in the Central and Eastern European countries. In particular, can it be said that the kind of policies now being implemented meet the needs for change? For example, undertakings have very often been privatised despite employees' reluctance. Also, the environment frequently ranks low down among policymakers' priorities, while road safety has deteriorated everywhere. All the countries are in the running for membership of the European Union and are therefore trying to import its competitive system. But is this system consistent with ways of thinking and realities in the former planned economies? The Round Table addressed all these issues in a three-step approach. After an overview of the general situation, the participants went on to discuss freight and then passenger transport.

2. GENERAL SITUATION

Some precautions have to be taken when assessing the real economic situation in the CEECs. The output of a rapidly developing private sector is

277

undoubtedly underestimated in the published statistics. According to estimates, the grey and underground economy is probably equivalent to between 10 and 25 per cent of official GDP. Bearing this caveat in mind, it seems that the economic situation of most countries in the region had greatly improved by 1995, with the confirmation and acceleration of the positive trends observed in 1994. Economic growth in the Central and Eastern European countries was rapid in 1995 and outstripped forecasts, with an average rise in their GDP of about 5.4 per cent as against 4 per cent in 1994. The best performances were recorded in the Slovak Republic, Poland, Romania and the Czech Republic. Despite the quite general improvement in the transition countries' situation, the fact remains that their output in terms of GDP is still far below the level achieved before the process of economic and political change started. In the countries which have been recently among the front runners, GDP is on average still 15 per cent below the 1989 level; in the Baltic States it is 50 per cent lower.

The structural changes are of a technological, economic, spatial and social kind. The major social changes are the rise in unemployment -- for many jobs have become unproductive -- and the advent of inequalities in incomes and standards of living, for there are winners and losers in the transition process.

The changes are greatly influenced by the macroeconomic environment. At present it can be said that the transition process is not yet over, even if the situation has stabilized, as seen in the few growth indicators mentioned above. The CEECs are now at the end of the first phase, that of unfettered capitalism. Inasmuch as transport and overall economic activity are very closely related, it is obvious that there can be no transport policy without a consistent general economic policy.

Differences and similarities across countries exist in the transport field. The similarities include:

- -- The difficulty of transforming major public enterprises;
- -- Rail's continuing role which is greater than in the traditional market economies;
- -- The magnitude of the psychological obstacles to be overcome;
- -- The scale of activities that are still subsidised.

The differences are to be seen in the private sector's share in the economy. In this respect, the transition is a very long process.

At present, policy shortcomings and limited public investment in transport are to be noted. The reason for this is the failure to take a comprehensive view of the economy and to analyse in detail the interactions within it. Transport must not be seen simply as a general policy instrument. It requires more resources and a more determined policy effort, particularly to overcome the resistance to change in government departments. A case in point is the environment which calls for sustained action, as the authorities do not show sufficient concern for external costs.

With regard to investment, which is one of the traditional levers in government action, it can be said that there is no justification for focusing exclusively on infrastructure. This applies particularly to rail, owing to the decrease in traffic and the resulting under-utilisation of capacity. Investment in telecommunications and in frontier crossing facilities is also extremely important. The possibilities of funding this investment must, moreover, be taken into account in its initial programming phase. There should be no illusions about purely private funding which is feasible only in a few cases. Tax revenue will therefore continue to play an extremely important role, particularly in public/private financing operations. When public funds are in short supply, private capital has an important role to play in financing the construction of infrastructure, but it is difficult to mobilise, since infrastructure use is limited by tolls that are not readily accepted by users unless their standard of living is high enough.

3. FREIGHT TRANSPORT

Any increase in transport activity depends on economic growth, and the decline in industrial output accompanying the changes in Central and Eastern Europe was bound to affect freight transport. The traffic of the ECMT countries in transition decreased by over 47 per cent in terms of tonne-kilometres between 1988 and 1993. But the fall in traffic slowed gradually as from 1993 as signs of an economic recovery appeared in some countries. The confirmation of this recovery in 1994 and the generalisation of the trend necessarily had a positive effect on transport. Owing to faster economic growth and higher industrial output as well as the return to peace in the former Yugoslavia, freight traffic expressed in tonne-kilometres rose by more than 8.5 per cent in 1995.

The freight traffic trend was positive in 1995 in all the ECMT countries in transition, except for Lithuania and Moldova. The greatest increases in tonne-kilometres carried were recorded in Croatia (up 23 per cent) and the Czech Republic (up 19.5 per cent). Road and waterway transport were the major beneficiaries of this development. However, not all transport modes benefited in the same degree from the growth of traffic. The road haulage sector had managed in 1993 to check a decline in traffic that had not been marked until 1990, whereas rail and the waterways, which had been confronted since 1989 with a continual decrease in their freight, did not see a return to growth until 1995.

In 1995, rail freight traffic rose by over 5.9 per cent in the ECMT's Central and Eastern European Member countries. This increase was mainly due to the international traffic generated by foreign trade, while domestic traffic marked time. Inland waterway results in 1995 improved greatly with the resumption of traffic on the Danube following the end to the blockade on the Yugoslav stretch of the river. Waterway traffic practically doubled in Bulgaria and Romania. Despite the pick-up in inland navigation in the CEECs, it should not be forgotten, however, that in 1995 their waterways still took less than half of the record volume of traffic carried by this mode in 1988. The same can be said of rail, which in 1995 also carried the equivalent of only 48 per cent of its traffic in 1988.

Great care must be taken when interpreting the figures for road transport. This sector is undergoing rapid change with the privatisation -- and split-up into small units -- of major public operators which previously had a quasi-monopoly. With the advent of a great many small private carriers and the lower volume of own-account transport operations carrried out by large industrial conglomerates, the statistical base for the observation of flows has changed. The statistical systems in use are not geared to these developments. For example, a change in the statistical base in 1994 in the Czech Republic to take account of haulage business of firms with fewer than 25 employees resulted in an increase of 185 per cent in transport for hire and reward in that country.

Quality of service is a real problem in freight transport. Owing to the split-up of the road haulage sector, the size of haulage firms is not sufficient to meet logistical needs. At a more basic level, this split-up of undertakings into smaller units makes the problem of return freight more serious, for the operators are prevented by their limited size from obtaining enough customers to carry complementary freight. The carriers could improve the use of transport capacity by forming associations. At the same time, regional freight offices would make it possible to match supply and demand in order to make up for the lack of return freight. Road hauliers in fact find that there is more pressure on them to haggle over transport prices than to cover their costs fully. This results in a great many bankruptcies along with market imbalances as the prices charged are too low. Rail cannot compete either with the prices offered by the newcomers. With such unbridled competition, it can be said that privatisation pure and simple is not necessarily the best or only choice. A degree of regulation must be maintained if competition is not to be ruinous. Capitalism in its unadulterated form cannot be seen as a model. A specific approach to suit each country has to be found.

In such a context, large undertakings are feeling the strain. They are finding the adjustment process difficult, particularly when they have to provide the quality of service expected by western firms. They are not up to the mark in logistical terms. Moreover, logistical training is required throughout the sector if it is to provide quality service. Otherwise the major international forwarders will monopolise freight flows and the value added of transport and logistical services.

Logistical training is not the only need in this sector, which also requires clear and stable rules. In particular, it has to observe accounting rules if it is to keep its costs under control. Appropriate tax measures also have to be used in order to stabilize public revenue and ensure fair competition. On the subject of taxes, a harmonized approach to transit charges would be necessary in order to avoid distortions between countries.

Regulatory action is also required to curb cut-throat competition. At present, competitive conditions are based on the use of old, poorly maintained and overloaded lorries. But, this being so, the Round Table participants wondered what could be done in response to a situation with potentially negative effects on road safety, especially as drivers often did not respect the rest periods required in Europe to maintain safety standards.

It would seem that privatisations have gone ahead and that markets have been allowed to develop spontaneously, without adequate structures being defined for intermodal competition, the integration of external costs and social policy.

These unsatisfactory competitive structures are detrimental to rail, especially when its many weaknesses are also taken into account. The rail system was not ready for the change. In particular, its infrastructure was not geared to the West but to the East. The Round Table participants, however, did not focus so much on its infrastructure as on its management deficiencies. In this respect, the reform of rail is essential. The Round Table stressed the need for energetic action, since the policies adopted so far have been lacking in clarity. In any case, they are not forceful enough to overcome the railway authorities' opposition to change. The lack of a logistical approach and of any relationship between prices and costs is detrimental to the future existence of rail freight. The first step should be to draw a clear dividing line between the role of rail and government so that the railways can become real commercial enterprises. Basic internal reorganisation is essential if a modern management approach is to be taken since, in addition to achieving real independence, operation and equipment have to be modernised. Maintenance is more of a requirement than new kinds of infrastructure, which is better than it is generally thought. Moreover, rail's main role, which is more important on the international network owing to the size of most of the countries, calls for the harmonization of railway policies by the countries concerned, and in particular for a solution to the problem of frontier crossings. But there are no examples that could be followed in the railway field. Reforms can be based on the objective of improving productivity, meaning that it must be possible to identify the services which are losing money by setting up a transparent accounting system. The entire sector must be given a strong policy lead, for it seems that it cannot be left to the railways to modernise themselves.

If combined transport is to play its full role, given that the necessary infrastructure is available, its organisation will have to be modernised and legal problems such as liability will have to be settled. The success of combined transport has been due so far more to the obstacles confronting road transport in certain areas than to its own efficiency.

As shown by the recent trend, most of the piggyback operators in the UIRR had a good year in 1995 and introduced many new services. A common denominator of these undertakings is that they operate only in the buoyant market for international traffic. Hungarocombi doubled the number of its consignments in 1995, with 74 per cent of traffic carried on the rolling road which now holds a key position in transit through Hungary. In Poland, however, Polkombi's traffic was not up from 1994 owing to problems with the opening of some services, while the Czech operator, Bohemiakombi, increased its rolling road capacity on services to and from Germany.

It may be added that rail container services contributed to a large extent to the decline in rail traffic in the first few years of the transition process. These services, with their particularly high volume of traffic to and from the former Soviet Union, have completely collapsed. Between 1989 and 1994, the number of containers carried by rail decreased by over 85 per cent, while their tonnage was down by 75 per cent. The pick-up in traffic in 1994, which became more pronounced in 1995, is giving good results on the Romanian, Czech and Slovene networks. This traffic trend, marked by a higher increase in tonnages than in container numbers, undoubtedly reflects the rationalisation of this type of activity.

Broadly speaking, growth in rail freight will be achieved by working out prices that will cover the economic and social costs of the services provided. Market mechanisms must be introduced on the basis of fair competition between modes and between operators. Privatisation seems to be the decisive step if operators are to be more dynamic and improve their ability to adapt to markets. At the same time, improved accounting systems would rationalise the railway management system by providing the kind of indicators needed by it.

As far as privatisation is concerned, it can be said that employees are not over-enthusiastic, since they are worried about their jobs. Productivity gains are therefore slow to materialise and, basically, ways of resolving these difficulties have to be found. According to some of the Round Table participants, however, privatisation in itself does not provide any solutions. What matters is the overhaul of the management system and the modernisation of methods by using EDI to track goods and organise the transport chain. This requires very high investment in training by freight transport undertakings, as was stressed at various times in the course of the Round Table.

Lastly, the possibilities of sea transport must be taken into account as a future alternative to inland transport for freight flows to and from the former CIS, with which trade is picking up. The importance of sea transport in the passenger field (Baltic countries) should also be remembered. Passenger transport was the next item discussed by the Round Table.

4. PASSENGER TRANSPORT

Travel was very cheap in the centrally planned economies. This resulted in high demand for private travel which was met by rail, and explains why this mode is still synonymous with the communist system. By contrast, the car has become a symbol of change and freedom. Owing to the rise in car ownership, the statistical system is even less satisfactory than for freight transport. Hungary and the Czech Republic are the only countries which have statistical data on car traffic in 1995. While car traffic in terms of passenger-km was up by 5 per cent in the Czech Republic, it was down by 4.5 per cent in Hungary. This decline for the second year running, despite the steady increase in the Hungarian car fleet, is to be explained by the less frequent use of cars owing to higher running costs, particularly since petrol is so expensive and by the pressures on household budgets caused by the austerity plan.

In the CEECs, it can be seen that the very marked increase in the car fleet has not been accompanied by a concomitant increase in car use. The transport policy which made it more expensive to run a car has therefore had an undoubted impact.

Bus and coach traffic expressed in passenger-kilometres fell by over 4 per cent in 1995 in the transition countries compared with the previous year. This decrease, which exceeded that for 1994, confirms the downtrend in this type of traffic which has lasted for several years (traffic down by about 40 per cent from 1989).

Rail passenger traffic again declined by 1995, by 3.6 per cent, thus marking a decrease of almost 50 per cent compared with the record year of 1989. Rail passenger traffic is therefore still falling, even if the rate of decrease is tending to slow down. This trend can be mainly attributed to the decline in individual mobility as a result of lower incomes and to the often steep increases in rail fares in the first few years of the transition process. It is also due to greater competition from the private car, following a marked increase in car ownership, which already exceeds 2 000 cars per 1 000 inhabitants in Poland and Hungary, and is even close on 300 cars per 1 000 inhabitants in the Czech Republic -- with particularly high rates in the latter country's major towns, since car ownership is mainly associated with the urban environment where increases in income are more frequent.

Car ownership will be influenced by the rise in incomes and by the population structure, i.e. the size of families and the age of their members. Saturation levels will depend on the use of cars and not so much on actual ownership.

The size of the car fleet and its modernisation suggests that an underground economy is at work and is generating income. This is confirmed by the expensive cars that are often seen, even though most of them are bought second-hand in the West. By comparison, public road and rail services have steadily deteriorated, resulting in a move to the car or airlines for intercity travel, with all the negative environmental effects this implies. Data on external costs are unfortunately lacking, but the internalisation of such costs would probably lead to higher taxes on fuel.

The question is whether public transport can still be subsidised to the same extent. According to the Round Table participants, public transport will continue to play a major role -- i.e. a social role -- by providing services for a whole section of the population who will still be without a private car, probably for a long time to come. It is an amenity that must be safeguarded, requiring firm action by the authorities. But spending must be kept under control. A multimodal approach to subsidies must therefore be taken to avoid waste, as subsidies must go to the most efficient undertaking -- perhaps a private operator -- for the services concerned. These subsidies must also be devised in such a way as to give operators an incentive to achieve productivity gains by reorganising themselves. Action by the authorities must be aimed at efficient management of the public sector, for example, by making regional bodies responsible for maintaining some services. At the same time, users can be given a wider choice of mode if better information is provided on services (timetables, for example). But, with regard to the basic issue, the Round Table participants said that the temptation to withdraw all subsidies for the operation of social services must be resisted. As in the case of freight, it must not be considered that there is only one solution or that the market is the panacea which will automatically resolve all problems. In this context, rail has a role to play, but not necessarily at its current level of activity.

Public transport is even more important if the environment and accidents are taken into account. As regards road safety, the overall picture in the transition countries was somewhat mixed in 1995, as the number of road accidents and injured users was at a record high in the CEECs, while there was a slight decrease in the number of accident fatalities. The marked improvement from 1991 to 1993 -- after a spectacular deterioration lasting three years --

therefore seems to have come to a halt, despite the often very energetic road safety measures taken by several governments and despite the downtrend in the use of private cars observed in some countries.

5. CONCLUSIONS

To sum up, it can be said that no single development model for the transport sector exists. Transposing the European Union model as it stands gives rise to social and environmental problems. Every country has its own specific characteristics that must not be disregarded.

Privatisation in itself is not the answer to everything. The first step must be to instil modern management methods in transport undertakings. Accordingly, principles of economic efficiency, such as achieving productivity gains in the public and private sectors, must be taken into account and training needs incorporated in the adjustment process. New thinking on the public sector's role is needed, for the market cannot regulate everything. The market must, in fact, be governed by rules that are stable and transparent. At the same time, an effort must be made to achieve greater efficiency in the public sector and provide greater freedom of choice for the award of subsidies. Lastly, the progress and effects of a policy cannot be analysed without reliable statistical information. Owing to the serious shortcomings in this field at the present time, action should be taken to improve the availability and quality of transport data.

LIST OF PARTICIPANTS

Monsieur Christian REYNAUD   **Chairman**
Directeur - DEST
Institut National de Recherche sur les
Transports et leur Sécurité - INRETS
2 avenue du Général Malleret-Joinville
F-94114 ARCUEIL CEDEX

Prof. Dr. Jan KOWALSKI   **Rapporteur**
Universität Karlsruhe
Institut für Wirtschaftspolitik
und Wirtschaftsforschung (IWW)
Postfach 69 80
D-76128 KARLSRUHE

Prof. Dr. Gerd SAMMER   **Rapporteur**
Head of the Institute of Transportation
Universität für Bodenkultur Vienna
Gregor Mendel Strasse 33
A-1180 VIENNA

Monsieur G. CHATELUS   **Rapporteur**
DEST - Département Économie et
Sociologie des Transports
INRETS
2 avenue du Général Malleret-Joinville
F-94114 ARCUEIL CEDEX

Prof. Dr. Katalin TANCZOS   **Rapporteur**
Technical University of Budapest
Faculty of Transportation Engineering
Department of Transport Economics
Bertalan Lajos u. 2
H-1111 BUDAPEST

Mr. Jan BURNEWICZ   **Rapporteur**
University of Gdansk
Chair of Comparative Analysis
Armii Krajowej 119/121
PL-81-824 SOPOT

Monsieur Wladimir ANDREFF
Directeur du ROSES
Université Paris I
90 rue de Tolbiac
F-75634 PARIS CEDEX 13

Dr. Gerd BAHM
ITF Intertraffic Berlin GmbH
Hohenzollernsdamm 150
D-14191 BERLIN

Mr. Grigore BUCHI
Deputy General Manager
Incertrans S.A.
Transportation Research Institute
Calea Grivitei 393 -- Sect. 1
RO-78341 BUCAREST

Monsieur Bernard GERARDIN
Gerardin Conseil
6 chemin du Bois d'Haucourt
F-60350 PIERREFONDS

Dr. Andris GUTMANIS
President
Latvian Transport Development and Education Association
Gogola Str. 3
LV-1743 RIGA

Dr. Derek HALL
Scottish Agricultural College
Department of Leisure and Tourism
Auchincruive
GB-AYR KA6 5HW Scotland

Prof. Wlodzimierz JANUSZKIEWICZ
Head of Department of International Transport
Warsaw School of Economics
World Economy Faculty
Al. Niepodleglosci 162
PL-02-554 WARSAW

Mr. Eamonn JUDGE
Faculty of Business
Leeds Metropolitan University
Bronte Hall
Beckett Park Campus
GB-LEEDS LS6 3QS

Mr. Andreas KÄFER
Raum- und Verkehrsplanung
Fillgradergasse 6/2
A-1060 WIEN

Mr. Olaf KRÜGER
Leiter des Bahnverkehrszentrums
Kühne et Nagel
Bahnvervehrszentrum Berlin
Wolfshagener Strasse 79
D-13187 BERLIN-PANKOW

Mr. Stig LÖFBERG
Consultant
LCG
Nörre Voldgade 82
DK-1358 COPENHAGEN K

Dr. Miroslav MALY
SRC International CS
Poceernicka 96
CZ-108 03 PRAGUE 10

Mr. Dominic PETREANU
Direction Générale des Transports Terrestres
Ministère des Transports
Rue Dinicu Golescu 38 - Section 1
RO-77113 BUCAREST

Mr. Peter SCHARLE
Deputy Secretary for Transport
Ministry of Transport, Communication
and Water Management
Dob u. 75-81
H-1077 BUDAPEST

Mr. Wladimir SEGERCRANTZ
Senior Research Scientist
Technical Research Centre
VTT Communities and Infrastructure
PO Box 1902
FIN-02044 ESPOO

M. Dinos STASINOPOULOS
Administrateur
Direction Générale des Transports
Commission des Communautés Européennes
200 rue de la Loi
B-1049 BRUXELLES

Mr. Andras TIMAR
Senior Banker
EBRD
1 Exchange Square
GB-LONDON EC2A 2EH

Mr. Arno VALMA
Department of Transportation Researches
Estonian Academy of Sciences
Institute of Economics
7 Estonian Avenue
EW-0100 TALLINN

Drs. Johannes VOGELAAR
Netherlands Economic Institute - NEI
P.O. Box 4175
NL-3006 AD ROTTERDAM

ECMT SECRETARIAT

Mr. Jack SHORT, Deputy Secretary-General

ECONOMIC RESEARCH, STATISTICS AND DOCUMENTATION DIVISION

Mr. Alain RATHERY, Head of Division

Mr. Michel VIOLLAND, Administrator

Ms Françoise ROULLET, Assistant

Mrs Julie PAILLIEZ, Assistant

TRANSPORT POLICY DIVISION

Mr. Ludomir SZUBERT, Consultant

ALSO AVAILABLE

13th International Symposium on Theory and Practice in Transport Economics. "Transport: New Problems, New Solutions" ECMT (1996)
(75 96 03 1) ISBN 92-821-1212-8   France FF450   Other Countries FF565   US$112   DM164

Express Delivery Services. Series ECMT - Round Table 101 (1996)
(75 96 04 1) ISBN 92-821-1214-4   France FF110   Other Countries FF 145   US$28   DM42

Changing Daily Urban Mobility: Less or Differently?. Series ECMT - Round Table 102 (1996)
(75 96 06 1) ISBN 92-821-1216-0   France FF260   £34   US$50   DM76

The Separation of Operations from Infrastructure in the Provision of Railway Services. Series ECMT - Round Table 103 (1997)
(75 97 02 1P) ISBN 92-821-1221-7   France FF295   £38   US$58   DM86

New Trends in Logistics in Europe - Round Table 104 (1997)
(75 97 05 1 P) ISBN 92-821-1224-1   France FF215   £28 $US42   DM63

Infrastructure-Induced Mobility. Series ECMT - Round Table 105 (1998)
(75 98 07 1 P) ISBN 92-821-1232-2   France FF400   £40 $US67   DM119

Prices charged at the OECD Bookshop.

The OECD CATALOGUE OF PUBLICATIONS and supplements will be sent free of charge on request addressed either to OECD Publications Service, or to the OECD Distributor in your country.

OECD PUBLICATIONS, 2, rue André-Pascal, 75775 PARIS CEDEX 16
PRINTED IN FRANCE
(75 98 10 1 P) ISBN 92-821-1235-7 – No. 50301 1998